HEART
OF A
SPARTAN

HEART OF A SPARTAN

THE STORY OF A MICHIGAN STATE FOOTBALL RENAISSANCE

JACK EBLING

photography by MATTHEW MITCHELL

SPORT COMMUNITY PUBLISHING
617 East Michigan Avenue
Lansing, MI 48912 USA

SportCommunityPublishing.com

Copyright © 2012 Sport Community Publishing, LLC

Trademarks of Michigan State University used with permission.

Photographs © Matthew Mitchell/Michigan State University Athletic Communications

All rights reserved. No part of this book may be reproduced in any form, electronic or mechanical, including photocopying, recording or by any information storage and retrieval system, without the express written consent of the publisher, except for brief excerpts in media reviews.

First Edition • July 2012

10 9 8 7 6 5 4 3 2 1   12 13 14 15 16

Book design by Traction • Lansing, MI

Library of Congress Control Number: 2012943035

ISBN: 978-0-9858312-0-2

PRINTED IN THE UNITED STATES OF AMERICA

ACKNOWLEDGEMENTS

ANOTHER WINNING TEAM

"WHEN DID YOU START writing the book?" the question came for the umpteenth time.

The easy answer? "An hour after 'Little Giants?'"

The correct one? "It started in 1896."

Without all that came before the past two seasons, *Heart of a Spartan: The Story of a Michigan State Football Renaissance* could never have come to pass.

From Henry Keep, M.A.C.'s first coach, to Matt Macksood, MSU's latest preferred walk-on, it's impossible to list every contribution.

But the first people who have to be mentioned are my dad and mom, Jake and Marge Ebling. Without them, there is no book. More than that, there is no me.

Jake taught me to love football back in Redford Township. He took me to high school, college and pro games at every opportunity. Long after I began writing for a living, he'd ask, "When are you going to get a real job?"

The first game I remember was the Detroit Lions' last NFL championship in 1957 at Briggs Stadium, a 59-14 clubbing of Cleveland. On our way back to the car, I said, "This was great, Dad! Can we do it again next year?" He never forgave me for jinxing the franchise.

We also saw a lot of college games at University of Detroit Stadium and Michigan Stadium. The obligatory joke: "What's the difference between those venues and programs?" The answer: "The Titans stopped playing football forever in 1964. The Wolverines waited 44 years, then stopped playing for three seasons."

But beginning with a 50-20 loss to The Ohio State University in 1961, I got a steady diet of Michigan football on Saturday afternoons. The Wolverines weren't very good in those years. Meanwhile, MSU was winning six national titles from the year I was born till my sophomore year in high school.

Two things happened in 1966, aside from the "Game of the Century" with Notre Dame. One, I developed a rebellious streak and questioned everything my dad said. Two, I visited East Lansing on a field trip to the MSU Planetarium. There, I bumped into Charles "Bubba" Smith – literally, nose-to-navel – when I wandered into the Union Building pool room.

My first reaction? What an amazing place! I didn't know anything about academic programs. But I knew it wasn't the hellhole it was reported to be. Every time my dad would talk about Ann Arbor, I'd tell him I wanted to be a Spartan – in part to be defiant, in part because I did.

From 1969-75, I threatened the Big Ten record for undergraduate credits in the quarter system and left with two degrees. If those years were the end of the line for Biggie Munn and Duffy Daugherty, they were the start of something meaningful for me.

As an English teacher and football and track coach at Lapeer West High in 1975, I got to know a great prep lineman, soon-to-be MSU mainstay Mike Densmore. After three years there, the most fun I ever had, I came back to Mid-Michigan and stumbled into a job at *The State Journal*, a p.m. paper in the typewriter days.

For some reason I'll never understand, Executive Sports Editor Ed Senyczko saw something in me I never saw in myself. He hired me for positions I didn't really want, taught me the business, gave me every opportunity and kept me from quitting twice.

I got to work with a lot of great people at the *LSJ*: Dave Matthews (still the best writer that department has had), James Tinney, Deb Pozega, Steve Waite, Jeff Rivers, Larry Lage, Joe Rexrode, writer's-dream editor Gerry Ahern and others who kept me from looking sillier than I did.

Without help from every coach and SID, someone else would have had to do this. Without the great John Hannah, Jack Breslin, Walter Adams, Duane Vernon, Doug Weaver, Muddy Waters, George Perles and Henry Bullough, there would have been no way to play catch-up.

But if two people made me say, "This program's

success isn't tied to the scoreboard," it was a pair of captains, No. 88 John Shinsky and No. 8 Kirk Cousins, two of the classiest, most caring individuals anyone could meet. Without their help in ways they can't imagine, you would be reading something else now.

Shinsky's humanitarian efforts with the Shinsky Orphanage in Matamoros, Mexico, have been well documented, as they should be. He's the dictionary definition of selfless. But his brave battle in overcoming neck cancer is almost as worthy of mention. It inspired me when I faced cancer of a different type and severity in December 2010.

The plans for this book, a much inferior version, were well under way when I was laid up for four weeks. One thing that was sacrificed was a trip to the Capital One Bowl in Florida, where MSU met Alabama, an angry team with arguably the nation's best coach, three-time national champ Nick Saban.

After a 49-7 pounding, it wasn't the best time for a season tribute, especially after surgery. But when I bumped into Cousins at a basketball game, he made it a point to apologize, saying, "I'm sorry we couldn't give you a better ending."

It was then that a follow-up comment changed the plan. The soon-to-be third-year captain promised that MSU had unfinished business and that 2011 would be just as good or better than 2010. Suddenly, the story of a breakthrough season morphed into a longer look.

That wouldn't have been possible without the support and patience of Sport Community Publishing owner Camron Gnass, a friend and partner from the earliest days of *Greater Lansing Sport Magazine*. His creative firm, Traction, is the best you will find. So is his wife, Lisa. And design genius Jon Eslinger is a gift to any project he touches.

No one is better with images than Matthew Mitchell of Matthew Mitchell Photography and MSU Athletic Communications. Without his artistic flair, attention to detail and awareness of what to shoot next, this book wouldn't be the same. His contributions are a comfort and a competitive challenge. Any writer would want his words to be worthy of Mitchell's pictures.

Thanks to Tom Izzo, our first and only choice to write the Foreword. It's hard to fully appreciate his commitment and dedication. Other than Hannah, no one has done more for his adopted school than Izzo has for 29 years.

Thanks to John Lewandowski and the Athletic Communications staff. They were a major help and understood the mission, even when it reversed its field. Without access to coaches, players and files, this would've been impossible.

And thanks to Head Football Coach Mark Dantonio for two illuminating, long-form interviews. His staff and players were cooperative, too, answering annoying questions. With 22 wins the past two seasons, they answered most of their critics, too.

Kudos to past historians like legendary SID Fred Stabley, longtime friend Lynn Henning, Ken Hoffman and Larry Bielat, neighbor Jack Seibold, first publisher Bruce McCristal, 17-year travel partner Steve Grinczel, Con and Steven Demos and Dr. David Young.

A special salute to Dan Kilbridge of 247Sports for his help with remembrances that explain the past and frame the present. And thanks to 247 publisher Dan Rubin for understanding why this was important.

Deep appreciation to all the media members who were there to exchange ideas, especially Grinz, Drew Sharp, George Blaha and best friend Earle Robinson. And thanks to John Braccio, Lynn Torrico and Nancy Keskeny, who helped keep me reasonably sane.

Thanks to Andy and Austin, Bing and Bemis and others who helped in countless ways, often without knowing. Everyone needs blockers and backup. We can all learn from Arthur Ray Jr. And the world needs more Muhsin Muhammads and Scott Westermans.

But no one did more for the finished product from this end than *Greater Lansing Sport Magazine* Assistant Editor Andrea Nelson. A gifted writer, she contributed in so many ways, from being my eyes and ears in Orlando to reporting to story generation.

Finally, my wife, Robin, and daughter, Alison, understood my moods and bizarre work habits. When things got tough, our son, Zach, was only a half-world away in Beijing. He didn't play football at MSU. He was a Kalamazoo College Hornet. But he bounced back from a devastating injury to excel in every way and has ... the heart of a Spartan.

TABLE OF CONTENTS

12 • FOREWORD BY TOM IZZO

15 • RED CEDAR REVIVAL

PLAYER VIGNETTES

18 • GEORGE GUERRE	40 • LORENZO WHITE
19 • DON COLEMAN	41 • BOBBY MCALLISTER
21 • HENRY BULLOUGH	42 • HARLON BARNETT
22 • EARL MORRALL	44 • JOHN LANGELOH
23 • DEAN LOOK	45 • COURTNEY HAWKINS
24 • SHERMAN LEWIS	46 • TICO DUCKETT
26 • CLINTON JONES	47 • NIGEA CARTER
27 • GENE WASHINGTON	49 • BILL BURKE
29 • GEORGE WEBSTER	50 • AMP CAMPBELL
30 • BOB APISA	52 • HERB HAYGOOD
31 • BRAD VAN PELT	53 • JOSH THORNHILL
32 • JOHN SHINSKY	55 • T.J. DUCKETT
33 • CHARLIE BAGGETT	56 • DREW STANTON
34 • KIRK GIBSON	58 • JAVON RINGER
36 • DAN BASS	59 • BLAIR WHITE
37 • CARL BANKS	63 • ERIC GORDON
39 • JIM MORRISSEY	

HEART OF A **SPARTAN**

67 • A FOOTBALL RENAISSANCE

2010

69 MARK DANTONIO A PATH WITH A PURPOSE	
JAN 02 • Almost Heaven (Unlike West Virginia)	
FEB 03 • Back To The Future	
APR 17 • Spring Forward	
APR 25 • No More Excuses	
JUNE 26 • Closer Than You Think	
JULY 19 • MSU's Pick Six	
JULY 25 • 1,000 Days	
AUG 10 • Still Unbeaten, Still Winless	
AUG 22 • Stability + Ability = Victories	
SEPT 04 • For Whom The Bell Toils	
SEPT 11 • Two Out Of Three?	

108 AARON BATES PUNT, PASS & POISE

- SEPT 19 • Hollywood Ending, Harrowing End
- SEPT 20 • You've Gotta Have Heart
- SEPT 25 • Let The Real Fun Begin
- OCT 02 • Proof Is In The Pounding
- OCT 09 • State-Meant Game

132 EDWIN BAKER ROCK READY TO ROLL

- OCT 16 • Se-Heaven-And-0
- OCT 23 • Eight Isn't Enough
- OCT 30 • Jekyll And Hydes
- NOV 07 • Daylight Savoring Time
- NOV 13 • There For The Taking
- NOV 20 • Second Chances ... First Place
- NOV 27 • Eleven Is Heaven

168 GREG JONES "ACTION" ATTRACTION

- DEC 11 • A Little Credit . Please

2011

- JAN 01 • Tide Rolls, Score Snowballs
- APR 16 • Beware Of False Starts
- APR 30 • Progress Comes Before The Fall
- JUNE 11 • One Title, No Entitlement

180 KESHAWN MARTIN "WHO'S HE?" A BIG KEY

- JUNE 18 • Looks A Little Bit Like ...
- JULY 30 • Quite The Experience
- AUG 03 • Larger Than Life
- AUG 13 • Three Is A Magic Number

198 B.J. CUNNINGHAM QUITE THE CATCH

- AUG 20 • Kool-Aid? Just A Hot Team
- SEPT 03 • Ray Of Hope

210 JOEL FOREMAN ALWAYS PROTECTING

- SEPT 10 • On Second Thought
- SEPT 17 • Maximum Exposure
- SEPT 24 • Chipping Away
- OCT 01 • Sack You Very Much
- OCT 15 • Four-Ever Yours

230 JEREL WORTHY WORTH EVERY SECOND

- OCT 22 • Hail, Yes!

240 KEITH NICHOL HAPPY HOMECOMING

- OCT 29 • "O" No!
- NOV 05 • T-Robbery ... T-Riffic
- NOV 12 • A Weekend Salute
- NOV 19 • Senior Moments
- NOV 26 • The Biggest 10
- DEC 03 • So Close ... All Class

262 KIRK COUSINS PERFECT PROGRESSION

- DEC 25 • ... And A Happy New Year

2012

- JAN 01 • On Your Mark ...
- JAN 02 • Bowled Over

276 WILLIAM GHOLSTON WHERE THERE'S A WILL

- JAN 05 • Program Wins

284 LE'VEON BELL A NICE RING TO IT

Spartan players Deon Curry (left) and Javon Ringer (right) douse Honorary Head Coach Tom Izzo after his team's last-second win in the 2008 Green and White Game, one of Izzo's favorite days in his 29 seasons at Michigan State

FOREWORD

BY TOM IZZO

I'VE SEEN THE HEART OF A SPARTAN. More than that, I've lived it.

It started when I first moved down here from the U.P. in 1983. I was a basketball coach, but my friends were all football guys. I lived with Bill Rademacher, the receivers coach. I knew Larry Bielat, the quarterbacks coach. I used to sit in the film room with Buck Nystrom, the best offensive line coach in the business, and pick his brain. I'd say, "Why would you do that on third-and-7 from the right hash?" And I used to get invited to George Perles' house. I loved every second of it.

There was just something about Michigan State, especially on football Saturdays. I used to come to campus and go for my jog at 7 a.m., just to go past all the tailgates. It was what a big-time environment should be. It was the absolute best.

Growing up in Iron Mountain, I always played basketball. My aunt and uncle had a court, and I'd shovel it off and play when it was 10 degrees. But I really loved football. Everything was Vince Lombardi and the Green Bay Packers. I had the plastic helmet and played an awful lot. I was on our first undefeated JV team as a freshman, and our varsity teams were very good, as you'd expect with Steve Mariucci at quarterback. My senior year was the year before the playoffs started, but I had football offers from St. Norbert's College and Michigan Tech. Northern Michigan wanted me as a walk-on, and I got letters from Central Michigan when Herb Deromedi was the coach. I always liked football more.

Coming to Michigan State to coach was perfect that way. I used to say the only place I'd take another coaching job was Wisconsin-Green Bay. Even when I was thinking of coaching in Cleveland, I knew I'd miss the folderol of football Saturdays. Then, a good friend, Pat Shurmur, got the Browns job. But it's still not the same as being on a Big Ten campus. There's just something about those seven weekends.

Magic Johnson once said a part of him wanted to buy an RV, travel around the country and go to all the football games. I'm the same way. I love the tailgating and the atmosphere. I don't like early games quite as much, but I'll come back and watch the other games until midnight. When it's a later game, I'll sit on the deck at my office in the Berkowitz Center and watch all the people. Nothing beats a football Saturday. I wish it would start on Thursday.

One of my greatest moments at Michigan State was a football game. When we beat Indiana in 1987 to go to the Rose Bowl, Matt Steigenga, Mike Peplowski and Mark Montgomery were visiting that weekend. After the game, they were running on the field, just having a great time. Mike and Mark committed in the parking lot after the game, and Matt committed later. They were the first big class we landed. And with Steve Smith, the first guy I recruited, they helped us win 28 games and a Big Ten title two-and-a-half years later. I still think that football game had a lot to do with it.

But football helps all of us. It helps everyone at this university. People thought it was easy for me to say that when we were up and football was down. Now that football is up and we've been a hair down, I don't feel a bit different. Football will always be the No. 1 program and the key to the whole athletic department.

If every program here won a national championship, it wouldn't do as much as if football won another one. The six Final Fours we've reached have given us something, but it's a lot tougher to survive without good football. I've told a lot of assistants when they've left here for other jobs, "Your first stop should be to see the head football coach." A couple of guys have gone to schools that didn't have football. I really felt sorry for them.

I don't just talk that way. I believe it. I got along great with George when he was here. He took me under his wing in a lot of ways. Nick Saban and I were assistants here together and became very close friends. And I love seeing the success Mark Dantonio has had. There's not even an inkling of jealousy. I'm so happy for all that he has done. He's more than a neighbor. He's someone I see and talk to all the time.

We've recruited a few players together. And we make a pretty good team that way. We like the same kinds of kids, quality people who want to be here and be the best they can be.

When we were looking for a new coach in 2006, I was part of that committee and made the trip to Cincinnati to interview Mark. I'd encouraged Mark Hollis to wait till we could talk to him, and that legitimately couldn't happen till after his team's last game, one of the classiest things I've ever seen a coach do. It was hard on everybody. We had to pick somebody and had to get moving, but I'm glad we waited and got the right guy.

Another coach can be the best friend you have when you're going through rough times, which all of us do. During the football season, Mark and I talk once or twice a week, and he calls or texts me before every basketball game. We don't need to spend a lot of time together. There isn't that much time to spend. But whenever there's a critical decision, he's a guy I feel very comfortable talking with and sharing opinions. We've hashed things out both ways.

Mark has the heart of a Spartan. When he asked me to speak to the football team, he said, "We don't have to bring anyone in here to speak. We've got a championship-caliber program right across Munn Field." And on the tape I did for him before the Big Ten Championship Game, I said our basketball team had to do as well as football has the last two years.

Mark and I are a lot more alike in some ways than people know. It's hard for another coach to

know everything about another program. But Mark doesn't make many quick decisions. He has discipline in his program, and he sticks up for players till it's impossible to do that. He knows they're not perfect and believes in second and sometimes third chances. In the end he also holds them accountable.

I've always said the greatest joy I get from coaching is when former players come back. Mark has done a great job of bringing them back, and Henry Bullough has done that with the Players Association, too. It's hard to have big reunions in football, but Mark has really embraced the past. Just with the honorary captains, he has had a lot of people back.

Mark has gone through a lot since he has been here, building a program, having the heart attack and putting Michigan State in position to be successful for a long time. When people go through tough times, you see a different side of them. He's a religious guy who really believes there's a right way to do things.

After the heart attack, I was in there to see him one day when he was talking to Don Treadwell, who was taking over till he got back. Mark told me how lucky he was to have such a good staff. He had no problem handing the reins over and said, "You know what to do, Tread." I knew a little bit about that from when Jud had his heart attack in '86. But I saw a guy who could deal with tough times, the same guy I saw when I flew down for his dad's funeral.

Everything isn't always smooth when you're winning , either. When Kirk Cousins went through some struggles and was getting criticism, Mark was always there for him. Sometimes it takes an iron fist and a mom's hug. Mark can deliver both of them, and that can be really hard to do. You know you need a guy to play better to win, but a coach has to stick up for his guy, too.

Though they're very different in some ways, Cousins is a little like Mateen Cleaves was for me. Mateen was at practice the week we played Michigan the second time. He knew it was Michigan Week and said, "Whatever it takes, I'm stopping by." I can see Cousins doing the same thing, though he'll have a pro football schedule to contend with.

Mateen was the guy who broke Jud's rule about not being able to be a great leader when you're struggling with your own game. He could have a bad game personally and still impact everyone else. He made winning the ultimate priority, and very few guys do that. It didn't matter if he scored two, four, 22 or 24 points. If we won, he was never anything but happy.

I remember during Mark's first year, he asked me if I thought Mateen would come and talk to the football team. I said, "Do I think that? I know that! Two-hundred percent. He'd jog here." He recruited for everybody. He even recruited a hockey player one time.

Now, I've had another leader with a lot of those traits in Draymond Green. "Day-Day" cares. He's a lot like Cousins that way, too. It's about more than just them. They're all about the program. They're Spartans. And they're not the first guys to do that.

There are other guys who've helped build this place.

In basketball I still see it with a guy who's bigger than big. I can go recruiting anywhere in the country and bring up Magic Johnson. He could've left here after his freshman year, but Jud always says he wouldn't have left after his sophomore year if it'd been anywhere else but the Lakers. He loved being on campus that much. And last year when he came back for a few days, what does Earvin do? He comes to practice with his dad, watches us for two hours, then talks to every guy.

I hope some day I can be as good to this place as those guys still are – the Mateens and Earvins and Steve Smiths. Steve is unbelievable, too. His value to this university can never be judged monetarily. When his mother died, we were in Minnesota. I asked Jud if I could fly back for the funeral. Steve's mother was so good to me.

The best thing she did was give us Steve, another blue-collar guy. And it's a blue-collar world. All the guys who've made the program, who've made the football program and who've made Michigan State University have had that in common. They've had the heart of a Spartan.

That's one of the reasons I'm excited about this book. I know a little more than most people about how special the last two seasons have been. And I've known Jack Ebling since I got here in 1983. He's a good friend. We've shared a lot of things, and nobody knows more about Spartan athletics. I know he'll do a great job of telling a great story.

But part of being a Spartan is staying humble. I was here when no one wanted my autograph. I remember when we were recruiting Drew Naymick, Bill Raftery from CBS was here for the weekend and came with me to Muskegon to see a game. I signed one guy's ticket stub and must've signed a couple of hundred. Bill was really impressed. When the game ended, they pushed the bleachers back, and there must've been 50 of them laying on the floor. I said, "Bill, see how important I am?"

The best people don't big-time anyone and don't even think they're big-time. That's how this place is. That's how it was built. And that's why I'm still here.

RED CEDAR REVIVAL

HISTORY HELPS SPARTANS WRITE NEW STORY

HEART OF A **SPARTAN**

MSC and MSU President John Hannah, always on the move

LONG BEFORE Mark Dantonio was born, the seeds of Michigan State football success were sown.

From M.A.C. to MSC to MSU, from Aggies to Spartans, from Green and White to Black and Gold then back to "the only colors" again, the story began in the 19th century.

It started before the first official game in 1896 and stretched for more than 110 years before Dantonio was hired late in 2006 – a rollercoaster ride wilder than any at Cedar Point.

To understand the significance of what just happened the past two seasons, it helps to know why that is so special and who and what made it all possible.

The following historical narrative, Red Cedar Revival, explains the trials and triumphs for a program that began without a head coach, grew with Hall of Fame leadership and bounced back with a Big Ten Coach of the Year.

It also highlights the memories and achievements of some of the Spartans' best players and leaders, with 33 vignettes covering the past 65 seasons.

From Guerre to Gordon, we visit with some of the program's greats to learn why they came to East Lansing and what they will always treasure.

CHERISH THE MEMORIES.

HISTORY HELPS SPARTANS WRITE NEW STORY

IT'S TOUGH TO CITE one signature moment in Michigan State's recent athletic renaissance. When a football team wins 22 games and two championships in two years, there are bound to be plenty of choices. But let's start with 12 of them — in honor of the Big Ten:

Back-to-back 11-win seasons, the first in school history.

· · ·

The program's first conference title in two decades.

· · ·

A 14-2 league mark and the first Legends Division crown.

· · ·

Four straight victories and new respect in a bitter rivalry.

· · ·

The first win over the league's top program in 13 years.

· · ·

A payback in a place where it hadn't won in 22 seasons.

· · ·

A berth in the inaugural Big Ten Championship Game.

· · ·

Five consecutive bowl appearances for the first time.

· · ·

A triple-overtime triumph for its first bowl win in a decade.

· · ·

A top-10 finish in a major poll for the first time in 12 years.

· · ·

"Little Giants" and "Rocket" and amazing walk-off wins.

· · ·

Career passing and receiving marks and dominating defense.

But before we revisit the glory against Notre Dame, Wisconsin, Michigan and Penn State in 2010 and Ohio State, Michigan, Wisconsin, Iowa and Georgia a year later, we have to understand why those nine games are so meaningful.

We need to understand where the Spartans had been in good years and bad, as a juggernaut and a joke, before we can appreciate what just transpired, when two inspired teams pulled together and raised the bar for a proud program.

The best way to categorize it is to think of four periods:

EXPLORATION
163-106-19 in 37 seasons under 12 head coaches from 1896-1932.

EXCELLENCE
206-78-16 in 34 years and 33 seasons under three coaches from 1933-66.

EXTREMES
216-224-9 in 40 years under 10 coaches from 1967-2006.

EXCITEMENT
44-22 in the first five seasons under Mark Dantonio's leadership.

Let's start at the beginning. The first official game was a 10-0 win for Michigan Agricultural College over Lansing High School on September 26, 1896, at Eltom Park. That was the only victory in a 1-2-1 season with no acknowledged coach and little resemblance to anything that followed.

More than four decades earlier, the Agricultural College of the state of Michigan was founded on February 12, 1855, with a faculty and staff of nine and a total annual payroll of $5,000. It became State Agricultural College six years later and the nation's first land-grant institution under the Morrill Act of 1862, signed on July 2 by President Abraham Lincoln.

Even then, there was a conflict with the University of Michigan. According to historian and lifelong Spartan J. Bruce McCristal in his definitive work, *The Spirit of Michigan State*, there were six legislative attempts to close the college and move all agricultural education to Ann Arbor between 1859-69. The first effort was defeated, 51-21.

Finally, the Michigan Regents realized that the plan to consolidate would "subject them to pressure from a group of rural leaders." Little did they realize that 150 years later they would be subjected to intense pressure from blitzing linebackers.

Actually, there was football on the East Lansing campus as early as 1884. A photo in the school yearbook proves that. And there is considerable evidence that a matchup with Albion that fall was the first collegiate game in the state. But that was when it was a club sport.

Fast-forward 12 years. Utah had just become the 45th state. Trouble was brewing in the Philippines, the precursor to the Spanish-American War. And at a little-known college in East Lansing, a course of study for women was introduced: home economics, natural sciences and liberal arts.

Against that backdrop, the first

1946-48

GEORGE GUERRE

No. 45 HALFBACK

On playing for Charlie Bachman and Biggie Munn after World War II:

"When I came back from Italy and North Africa, I'd already spent one year at Michigan. I was 5-foot-5-1/2, 157 pounds. After talking with Johnny Pingel, Charlie's backfield coach, I came to Michigan State. But John Hannah wanted to get into the Big Ten in the worst way and thought he needed a different coach. It was a surprise to all the players, and a few left. I think a lot of Biggie. He was the kind of coach you'd break a leg for. And I did that in '47 on a touchdown vs. Kentucky. Biggie had been at Michigan, too, as an assistant to Crisler. He knew Fritz would do everything in his power to humiliate him. When the sewage backed up into the visitors' locker room there in '47, we had to stand on benches to get dressed."

official game was played. The first game story in the *Lansing Republican*, later to become the *Lansing State Journal*, forgot to include the final score. But we know the game started at 4 p.m., setting the stage for all late-afternoon kickoffs. And from a more in-depth story in the *M.A.C. Record* the following week, we know that George Wells of Ithaca scored the school's first touchdown — worth four points — and a history of shutouts was born.

The first loss came in the Aggies' second game, a 24-0 drubbing by Kalamazoo three weeks later. After a tie and a loss to Olivet, it was time to regroup for 1897 and to name a coach. Henry Keep, an engineering student, earned that distinction and went 8-5-1 the next two years. But his 1898 team lost back-to-back games to Michigan and Notre Dame by a combined score of 82-0. Even then, that couldn't be tolerated.

Thus, Charles Bemies, a Presbyterian minister and the school's first "Professor of Physical Culture," took over in 1899 and was 3-7-1 in two seasons. But according to Fred Stabley's book, *The Spartans*, a young alumnus named L. Whitney Watkins triggered a facilities race in 1900 that continues to this day. Watkins, a member of the State Board of Agriculture, proposed the purchase of 13 acres of land south of the Red Cedar River, which soon became Old College Field.

When George Denman's teams were 7-9-1 in 2001-02, including a 119-0 loss to Fielding Yost's point-a-minute Michigan machine, President Jonathan Snyder had seen about enough. When he walked over to encourage the team after a tough first half in another game, he found more than a dozen players sitting a circle, passing around a bottle of Duffy's Malt Liquor. The pep talk was cancelled. A coaching search was under way.

Enter Chester Brewer, a four-sport letterman at Wisconsin and

1949-51

DON COLEMAN

No. 78 Tackle

On overcoming adversity and being a Hall of Famer on and off the field:

"Bob Reynolds, the broadcaster, helped me get from Flint to Michigan State. If not, I would've had a music career in some fashion or an opportunity in an auto factory. At 175 pounds, I was still able to excel as a lineman under Biggie and Duffy. I was also able to earn three degrees there and have a long career in administration. I remember taking a physical beating from a Penn State player with a cast on his arm. My nose needed eight stitches. I played against guys who hollered, 'You black so-and-so!' But Biggie always believed you kept your mouth shut and did your talking with your play. And I remember Bear Bryant coming up and saying, 'You could've played for me any time.' I always wanted to set an example."

a recognized defensive genius. His teams were 54-10-6 in eight seasons from 1903-10, including a scoreless tie with the mighty Wolverines in 1908 and a 17-0 win over the Fighting Irish two years later. Counting two ill-advised returns in 1917 and '19, his defenses posted 49 shutouts in 88 games.

"No man did more to persuade the faculty, the Board, and the older alumni that organized athletics could be compatible with higher education," Madison Kuhn wrote in *Michigan State — The First 100 Years*.

After Brewer's first season, a 6-1-1 breakthrough, the school dropped out of the Michigan Intercollegiate Athletic Association and was an independent in football for the next 49 seasons. But the first big game was clearly the tie with Michigan in East Lansing. Before an estimated crowd of 6,000, the improbable became reality. A headline read "Farmers Hold Yost's Eleven." And the ROTC band played a new tune, "Rub It Into Michigan."

Two years later, the Aggies lost 6-3 in Ann Arbor in the series' first example of — take your choice — home cooking, referee intimidation or sour grapes. According to Stabley's must-read pigskin history, Leon "Bubbles" Hill kicked a field goal for a 3-0 lead, then returned a punt 70 yards for an apparent score. That was when Yost raced onto the field and convinced the officials that they had missed a holding call. The penalty kept Michigan alive. And after the game, the Wolverine who was supposedly held said he hadn't been within 15 yards of the play.

But the real fun came in the second half when Hill correctly diagnosed a fake field goal on a then-illegal direct pass from the quarterback to the fullback. Hill made the hit well short of the goal line, then delivered a more satisfying sock to the jaw of the official who ruled otherwise and gave the hosts the game's only touchdown.

"I nailed this Magnuson on the 2-yard-line and had him boxed in," Hill was quoted as saying. "He couldn't go one way or the other. Then, this official came tearing over there, picked up the ball and said, 'Touchdown for Michigan.'

"'What do you mean, touchdown?' I asked.

"'You pushed it back,' the umpire said, and I hauled off and kissed him one right on the chin. And I never got put out of the game."

That blow created an incredible buzz for Notre Dame's visit two weeks later — if not the equivalent of the "Game of The Century" hubbub 56 years later, certainly a new phenomenon. Special box seats were installed at the princely price of $1.50. And though the Irish left with an $800 guarantee, $300 more than the Aggies made, the best team in the West for a second straight year also left with a whippin'.

"We were simply outclassed," Notre Dame coach Shorty Longman said of the 17-point loss. "M.A.C. is vastly underrated. There is no team in the West that can defeat the Farmers on their own field. We were licked, and the sting of defeat is allayed by the fact that we lost to such a sportsman-like bunch."

As Stabley recollected, that was just after the Aggies nearly became the Bears or the Bruins — or even the Cubs. A brown bear cub, captured by graduate foresters and seniors that summer in Montana, made his new home in a cage on campus. Montie, or "Brewer's Bruin" as he become known, was the school's first mascot. Then, just as suddenly, he disappeared. Bear-napped? Tired of football? We'll never know.

When Brewer stepped down in 1911, there were big shoes to fill. No one could have filled them better than John Macklin, a 6-foot-5, 250-pound giant who had starred at Pennsylvania. He was bigger than any player the program had dressed or faced in its 20 seasons. His M.A.C. mark of 29-5 was an .853 success rate, the best in school history.

A poem that ran in *The State Journal* before the 1913 game at Michigan suggested that Macklin was really 6-7, 275. But it was clear that he was the third choice for the job. Hugo Bezdek, a star under Amos Alonzo Stagg at Chicago, was hired but promptly disappeared like Montie the bear. He later became a successful coach at Penn State. And Wabash College coach Jesse Harper said he would come to East Lansing for $2,200 a year, more than Macklin had made. When the State Board of Agriculture said no, Harper went to Notre Dame and helped popularize the forward pass. More on that momentarily.

First came Macklin's first big victory, a 35-20 season-ender at Ohio State in 1912. The following year, with just 15 players, he took the team to training camp at Pine Lake, now known as Lake Lansing, and built a bond that was breathtaking to behold. M.A.C. finished 7-0 and outscored its opponents 181-28, including back-to-back road wins over Michigan and Wisconsin.

The week of the game in Ann Arbor, Macklin scrimmaged his team on Tuesday, Wednesday and Thursday, installed 12 electric lights for extra evening practices on Old College Field and had uniformed ROTC members stand guard to keep everyone else north of the Red Cedar River, for fear of spying. On October 13, 1913, giving up 25 pounds per man up front, the Aggies stood their ground like Spartans in one of the greatest upsets in college football history.

When George Gauthier completed an unheard-of seven throws for 100 yards, newspaper accounts referred to M.A.C.'s "basketball tactics" and said the win was "a demonstration that Yost's men are unable to cope with a team that uses the forward pass as a primary offensive weapon." It also proved that bright beats might, even when a star like end and halfback Blake Miller is hospitalized and partially paralyzed for a brief period.

Tackles Gideon Smith, the school's first black player, and Hugh Blacklock were heroic in the five-point win. Carp Julian and Hewitt Miller, Blake's brother, scored touchdowns. And M.A.C.'s ROTC Cadet Band marched through the streets of Ann Arbor playing "The Victors" because the Aggies didn't have a song of their own. Nearly a century later, some suggest that confusion has led Wolverines to believe they have never lost in the series.

Back in Downtown Lansing that night, there was free admission to the Bijou Theatre, a snake dance in

1952-54
HENRY BULLOUGH
No. 67 Guard

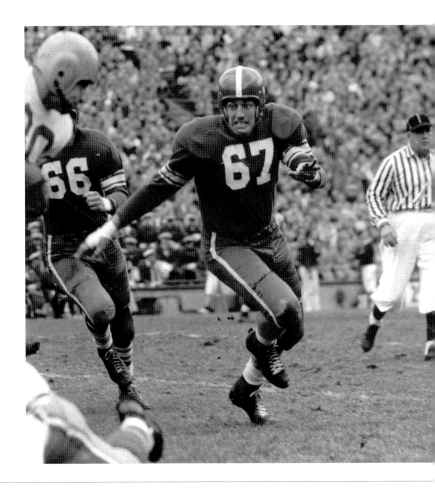

On his days as a player in the early '50s and a coach in the mid-'60s:

"When we were winning 28 straight under Biggie, winning was nothing. The only question we asked was: 'Where's the party tonight?' We beat Notre Dame and Michigan every year. We beat Notre Dame 35-0 and had Woody Hayes decorating his locker room in green-and-white. We finally lost to Purdue 6-0 when they called a late clip on Tommy Yewcic. LeRoy Bolden had scored on a return and was running off the field when the flag came out. But our best defenses were in '65-66. We were way up on Penn State with the subs in the game in '66 when the players all said, "Let's get the shutout!" I put the first team back in until Duffy pulled them out again. We wound up winning 42-8 – Joe Paterno's first loss."

front of the Capitol and a bonfire – planned and without altercations or couches. Classes were cancelled on Monday. And the big concern heading into an equally tough challenge against the unbeaten Badgers was supposed to be "a bad case of conceit," according to a Detroit paper. Instead, the result was exactly the same.

In the spring of 1915, yellmaster (cheerleader) Francis Irving Lankey composed the music for what we now know as the "MSU Fight Song," inspired by the wins over Michigan and Wisconsin. Classmate Arthur L. Sayles contributed most of the original lyrics:

On the banks of the Red Cedar,
There's a school that's
known to all.
Its specialty is farming,
And those farmers play football.
Aggie teams are never beaten,
All through the game
they'll fight.
Fight for the only colors,
Green and White.
Smash right through
that line of blue,
Watch the points keep growing.
Aggie teams are bound to win,
They're fighting with a vim!

Rah! Rah! Rah!
Michigan is weakening,
We're going to win this game.
Fight! Fight! Rah! Team, Fight!
Victory for M.A.C.

When the Aggies returned to Ann Arbor in 1915, most writers and fans expected a payback of ridiculous proportions. What they got was another shocker, a shutout and blowout in a battle of unbeatens. Fullback Jerry DaPrato, the school's first major-team All-American, scored every point on three TDs, three extra points and a

RED CEDAR REVIVAL

1953-55

EARL MORRALL

No. 21 QUARTERBACK

On a career that made him a fourth-place Heisman Trophy finisher:

"It came down to Michigan State and Michigan for me. I took a look at Notre Dame, too. Jim Morse and I lived five houses apart. But after meeting the coaches – Biggie, Duffy and Sonny Grandelius – I felt more comfortable in East Lansing. We didn't throw that much. I think I threw 68 times my senior year. Now, they throw 60 times in one game. I punted almost as often as I passed. But we went to the Rose Bowl twice and beat UCLA both times. My senior year, it took Dave Kaiser's field goal. He could've backed up another 10 yards. It still would've been good. Then, I was the No. 1 pick of the 49ers and signed for $30,000. I got to play another 21 years."

field goal. And his 153 yards from scrimmage didn't include several big gains nullified by penalties.

"What was the score?" Eddie Batchelor wrote in the *Detroit Times*. "Just coming to that. It read 24 to 0 on the official blackboard, and the men who possessed the two-dozen points were the Aggies. Michigan claimed ownership of the zero, and if there had been any numeral lower than that to hang up on the scoreboard, they would have been forced to display it to indicate the Wolverines' accomplishments."

Less than five months later, the schools went at again with similar results. This time, it was a game of survival for an M.A.C. academic department following a fire that roared through the Engineering Building in 1916. As McCristal wrote: "University of Michigan advocates pounced on the crisis as an opportunity to move all engineering education to Ann Arbor. They argued it would be less expensive to enlarge the engineering facilities there than to rebuild in East Lansing."

Ransom E. Olds came to the rescue with the first substantial gift to the college, a whopping $100,000. But there was nothing he could do over the next 15 seasons to keep the fire burning in the football program. Macklin's last game in a 5-1 farewell was a 68-6 win over Marquette. But when his hand-picked successor, Frank Sommers, went 4-2-1 in 1916, the decision was made to try again. And new President Frank Kedzie knew just the man to hire. His name was Knute Rockne.

At that point in 1917, Rockne was best known as the end who had caught Gus Dorais' revolutionary forward passes for Notre Dame four years earlier. But the Aggies saw the Irish assistant as an up-and-comer and almost had his commitment to come to East Lansing. Instead, Harper, the coach M.A.C. had tried

1957-59

DEAN LOOK

No. 24 Halfback/Quarterback

On deciding to stay close to home and becoming an All-American:

"We used to take the bus from Lansing to East Lansing when we were 10. We'd stand around Macklin Stadium and look sad, waiting for someone to give us a ticket. Or four of us would charge the gate. Actually, I almost went to Michigan. But I was sitting behind the bench at the Ohio State game in '55 when Hopalong Cassady got loose on a punt return. I stood up and yelled 'Go, Hoppy, go!' I sat back down and said, 'I can't possibly go here.' I went to Duffy's house the next day and committed. Three years later, I had a 92-yard runback against Michigan. I went from one side of the field to the other four times. I didn't become a quarterback till I was a senior."

to hire in 1911, convinced Rockne to stay in South Bend and take over the program the following year.

That brought Brewer back in a disastrous rescue attempt in 1917. The Aggies went 0-9 in the worst performance in school history, never posting more than seven points and being outscored 179-23. When M.A.C. turned to Gauthier, its former quarterback and the first alumnus to serve as head coach, the record improved to 4-3, including one of the most astounding, mysterious games ever played.

A 13-7 Homecoming triumph over Notre Dame in 1918 was Rockne's first loss and the only defeat in his first three seasons. We know that legendary halfback George Gipp had a TD for the Irish in a return to his home state. But the story in *The State Journal* only said, "The game was played in a sea of mud, but Michigan State won without flukes or horseshoes." Perhaps the mud explained why no one was ever identified as scoring the winning TD. If any of your ancestors did, this might be the time to identify him.

Gauthier immediately moved on to Ohio Wesleyan, where he served as head coach and athletic director for 34 years. So Brewer had to take over again, going 4-4-1 in 1919. And the decade that followed was important for five reasons: Rockne's second flirtation with the Aggies, the arrival of the most important figure in school history, a stadium dedication, another renaming of the institution and the choice of a new nickname.

"Things might have been so different in football at Michigan State," *Detroit Times* columnist George Van wrote in 1957. "They might have been known as the Fighting Farmers … But there was a time back in 1921 when Knute Rockne signed a contract to coach State, then known as the Aggies.

RED CEDAR REVIVAL

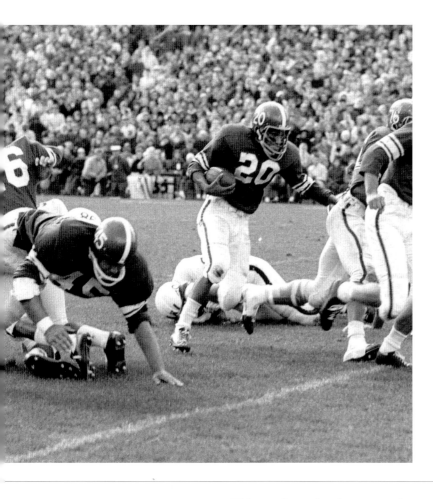

1961-63

SHERMAN LEWIS

No. 20 HALFBACK

On seizing his opportunities en route to a third-place Heisman finish:

"Being from Louisville, I wasn't recruited by many big schools. I couldn't play from Kentucky south. And I weighed 152 on a good day, 148 on a bad one. I'd watched Michigan State on TV and knew African-Americans were playing. When I got there, Dean Look was my freshman coach. They were a little scared to even put me in drills. But I never missed a game there. Running track helped me break big plays. We won a lot but never made the Rose Bowl. We'd have gone but lost to Illinois in '63 after the Kennedy assassination. We had to play our third-string quarterback and had six or seven turnovers. Against Dick Butkus and those guys, you couldn't have one."

"It's rather shocking to the Rockne tradition to know that the ambitious young Norwegian was still shopping around for bigger dough after those first few years coaching at Notre Dame. The Rock decided to stay in South Bend, and the Fighting Irish legend was on its way."

That signed contract remained in the desk drawer of business manager Lyman Frimodig for more than three decades. It called for Rockne to get $4,500 in 1921 and a $500 raise in each of the next two years. But instead of having the coach with the highest winning percentage in history, M.A.C./ MSC had five coaches in a 10-year span and a record in the not-so-Roaring '20s of 36-45-4.

George "Potsy" Clark was 4-6 in 1920 before moving on and leading the Detroit Lions to an NFL title 15 years later. Albert Barron, a fall-back when the Rockne deal fell apart, was 6-10-2 in 1921-22. Ralph Young, better known as the school's athletic director for 32 years, went 18-22-1 from 1923-27. Lansing native and Wolverine All-American Harry Kipke was 3-4-1 in 1928 before returning to Ann Arbor. And "Sleepy Jim" Crowley began with a 5-3 mark in East Lansing.

At the start of the decade, it dawned on more than a few people that part of the problem was an antiquated facility. Old College Field had seats for 6,000, not nearly enough to schedule quality teams or convince many of the state's best high school players to see MSC as an acceptable option. And unless that changed, the idea of ever being asked to join what was then called the Western Conference was a ridiculous notion.

Luckily, Michigan Gov. A.J. Groesbeck understood and said, "It is absolutely necessary to provide a stadium on the campus, and I think a way can be found to make the general desire for one a real accomplishment within a comparatively short time."

Groesbeck urged the state to lend the school enough money to build a 14,000-seat concrete facility south of the Red Cedar, precisely where it stands today, several expansions later. When the 1923 Legislature approved a $160,000 loan for just that purpose, the project was completed in near-record time, before a 21-6 win over Lake Forest in the home opener.

When the Legislature acted on a broader issue and approved a name change to Michigan State College of Agriculture and Applied Science on May 15, 1925, it was time to retire the Aggies moniker. In a naming contest, the Michigan Staters was the popular choice, though it sounded more like a choral group. For *The State Journal's* Sports Editor George Alderton, the most influential media member in school history, that decision was unacceptable.

Alderton and Dale Stafford of the *Capital News* dug through the garbage, found all the rejected entries and settled on a name submitted by former M.A.C. athlete Perry J. Fremont: "Spartans." It was first used on MSC's first Southern tour in 1926 and was misspelled initially as "Spartons". When that error was corrected and *The State News* began using the term, it stuck as a distinctive brand.

"When the young men of ancient Sparta went off to war, they were told to come home with their shield on high or come home carried on it," Alderton was quoted as saying in *The Spirit of Michigan State*.

Amazingly, Vermont Congressman Justin Morrill had promised back in 1858 that the Morrill Act creating land-grant colleges "would found schools like those in Michigan, schools like those of ancient Sparta whose graduates would know how to sustain American institutions with American vigor."

Enter John Alfred Hannah, a Grand Rapids native and an entrepreneur from the age of 6. Entrusted with the family's poultry flock, he began attending shows around the state almost immediately and traveling alone by train to build a successful chicken business by the time he was 13.

Hannah was so exceptional that after two years of study at Grand Rapids Junior College, he was admitted to the University of Michigan Law School in 1921. An accelerated academic plan would have left him with a prestigious law degree after just five years of higher education.

But that winter, E.C. Foreman, the head of the poultry department at M.A.C., paid a visit to Hannah in Ann Arbor and changed the face of both schools forever. His pitch? If Hannah would transfer and earn a degree in agriculture, he would be guaranteed a job at the princely salary of $2,500 a year.

If Earvin Johnson's recruitment as a basketball prospect was crucial 55 years later, Hannah's decision concerning the same two schools was the most important moment the institutions have shared. Without that move to East Lansing, Pittsburgh probably would have become a member of the Big Ten.

Graduating in just one year, Hannah began his career as an extension poultryman in June 1923. During a leave of absence 11 years later, he accepted an offer from Michigan State College President Robert Shaw to meet in Chicago, the site of one of the first national high school all-star football games.

When Shaw offered Hannah an annual salary of $4,200, it was much less than he was making with the National Recovery Administration in Kansas City and roughly one-fifth of a pending offer from a poultry packing company in Chicago.

The decision would have been a no-brainer for most people. Hannah was no exception — just exceptional in every way, as his rationale in *A Memoir* explains.

"I had already concluded that there were things more important to me than making money, and I had about made up my mind that I would rather return to a university — particularly to Michigan State College — than do anything else," he wrote in 1980. "It seemed to me that when a person gets old and looks back over his life, what is important is not prestige or the amount of money in the bank, but rather whether or not he feels his life has been useful."

As Secretary of the Board of Agriculture, Hannah was more than useful. He was as close to irreplaceable in Shaw's eyes as anyone could be. Taking on additional duties, Hannah was able to get a new Farm Lane bridge built and a Macklin Stadium

RED CEDAR REVIVAL

1964-66

CLINTON JONES

No. 26 HALFBACK

On a brotherhood with teams that made history on and off the field:

"None of us had any idea what this was about 45 years ago. We came together and did something that was sustainable. We had one defeat in the Rose Bowl and a tie in the 'Game of the Century.' But we opened the modern era of NCAA football. The schools in the South were all segregated. Michigan State University broke the mold of separatism and brought together different cultures. We were all about each other. The timing was right. And the feeling is stronger today than it was then. We are a band of brothers. Nothing changes the relationships we had with each other. The energy is very infectious. We're different bodies with one mind and one heart."

expansion completed through the Work Progress Administration as the U.S. emerged from the Great Depression.

He also realized that MSC had to evolve from an A&M-type school to a traditional institution of higher learning to reach its vast potential. One of Hannah's ideas was a different way of funding dormitory construction that led to the largest on-campus housing system in the world when the G.I. Bill created a new pool of students.

Hannah made things happen instead of asking, "What happened?" And in the process of acquiring more than 7,000 acres of new land for a massive campus, he landed a new job. On July 1, 1941, Hannah took over as MSC's president, succeeding Shaw and serving brilliantly in that role for 28 years.

By the time he left to head the U.S. Agency for International Development in 1969, enrollment had risen from about 6,000 to 44,000, and a small, sleepy, land-grant college had become a huge, world-respected Big Ten university.

Hannah is Michigan State's mastermind, as much as anyone ever could be. His green-print for growth is today's campus map. And without his leadership, Spartan teams likely would be playing in the Mid-American Conference this season.

Besides being one of the most important educators of the 20th century, he served in a myriad of national and international leadership positions under U.S. presidents Harry Truman, Dwight Eisenhower, John Kennedy, Lyndon Johnson and Richard Nixon in agriculture, education, international development, defense and civil rights.

Hannah also loved athletics — ironically, a passion that began in 1921 when he enrolled at Michigan

1961-63
GENE WASHINGTON
NO. 84 SPLIT END

On beating his rivals and MSU's role in integrating college football:

"We had four of the first eight picks in the '67 NFL Draft. Three of us are on the stadium wall as Hall of Famers. Now, we have to get Clinton up there. We ran track together, too. And I never lost a race to a Michigan or Notre Dame guy in my entire career. None of that would've happened without Bubba and Duffy. I knew Bubba in Texas. He told Duffy he should take me. I'd been denied admission at Texas and Houston. Those were the days of segregated water fountains. So I'm certain my life would've been totally different if I'd had to go to an all-black school. I didn't want that to happen. Right away when I got there, he said, 'I want you to call me Duffy.' That meant a lot. Before, everything had been 'Mister' and 'Sir'."

and became friends with several athletes. He hadn't participated in high school sports. That would have been impossible with his farm obligations, even if he hadn't graduated at age 16. So he channeled his competitive instincts into other areas and won far more often than he lost.

If recruiting was supposedly illegal in the Big Ten in those days — wink, wink — it's a good thing MSC wasn't a member of the conference in the 1930s. Hannah was a proud and persistent violator of that rule while pursuing prospective agriculture students, especially after the coaching hire of Crowley, a member of the fabled "Four Horsemen."

"That relationship encouraged me to visit high school athletes in Michigan, particularly in the more remote and rural areas of the state, to try to persuade as many of them as possible to attend Michigan State," Hannah wrote of his friendship with Crowley, 22-8-3 in four seasons.

Whether or not he was the Spartans' first recruiter, Hannah was clearly their best. As he crisscrossed the state, his only dead period was the few hours each night he closed his eyes. He accompanied the team to every football game, home and away.

MSC went 5-1-2 in 1930, including a scoreless tie at Michigan. But on the season's only other road trip, the Spartans lost 14-13 at Georgetown. The following year, when Crowley's team got a 6-0 payback, he was wowed by the work of Hoyas first-year assistant coach Frank Leahy and persuaded him to move to East Lansing.

Leahy only stayed one season before he and Crowley left for mighty Fordham in 1933 and built the famed "Seven Blocks of Granite," including another member of a great coaching tree, Vince Lombardi. But before leaving the banks of the Red Cedar, Leahy nearly got a different promotion.

"Frank Leahy wanted to succeed Crowley, but President Shaw thought he was too young and inexperienced," Hannah wrote. "At that time, I didn't know President Shaw very well, but I did muster enough courage to suggest that Mr. Leahy had some qualities that ought to be examined and considered. Instead, President Shaw and his advisers chose Charlie Bachman, who was head coach at the University of Florida."

The Spartans would see Leahy again — five times on the opposite sideline and as an integral part of a great relationship with Notre Dame. More on that in a moment.

The Bachman era lasted 13 seasons from 1933-46, when MSC won 70 games, lost 34 and tied 10. Like Crowley and Leahy, he had played for the Fighting Irish and had been coached by Rockne, then a Notre Dame assistant. So it was no surprise that his teams employed a similar system.

It remains a surprise to many, however, that the Spartans wore black-and-gold uniforms in those years and sported a winged helmet before Fritz Crisler brought it from Princeton to Ann Arbor in 1937. MSC's single-stripe version had a small block "S" on the front. But that look went away when Bachman did, allowing players to again"… fight for the only colors, green and white," after a decade-and-a-half of battling the Great Depression, then Japan and Germany.

"We had few inducements to offer prospective students except our enthusiastic desire for better teams," Hannah wrote. "We had no scholarship funds, no gifts or blandishments of any economic value. It was the depths of the Depression and all that Michigan State could offer was an opportunity for a young man to come to college. If he had no funds or family help, he might be able to borrow enough to pay his tuition and we might be able to get him a part-time job. The going rate for student jobs was 35 cents per hour."

Somehow, that offer was more than enough to produce teams that beat Michigan four straight years from 1934-37 by a combined score of 81-27. The '34 team lost only at Syracuse. The '35 team featured guard Sid Wagner, the school's first All-American in 20 years. The '36 team was led by All-America fullback Art Brandstatter. And the '37 team, led by Hall of Fame halfback John Pingel, took an 8-1 record into the Orange Bowl, the school's first postseason game, but lost 6-0 to Auburn.

Bachman's Spartans, also known as "The Black Knights of the Red Cedar," finished with one defeat in '34, '36 and again in '44. The latter team included soon-to-be captain and Hannah protégé Jack Breslin, after the sport had been suspended due to the war the previous year. When the servicemen came flooding home, MSC took full advantage of the G.I. Bill to increase enrollment and trigger a massive expansion.

The included the completion of "The Spartan," the largest free-standing ceramic sculpture in the world, just south of the Kalamazoo Street Bridge. The distinctive work of art professor Leonard Jungwirth was dedicated on June 9, 1945, and has been the scene of more cap-and-gown photos than any spot in the state over the past 67 years.

By the end of the following season, Hannah knew there had to be a coaching change. They had gone 10-8-1 in 1945-46. But they had lost 40-0 and 55-7 to Michigan. They were having difficulty with scheduling and facilities. And they were hoping to gain an invitation to join the Big Ten when the University of Chicago withdrew from membership in '46.

That set the stage for three of the most important events in the school's football history, with full appreciation of the glory of the mid-'60s and the success of the past two seasons. Without the hiring of Clarence Lester "Biggie" Munn as head coach, the agreement to play Notre Dame home-and-home and the chance to join the nation's most prestigious league, the rest of the story would change dramatically.

While Hannah had laid the groundwork for Big Ten consideration before most presidents and faculty representatives realized they were being lobbied, he worked every angle of the Notre Dame relationship from the governor down, then set out to hire the coach who could make his athletic dreams a reality.

The first name on the list of candidates was Munn's. The second was Bud Wilkinson, who would soon be promoted at

1964-66
GEORGE WEBSTER

No. 90 ROVERBACK

On starring for college football's best defense and feeling Spartan love:

"We went to South Bend in '65 knowing they couldn't score. I'm still upset they didn't try to win at the end the following year. But we had a better team my junior year – as good a defense as any team that has ever played. We had hitters and great leaders. Other than calling signals, I never said much. It was never about me. That's what people didn't understand. We had so many guys – (Robert) Viney, Mad Dog (Thornhill), Bubba and the rest. We were a team! And we still are. Being at Michigan State was the best time of my life. Now, it's important we help others get their degrees. We can do that with this (Webster) scholarship fund. We can give them something that'll last the rest of their life – just as being a Spartan will."

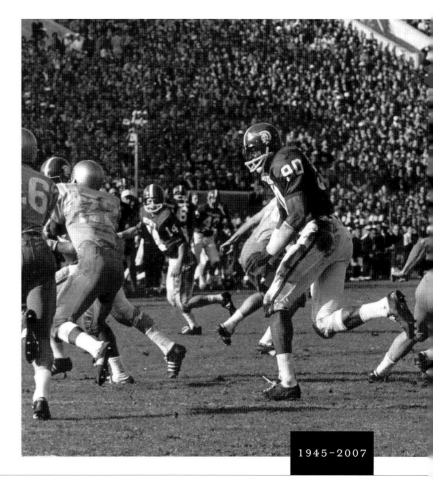

1945-2007

Oklahoma, where he would go on to a Hall of Fame career. And the third was Wes Fesler, who would become the head coach at Ohio State before Woody Hayes.

Munn, a former Minnesota All-American under Fritz Crisler in 1931, knew football and was tough enough for any challenge. He also knew the competition, having worked as an assistant for Crisler at Michigan from 1938-45, before becoming the head coach at Syracuse for one year.

The Munn-Crisler relationship was complex and highly competitive – similar in many ways to the teacher-pupil problem Hayes had 21 years later with the Wolverines' equally fiesty head coach, Glenn "Bo" Schembechler. But unlike that decade-long combat, Munn and Crisler only met once as head coaches — once more than Crisler had ever imagined and Munn could ever forget.

When Munn was hired at MSC, the smoke that came from Crisler's head wasn't sent to signal the naming of a pope. It was a reaction to a perceived betrayal by a once-trusted disciple. To make things worse, Munn was taking Michigan great Forest Evashevski to East Lansing with him, along with assistants Kip Taylor and Duffy Daugherty.

Needless to say, there hadn't been a congratulatory letter or phone call. When they met for the first time at a public affair before the first game in 1947, Crisler barely acknowledged his former aide, then gave him an icy stare and said, "And what are you doing back in the state of Michigan?"

Crisler knew the answer to that question. Munn had come to do a job. If that meant going through the Wolverines instead of around them, that's what would happen. And happen it did. Starting with a major disadvantage in talent and dropping the first three meetings, twice by a total of 10 points, Munn

RED CEDAR REVIVAL

1965-67

BOB APISA

No. 45 FULLBACK

On the MSU melting pot and becoming the first Samoan All-American:

"For me, it was Michigan State, USC or Penn State. But Penn State was an independent. I wanted to be in a conference and play in the Rose Bowl. And the coach from SC missed his flight to Hawaii. Duffy did a great job of recruiting there, then meshing players of different ethnic backgrounds and locations. I'd never seen snow till I got there. But I got to play in the Rose Bowl my sophomore year and on two National Championship teams. I played three years with a bum knee and had three surgeries. It was worth it to have the relationships I've had. And the '66 tie with Notre Dame was the first live telecast on the Islands. I'm proudest of that – helping to bring Hawaii into the 20th century."

won his final four games against Michigan and Crisler's successor, Bennie Oosterbaan.

But it was his first game as a Spartan that shaped the remaining 64 - of them victories. It wasn't just that MSC was clobbered 55-0 in Ann Arbor. Munn always believed that Crisler made the sewage back up and flow into the visitors' locker room at halftime, forcing his players to stand on benches to get dressed after the game.

"So help me, this will never happen again!" a teary, red-faced Munn told his team before it left the stadium. And it never did. The Wolverines couldn't score more than 13 points in the next six meetings and averaged 7.7 per game. Munn left as one of the very few Big Ten coaches with a winning record against Michigan — something Daugherty and Dantonio also can claim.

None of that would have mattered if the Spartans hadn't gone from irrelevance to national champions and winners of two Rose Bowls in the next 10 years. That never could have happened without conference membership. And many thought MSC was out of its league when it approached Notre Dame for support.

The Spartans and Fighting Irish already played in everything but football. In fact, there was a basketball series in progress, one that has been dormant since the Elite Eight of the 1979 NCAA Tournament. So when Michigan said there was no assurance it would continue to play MSC after World War II, it was time for some Hannah magic.

His close friend, Michigan Gov. Harry Kelly, was a proud Notre Dame alumnus. And Father John Cavanaugh, Notre Dame's distinguished president, just happened to be a native of nearby Owosso. So when Kelly arranged a luncheon at the governor's home,

1970-72
BRAD VAN PELT

No. 10 SAFETY

On a Hall of Fame college football career and its impact on his life:

"Coming from Owosso and playing at Michigan State was one of best decisions of my life. When we opened our place in Santa Barbara, we even named it Duffy's. It was great to win the Maxwell Award my last year and get to play three sports for the Spartans. I only have two regrets in life. One of them is that I wish I would've waited to sign my first pro contract. I would have loved to play basketball and baseball as a senior and earn nine letters. And I really wish I could've coached there. I have a lot of love for that place. But it's really all about the people – the Joe DeLamielleures and the John Shinskys. They're what I'll remember more than any games or honors."

1951-2009

Hannah convinced Cavanaugh that the schools should play a home-and-home series for an indefinite period.

Nearly every school in the country would have loved to play the Fighting Irish, the gold standard in college football. That contract allowed MSC to expand Macklin Field into Macklin Stadium in 1948 and increase its capacity from 26,000 seats to 51,000, roughly two-thirds of what it is today.

As much as anything else, that validated Munn's rapidly developing program. It also set the table for Hannah's greatest feat, convincing the nine remaining Big Ten schools — or at least five of them — that the conference needed another member and that East Lansing was a better place to look than Western Pennsylvania.

The biggest problem? That all depends on what you believe. The league was run by faculty representatives in those days, not by presidents. In fact, its official title from its earliest days in 1895 was the Intercollegiate Conference of Faculty Representatives. And no one was more powerful than Michigan law professor Ralph W. Aigler, who opposed all athletic scholarships.

Likewise, no one has done a more thorough job of researching MSC's acceptance than David J. Young, a physician and historian from Holland, Mich. In his 2011 treatise, *Arrogance and Scheming in the Big Ten*, the Notre Dame graduate laid out the arguments and drew conclusions after visiting every campus and nearly moving into the Bentley Historical Library in Ann Arbor.

After being rejected in three attempts to gain an invitation to join, Hannah was denied so much as a chance to meet with the faculty reps in 1946. But when Verne Freeman of Purdue took over as chairman, Hannah tried again and was allowed to speak at

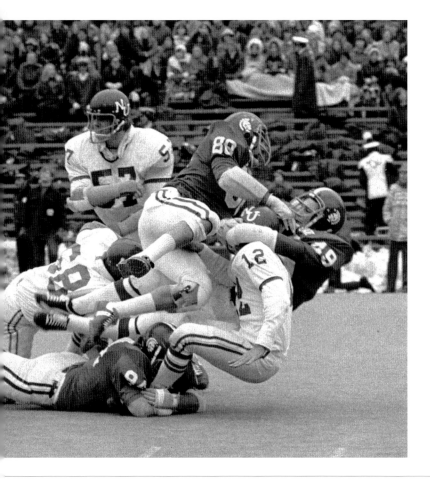

1970, 72-73

JOHN SHINSKY

No. 88 DEFENSIVE TACKLE

On Daugherty's influence and what it means to be a Spartan forever:

"Duffy gave us an opportunity to participate in an environment I never imagined I could be a part of. It's more than football. It's so much more than that. When you're a part of Michigan State, you're part of the family. Coach Bullough recruited me from high school, and he's still supporting me with my orphanage right now. We're family. All my player friends, my professors, we're family, too. And that's what Michigan State is about. I think every one of us takes pride in the history and contributions of people that have been made off the field. We take pride in this University, what it has been and what it will be in the future. And I'm not just talking about football."

a special meeting in May 1947. As expected, he put on quite a performance, then was escorted out of the room.

At that point, the Big Ten athletic directors were polled on the idea of expansion. A majority said no. But to Hannah, that meant, "So you're saying there's a chance!" A strong alliance with Minnesota President Lew Morrill paved the way, with Hannah railing against the hypocrisy of holier-than-thou programs – no names mentioned but clearly implied – as early as a January 1946 address to the NCAA.

One key development was an endorsement that year from Michigan President Alexander Ruthven, who feared the political consequences of denying another state institution whatever it deserved. That seemed to stifle Aigler and Crisler, at least publicly. Behind closed doors, both expressed doubts, bordering on outrage, when the Spartans kept inching closer to an invite. But when it finally came time to say yea or nay, Aigler had little choice in how to vote.

MSC had other adversaries, none more vocal than long-time Ohio State athletic director Lynn St. John, who was losing his clout in the conference as he was about to turn 70. According to Young's research, St. John still saw fit to fire off this salvo against the Spartans and in favor of the Panthers to Commissioner Kenneth "Tug" Wilson, no friend of MSC, in '46:

"I have no hesitation in saying that I see no justification whatever for taking on Michigan State. They would fundamentally and of necessity be another more or less weak sister, trying to 'keep up with the Joneses' and definitely not add anything of particular value to the Conference. Pittsburgh, because of its location and facilities, is the only institution

HISTORY HELPS SPARTANS WRITE NEW STORY

1973-75
CHARLIE BAGGETT

No. 16 QUARTERBACK

On going from North Carolina to MSU and learning a life lesson:

"I think Spartan Pride is something we learn when we first come to campus. It's all about toughness, because the Spartans were warriors. That was something we were told as soon as we came to Michigan State. Even on offense, we always played with toughness and heart and desire. I think it was something that was kind of handed down over the years. Guys were taught and told all about it. I think it even helped me later as a coach. I had a real advantage, being able to relay that from another perspective. The guy I worked for, George Perles, was always talking about toughness anyway. He always preached that, and our teams played with toughness. We both tried to instill that in all the players we coached."

that can possibly add anything to the Western Conference."

Most athletic directors and football coaches were against either move. And while Hannah was maneuvering and massaging egos, his head coach, never known for his patience, finally let loose on MSC's critics. Munn had had enough of the gripes about the school's Jenison Awards while others pontificated about amateurism. If you wanted the truth, at least as he knew it, Munn was your man. If you needed a little tact, you probably had the wrong guy.

"Why should we have to do like a hell of a lot of them do — pay their athletes under the table?" Munn asked, as reported in *Arrogance and Scheming*. "In some Big Nine schools it is a practice to hand it to the players under the table and then take them into another room and make them sign a paper to the effect that they haven't received anything....We're not going to push the issue any further. I don't believe we'll get anywhere by apple polishing. If they want us, they'll ask us now."

Hannah had a Ph.D. in diplomacy as well as in agriculture and was able to calm things down just in time for friends and allies to take care of the rest. On Sunday afternoon, December 12, 1948, his plan came to fruition with Morrill's invaluable aid. After MSC Dean Lloyd Emmons made a brief statement and answered a series of questions, a 12-year effort with five rejections finally paid off at the University Club of Chicago.

Minnesota law professor and faculty rep Henry Rottschaefer moved "that Michigan State be admitted, the admission to take effect at such time as a Committee of the Faculty Representatives shall have certified to the conference that the rules and regulations of the conference are completely in force at that institution."

1975-78
KIRK GIBSON
No. 23 FLANKER

On becoming a two-sport star and competing with Spartan pride:

"I came here for football. Darryl Rogers suggested I go out for baseball. And Danny Litwhiler convinced me not to quit. But the guy who got me here was Andy McDonald, a Denny Stolz assistant. When they brought Darryl in, he was thinking of making me an outside linebacker. I was 6-3, 220. Then, he saw I could run and said, 'Man, we better keep him on the other side of the ball.' What am I most proud of? All of it. But I don't claim I did it by myself. I never will. I support the program. We've remodeled the baseball, softball and soccer fields. The people who donated money are friends of mind. I had a little something to do with it. And I'm connected here forever. My son, Cam, will be here next year to play baseball."

That additional wording after an Aigler-Crisler amendment would force Hannah to make a painful-but-prudent decision about the eligibility of those who had received Jenison aid. His choice to keep those players in the program meant a delay in football competition until 1953, nearly three years and 10 months after the Spartans' Big Ten basketball debut at Iowa. But it was enough to carry the day and lift MSC into a new realm with national respect.

Purdue's Freeman seconded the motion, Young's research shows. That motion also may have come with a presidential push, as Fred Hovde, a former Golden Gophers football player, had a personal vendetta with the Faculty Representatives Committee and may have seen this as a slap at Aigler and mighty Michigan.

What happened next is open to debate. The official vote was reported as 9-0 in favor. But it seems clear from multiple sources that Iowa voted against the motion, making the tally 8-1 for admission with conditions. If that put MSC under greater scrutiny and kept the Spartans from representing the league in the Rose Bowl after winning a share of the national title in 1951 and the consensus crown in '52, the bargain was worth it in Hannah's eyes and those of his staunchest supporter.

A letter from Morrill nine days later said: "I haven't yet had a chance to hear the 'inside story' of the Chicago meeting — except that George Hauser, our assistant football coach who represented (Bernie) Bierman at the (nearby coaches) meeting, told me that the University of Michigan people worked very hard undercover to block the admission. This makes it all the sweeter, so far as I'm concerned."

Aigler's papers from the Bentley Historical Library prove beyond a doubt that he distrusted Hannah and MSC and considered them to be barbarians at the gate. His main concerns: financial aid based on athletic talent instead of academic merit, off-campus recruitment by coaches — another supposed no-no — and eligibility questions.

But in a letter to Illinois faculty rep Frank Richart the same day as Morrill's message to Hannah, Aigler gave another insight: "I have every confidence that with Michigan State compelled, if we can accomplish that desirable end, to observe conference rules, Michigan will have more good material. You have, of course, no way of knowing how much good athletic material has chosen Michigan State under the influence of her program of financial aids."

None of that would have surprised Hannah, who summarized the relationship between the schools and a neighbor's near-constant obstruction, including resistance to a name change and the establishment of med and law schools, in an extended interview and in *A Memoir* more than 30 years later.

"We knew from the beginning that there would be no friendly consideration of Michigan State's cause by the Big Ten if the University of Michigan had its way," Hannah wrote. "We anticipated that Ann Arbor would be unfriendly and critical and obstructive, and that's exactly what they were, not only when we hoped to join the Big Ten, but later when we were being considered for membership in the American Association of Universities. But several other universities, particularly the University of Minnesota, helped us a great deal."

When the Committee of Three made its inspection trip to East Lansing and found a move toward compliance but some lingering concerns, Aigler was incensed. Yet, on May 20, 1949, it became official. Though it was recorded and reported as unanimous support, there is every indication that it was actually a 5-4 verdict, as revealed first in a piece by columnist Watson Spoelstra in *The Detroit News* the following day.

Minnesota, Purdue, Indiana, Ohio State and, yes, with Aigler having no choice, Michigan were the five affirmative votes. Iowa, Illinois, Wisconsin and Northwestern not only voted against the Spartans, they refused to schedule MSC in football from 1950-52, as Young discovered.

Until his death, Hannah thought otherwise. He was convinced that Minnesota, Purdue, Ohio State, Illinois and Wisconsin had voted yea and said, "The University of Michigan opposed us strenuously."

Once Munn's "Green Machine" got rolling in his fourth season in East Lansing, the opposition was helpless. After going 7-2, 6-2-2 and 6-3, the Spartans went 8-1, 9-0, 9-0 and 8-1 from 1950-53. Their winning streak reached 28 games. They were 4-0 against the Wolverines, 3-0 against the Irish, 2-0 against Ohio State and 1-0 in the Rose Bowl. Individually, Munn wound up 3-2 against Leahy and 2-0 vs. Hayes.

A running joke in the 1950s was that Hannah wanted a university that would make its football team proud. He always disputed the notion that there was any sort of misplaced priority. The school's phenomenal growth couldn't have come from a football factory. But there was a reason that No. 46 was retired, commemorating his years of service to the school.

The list of All-Americans in Munn's years would have filled a lineup with subs to spare. Hall of Fame tackle Don Coleman was arguably the best small lineman in college football history. And there were 18 first-team national selections in a seven-year span:

1949 — Outland Trophy winner Ed Bagdon and Don Mason at guard and Lynn Chandnois at halfback.

1950 — halfback Sonny Grandelius and end Dorne Dibble.

1951 — Coleman, end Bob Carey, quarterback Al Dorow and halfback Jim Ellis.

1952 — guard Frank Kush, halfback Don McAuliffe, center Dick Tamburo, quarterback Tom Yewcic, end Ellis Duckett and Jim Ellis for a second time.

1953 — end Don Dohoney (Eric Gordon's grandpa), halfback LeRoy Bolden and tackle Larry Fowler.

And if MSC didn't have "The Four Horsemen," it did just fine with "The Pony Backfield" of Yewcic, Bolden, fullback Evan Slonac and halfback Billy Wells, the MVP of a 28-20 comeback win in Pasadena and Debbie Reynolds'

RED CEDAR REVIVAL

1976-79
DAN BASS

No. 49 LINEBACKER

On setting MSU tackles marks and his 99-yard interception TD:

"Being from Bath, there wasn't much of a recruitment. I had to beg them to take me. If they hadn't gone on probation, I never would've had the chance. A week before my first game, Darryl Rogers said, 'We're going to start you at Ohio State. Just promise me you won't piss your pants in front of 85,000 people.' I wound up making 32 tackles. That meant our defense was on the field a lot. Instead of reading the guards, I shot the gaps and just made plays. The long return against Wisconsin was different. When I got to the 50, I thought I had a piano on my back. After I dove into the end zone, everyone jumped on top of me, and I couldn't get any air. But I thought Greg Jones might get my career record. It was made to be broken."

postgame date. If Duckett's blocked-punt TD started that surge, Wells' 62-yard punt return in the final five minutes sealed the deal and sent Munn off with a record of 54-9-2.

"Midgets. Comparative midgets," wrote Dick Hyland in the *Los Angeles Times* of the last group of ballcarriers in Munn's famed Multiple Offense. "When the Spartans lined up for the photogs yesterday, everyone in the backfield except quarterback Tom Yewcic seemed to be standing in a hole."

With Munn sliding into the athletic director's chair until he suffered a stroke in 1971, it seemed like a seamless transition when line coach Hugh Duffy Daugherty, named after the all-time baseball great, took over in 1954. And from 1950-69, the pair combined to earn six national titles and go 14-4-2 against Michigan and 13-4-1 against Notre Dame.

Under Daugherty, arguably the national media's all-time favorite head coach, the steady stream of All-Americans continued, with four of them — roverback George Webster, defensive end Bubba Smith, split end Gene Washington and safety Brad Van Pelt — joining their coach in the College Football Hall of Fame. Daugherty's Spartans had 36 first-team selections, with seven players recognized twice:

1955 — quarterback Earl Morrall (fourth in the Heisman Trophy balloting), tackle Norm Masters, guard Buck Nystrom and fullback Jerry Planutis.

1957 — halfback Walt Kowalczyk (third for the Heisman) and center Dan Currie.

1958 — end Sam Williams.

1959 — quarterback Dean Look.

1961 — center Dave Behrman.

1980-83

CARL BANKS

No. 54 LINEBACKER

On being MSU's first three-time All-Big Ten position player:

"The guys who really recruited me were Magic Johnson and Sherm Lewis. Magic told me it was a great campus and a great opportunity. And I connected with Sherm right away. Still, I almost went to Oklahoma. We never had a winning season while I was there. But I never got used to losing. It was tough. I'd be lying if I said it wasn't. Yet, I wouldn't trade it for anything in the world. Earvin didn't lie about that. After playing three years for Muddy, I had the good fortune of playing for George Perles. He put me on track to be the No. 3 pick in the NFL Draft. Winning at Notre Dame in '83 was great, too. I had a lot of friends who went there. And I never let them forget it."

1962 — fullback George Saimes, guard Ed Budde and Behrman.

1963 — halfback Sherman Lewis (third for the Heisman) and guard Earl Lattimer.

1965 — Webster, Smith, Washington, halfback Clinton Jones, fullback Bob Apisa, middle guard Harold Lucas, quarterback Steve Juday and linebacker Ron Goovert.

1966 — Webster, Smith, Washington, Jones and Apisa, all repeaters, and tackle Jerry West.

1968 — two-way end and safety Allen Brenner.

1969 — guard Ron Saul.

1971 — Van Pelt, halfback Eric Allen and defensive tackle Ron Curl.

1972 — Van Pelt again, guard Joe DeLamielleure and tight end Billy Joe DuPree.

Daugherty's recruiting skill was legendary. And though he got the most publicity for bringing Apisa and other Hawaiians to East Lansing, his greatest contribution to football was playing a major role in the integration of the sport, continuing what Munn had done. The Spartans and Minnesota, more than any other schools in the Big Ten, recruited and signed the best black athletes in the land, as often from the South as the Midwest.

Daugherty didn't believe in stacking, a popular trick to limit the number of black starters. He believed in winning. And he did that well enough to be a four-time national champ and a two-time Coach of the Year. In 19 seasons from 1954-72, his teams were 109-69-5. Finally, in 1984 the pride of Barnesboro, Pa., joined his predecessor in the College Football Hall of Fame.

"You can credit me for getting Biggie in the Hall of Fame," Daugherty said in 1959, midway through a 26-year hot-and-cold working relationship. "After six years of my coaching, they appreciate what a great coach he really was."

The "Duffyisms" are seemingly endless, and if you can find a copy of *Duffy: An Autobiography* by Daugherty and long-time Detroit writer and broadcaster Dave Diles, be prepared to laugh and smile:

"I like those goal-line stands of ours, but I wish they'd make them around the 50-yard line where I can see them better."

. . .

"I just want to say that I could have been a Rhodes Scholar, too — except for my grades."

. . .

"The object of the triple-option is to bypass the defensive tackle and end in the flow of the play without blocking them. That's easy for us. We never blocked them anyhow."

. . .

And when asked at the start of a season, "Who are you happiest to see returning this year?" the answer was instantaneous: "Me."

But things weren't so funny in 1954, a 3-6 head coaching debut. And when Munn barged into a coaches meeting at Spartan Stadium and began to rip the assistants, Daugherty told him to shut up and get out, emphasizing that he was in charge. That blowup let everyone know he was about more than just punch lines. It also began the disintegration of a relationship that was never the same.

The following year brought lower expectations record-wise, another new name: Michigan State University of Agriculture and Applied Science — again over Michigan's objections in the state legislature — and surprising success. The Spartans lost their second game to the Wolverines but won the other nine, including a rematch with UCLA in the Rose Bowl, 17-14. That matched the most points MSU allowed in 10 games en route to a share of the national title.

In one of the strangest finishes in bowl history, it was 14-all with :07 left when Morrall called on end Dave Kaiser to kick the first field goal of his career from 41 yards. The far-sighted Kaiser had left his contact lenses in the locker room. And just as he started a practice leg swing, the ball was snapped. Stepping back and swinging through again, he delivered the most dramatic kick in school history. Who cared that the official play-by-play in the press box and hundreds of newspaper stories gave credit to Planutis, the usual kicker?

The Spartans were 7-2 in 1956 and 8-1 the following year, falling 20-13 to Purdue in a game when a TD was taken off the scoreboard incorrectly. A dead-ball penalty should have been administered on the ensuing kickoff, as an apology from the Big Ten office the following week confirmed. Despite losing out on a third trip to Pasadena in five years, MSU earned another share of the national crown.

The 1958 season began with two wins and a tie against Michigan. But a five-game losing streak, capped by a 39-12 defeat at Minnesota sent Munn over the edge. He told *The Detroit News*, "When you throw the game away like we did today by losing the ball 10 times, it's terrible... just terrible. It was the most futile display I've ever seen. Utter futility. I've never taken losing so bad, but I cried after this one. When you've scratched and clawed an inch at a time to build an empire, although it's a small empire, it takes a lot out of you to see it crash."

It took all of Hannah's people skills to keep Munn and Daugherty from picking up dueling pistols at that point. And Daugherty reported directly to Hannah from that day forward, a relationship that probably kept him from going to Notre Dame as head coach five years later, when Ara Parseghian was the fall-back choice. The joke was the Irish wouldn't have been able to tell Daugherty apart from their leprechaun mascot.

A 5-4 finish in 1959 didn't do much to restore the fans' confidence. But MSU went 6-2-1 and 7-2 the next two seasons. In 1963 they played an assassination-delayed season-ender against Illinois for the conference title and a trip to California. The day after Kennedy was shot, the Spartans held a full-scale scrimmage in the dirt arena in Jenison Field House and had the best practice anyone could remember. When Illinois returned to East Lansing five days later, Dick Butkus & Co. took

1981-84

JIM MORRISSEY

No. 40 LINEBACKER

On going from a last-chance signee to MSU's last solo captain:

"My brother was a linebacker at Central. I wanted to play at a higher level. I'd gone to a lot of Michigan games. They didn't offer. At the last minute, a scholarship opened at Michigan State. When we won at Notre Dame in '83, we had all their signals down. I was yelling run or pass before each play. Winning in Ann Arbor the next year was an unbelievable feeling. And we stopped Chuck Long on a two-point conversion to win in Iowa City. We knew he didn't get in. I got thank-you letters for that from Ohio State alumni. A few years later at Jim Harbaugh's golf tournament, Bo came up to me. He'd asked me to walk on. And he said, 'You're the biggest mistake we ever made.'"

advantage of seven turnovers for a 13-0 Thanksgiving Day win.

A 4-5 season in 1964 set the stage for two of the most spectacular seasons any team has had. MSU went 10-1 and 9-0-1 but could have been 21-0 in that span. It will have to settle for two outright Big Ten titles and back-to-back shared national championships.

The 1965 team most resembled the 1985 Chicago Bears with its efficiency on offense and incredible ferocity on defense. No opponent scored more than 14 points. After winning 23-0 at Penn State, coordinator Hank Bullough's defense held Michigan to -51 rushing yards, Ohio State to -22 and fourth-ranked Notre Dame to -12 in South Bend — a combined -85 on the ground, mostly on sacks.

The last thing a team wanted to do that year was to make Webster and Smith and Lucas and Goovert and especially Robert Viney mad. When the Spartan Marching Band was roughed up before a 12-3 win over the No. 4 Irish, it was kerosene on the campfire. So when it was time to take the field, linebacker Charlie "Mad Dog" Thornhill actually took the door off its hinges.

All that remained was a rematch with the Bruins in the Rose Bowl. Perhaps because it had beaten UCLA by 10 points in September and because the West Coast media made MSU seem like the Green Bay Packers, that wasn't going to be easy as anyone across the county imagined. Daugherty knew that, putting the team up in a monastery to try to curb the SoCal distractions.

It didn't work. Soon-to-be Heisman quarterback Gary Beban made just enough plays, sure-handed Spartans captain Don Japinga fumbled a punt at the 6-yard line, and suddenly the deficit was 14-0. After four first-half turnovers, MSU came alive midway through the fourth quarter and made it 14-6 on a 38-yard run by Apisa. But when

RED CEDAR REVIVAL

1984-87

LORENZO WHITE

No. 34 TAILBACK

On a feeling that means more than records and trophies could:

"For me, being a Spartan is everything. When I think about Michigan State and the times that I had there, once you learn the dedication of 'Go Green, Go White,' that's what I live by. The Rose Bowl game was great. But the game against Indiana at Spartan Stadium to put us in the Rose Bowl, that was when I really understood about being a Spartan family. I talked to so many people in the week leading up to that game, and everybody was so excited. I'm talking about the whole town of East Lansing. It felt to me that we weren't fighting by ourselves. If I had to do everything all over again, I wouldn't change a thing about coming to Michigan State and being a Spartan. That's how much that means to me. Now and always."

Juday scored again from the 1 with :31 left, the best it could do was tie. That chance disappeared when Apisa was stopped on a pitchout attempt for two points.

With eight-and-a-half months to think about the loss, the Spartans were ready for anyone in 1966. A 42-8 shellacking of the Nittany Lions in the second game was notable for two reasons. It was the first loss in Joe Paterno's 46 years as the head coach in Happy Valley. And that was the game when the starters on defense kept wanting to return in the second half to post another shutout.

With the Big Ten's archaic no-repeat rule for bowl participation, MSU had to settle for what it could accomplish in the regular season. But aside from a 41-20 Homecoming win over Bob Griese and Purdue, the Big Ten's second-place Rose Bowl representative, it was clear by the end of September that the Spartans and Irish would meet on November 19 in East Lansing as the No. 1 and 2 teams in the country, the first time that had happened in a season finale.

MSU fell from first to second in the polls after an 11-8 escape in the rain on October 15 in Columbus, while Notre Dame was beating North Carolina 32-0 for one of its five shutouts. From that point on, the five-week buildup seemed more like five months. ABC publicist Beano Cook didn't help by billing the game as "the greatest battle since Hector fought Achilles." And when the NCAA insisted the game couldn't be nationally televised because both teams had been on previously, one Southerner sued and got the policy changed.

Ticket demand had never been higher for a college football game. But one clever Ohioan scored big by enclosing the $5 cost with this letter: "If President Johnson phoned or wrote you asking for a ticket, I'm sure you would be able

HISTORY HELPS SPARTANS WRITE NEW STORY

1985-88

BOBBY MCALLISTER

No. 8 QUARTERBACK

On his choice of schools and two chances to make bowl magic:

"Growing up in Pompano Beach, I didn't know anything about Michigan State. Just Michigan. Charlie Baggett did a tremendous job recruiting me. He talked about the '66 team and said, 'You can help us get back to the Promised Land.' It didn't hurt when Coach Perles walked in with four Super Bowl rings. I visited Michigan, too. But I came from humble beginnings. I'd be lying if I didn't say I had moments when I wondered if I'd made the right choice. If I'd had a chance to throw the way they do now…are you serious? You saw what Andre Rison and I could do in our last game against Georgia. But people still ask about the jump pass the year before in the Rose Bowl. They say, 'Did you practice that?' How could you?"

to send him one. Well, President Johnson will not be there, I'm certain. So why not send me the ticket you would have him for him?" MSU Ticket Manager Bill Beardsley had to agree and gave him a seat on the 48-yard line.

ABC headquarters in New York caught a lot of flak for showing the "Kill, Bubba, Kill" signs around campus, plus messages like "Even the Pope has no hope" and "Hail, Mary, Full of Grace, Notre Dame's in Second Place."

Actually, the Irish arrived in first place and left the same way after a frustrating 10-10 tie — a bruising, mistake-filled matchup commemorated in Mike Celizek's book, *The Biggest Game of Them All: Notre Dame, Michigan State and the Fall of 1966*. A cold, cloudy day got considerably grayer when the ending was so unfulfilling.

The Spartans took a 10-0 lead on a 4-yard run by Reggie Cavender and a 47-yard field goal by barefoot Hawaiian booter Dick Kenney. With Irish halfback Nick Eddy sidelined by a fall as he stepped off the train the day before the game, another injury to quarterback Terry Hanratty on a big hit by Smith seemed to put MSU in great shape.

But backup QB Coley O'Brien came on and played like a champion that day. His 34-yard pass to Bob Gladieux cut it to 10-7 at halftime. And Joe Azzaro tied it with a 28-yard field goal on the first play of the fourth quarter. Azzaro just missed another chance to put his team ahead moments later. And with the ball on their 30 in the last two minutes, Parseghian called six straight running plays and left with the tie — a wise decision after his team smashed USC 51-0 the following week as its closing argument.

Smith in particular taunted the Notre Dame players, calling them sissies and much worse. "Tie One for The Gipper" was the headline

RED CEDAR REVIVAL

1986-89

HARLON BARNETT

No. 36   Cornerback/Safety   Coach 2006-present

On being the Spartan with a Rose Bowl ring and an 11-win season:

"I was hosted on my visit by Lonnie Young, whose best friend was Carl Banks. Carl had just finished his rookie year with the Giants. Hanging out with those two guys, it just felt right. I could've gone to Tennessee, Notre Dame or West Virginia. But I knew in my heart where I wanted to be. My redshirt-sophomore year we beat Michigan 17-11 and had seven interceptions. John Miller had four all by himself. Demetrius Brown liked throwing to the Green, I guess. I read his eyes on the last one and cut in front of Greg McMurtry. The following year I moved back to safety and broke my foot. I heard it break but made it back for the Gator Bowl. The best team I was on was in '89. Nine guys on that defense played in the pros."

of the day. And Dan Jenkins' cover story in *Sports Illustrated* led with the line, "Old Notre Dame will tie over all." All they needed was for the Band of the Fighting Irish to play "The Notre Dame Who-Cares-About-Victory March."

Neither team could go to a bowl game. The Irish never did in those days. And the Spartans wouldn't go again until 1984, a maddening drought of 19 seasons. But on one unforgettable day, the attention of the entire sporting world, reflected in record TV ratings, was focused on East Lansing. As Clinton Jones still insists, maybe it's better it ended that way. The debate will never end.

The end of Daugherty's glory was closer than anyone could have known, even after a 37-7 loss to Houston and his former assistant, Bill Yeoman, in the 1967 opener. MSU was 3-7 that year and followed by going 5-5, 4-6 twice, 6-5 and 5-5-1 for a 27-34-1 mark in a six-year span. An end to segregation in the South, the loss of some key assistants and tough luck with injuries were significant factors.

Yes, the Spartans still had big wins: a 21-17 upset of Notre Dame with goal-line stands in 1968, a 23-12 victory over the Wolverines when Daugherty stunned Schembechler by shifting from the Veer to the Power-I in '69, an NCAA-record 350-yard rushing day by Allen at Purdue in '71 and back-to-back triumphs over the Buckeyes in '71-72. The latter game featured four field goals by soccer-team loaner Dirk Kryt, whose name wasn't even in the program or the press notes. When he lit up a cigarette in the locker room and suggested Duffy join him for a few beers, it capped an amazing day.

His final team had plenty of talent. And when Daugherty decided to resign at mid-season after a 6-6 tie at Iowa, he tried to keep it a secret. His lone regret was that the story had leaked from an assistant coach to a member of the media before he had told his team. Retirement in sunny Santa Barbara, Calif., wasn't a bad option, after all.

Munn's successor as A.D., Burt Smith, was the point man in the Spartans' first football coaching search in 26 seasons. And his final four candidates were high-octane Oklahoma assistant Barry Switzer, Iowa State head coach Johnny Majors, Louisville leader Lee Corso and Daugherty's defensive coordinator Denny Stolz, who had been highly successful at Haslett High and Alma College.

The job appeared to belong to Switzer. In fact, WJR radio Sports Director and MSU insider Bob Reynolds had gone on the air to announce the Arkansas native's hiring. All that remained was what he believed to be a mere formality: an interview with President Clifton Wharton, Vice President Jack Breslin, Faculty Representative John Fuzak, Smith and Assistant A.D. Clarence Underwood.

But when Switzer started making what were seen as demands and asked about the number of private jets available for recruiting trips, then talked about credit-card arrangements for coaches on the road, his Sooner Schooner was about to blow a wheel.

As Lynn Henning explained in *Spartan Seasons,* Majors' candidacy was hurt by his concern about how many non-predictors with academic deficiencies the Spartans could take. Instead, he was hired at Pittsburgh where he won a national championship four years later with Tony Dorsett. Meanwhile, Corso was seen as a bit slick and not quite ready for the Big Ten. Before long, he would be hired at Indiana, where he lifted a moribund program to bowl games.

That left Stolz — solid, stable, youthful and familiar with the area, having grown up in nearby Mason. He knew MSU was losing a terrific senior class, with 11 players going in the NFL Draft. And he didn't care about jets or non-qualifiers. He knew he had the qualifications to win in a job he had wanted for almost 30 years.

On December 13, 1972, Stolz would get that chance at an annual salary of $25,000 and with a new quarterback, a sophomore transfer from North Carolina named Charlie Baggett, to run his I-formation option attack. After a 1-5 start in '73, his team closed strong to finish 5-6. The only discouraging notes: a 31-0 loss to Michigan in a monsoon and a 35-0 loss at Ohio State.

It just so happened that those two unbeatens had played a 10-10 tie of their own in the final regular-season game in Ann Arbor. Wolverines quarterback Dennis Franklin had broken his collarbone that day. And when the Big Ten A.D.s cast their ballots on Sunday for the league's Rose Bowl representative, the vote was destined to be close.

Michigan assumed it would have Smith's vote since he had competed for the Wolverines in hockey, baseball and freshman football. But it didn't turn out that way. Let's just say that Breslin helped him make up his mind. "Tiger Jack," also known as "Mr. MSU" for his many years of distinguished service, had no love for the school 63 miles away.

The vote was 6-4 in favor of the Buckeyes, who had been badly outplayed in Ann Arbor. But with Franklin's injury, OSU's higher ranking and the Spartans' lack of success against both teams that season, Smith's vote was hardly the abomination it was seen as being in the state. In fact, a bigger surprise was the pro-Ohio vote from Wisconsin A.D. Elroy "Crazylegs" Hirsch, a Michigan All-American and the school's only four-sport letterman in one season.

Nonetheless, a teary Schembechler was livid when the vote was announced and said Big Ten Commissioner Wayne Duke had "engineered" the vote, telling Sports Editor Wayne DeNeff of the *Ann Arbor News*: "He's the guy who took it away from us....I would really like to know how those schools voted and particularly how our sister school voted."

MSU had voted in its own self-interest, just as Michigan had many times, whether the question was membership in the prestigious American Association of Universities or the establishment of a law school or a med school in East Lansing. But that ballot would have long-lasting ramifications.

The 1974 Spartans were a much-improved team and finished 7-3-1 with a 5-0 finish. If not for a 21-all tie at Illinois, Stolz's team would have been 7-1 in league play and would have been in Pasadena. The reason for that was one of the greatest upsets in Big Ten history, a 16-13 jolt to the

RED CEDAR REVIVAL

1987-90

JOHN LANGELOH

No. 10 PLACEKICKER

On booting two field goals that beat USC in postseason play:

"I was going to Boston College. State didn't offer till the last weekend. I'd gone to every camp and outkicked everyone. But nothing happened till the 11th hour. I redshirted in '86 when we lost close games. Percy Snow was the only freshman who played. I had two field goals in my first game against USC, then two more in the rematch in the Rose Bowl. Kickers are all goofy. I liked to watch the game. When Andre Rison caught that pass, I was ready. But I missed a couple, too. I had one blocked when we tied Illinois in '87 and hooked one when we lost to Michigan in '89. We beat U-M again my senior year, then beat the Trojans in another bowl game. My last kick was perfect. It would've been good beyond 60. We won, 17-16."

top-ranked Buckeyes and Archie Griffin. After an 88-yard sprint by fullback Levi Jackson with 3:12 left, the MSU defense made a miraculous goal-line stand as the final seconds ticked away.

When the game ended with a false-start penalty against Ohio State, no one was sure exactly what had happened. The line judge signaled a touchdown after halfback Brian Baschnagel recovered an errant snap and dove into the end zone. The referee signaled time was up. Then, the officials left, running through the tunnel at the north end of Spartan Stadium and heading back to Kellogg Center, where they showered, turned on a television and saw that the stands were still full nearly 40 minutes later.

Both teams thought they had won. But the commissioner told Stabley not to say anything until he tracked down the crew and got answers. When the score was finally announced, there were marriage proposals and pandemonium on the field. And when Duke finally broke the news to Hayes, he nearly got punched — without even looking like a Clemson linebacker.

Across the tunnel in the winners locker room, a wild celebration came to a screeching halt with the news that MSU equipment manager and player favorite Troy Hickman had been killed in the on-field commotion, his head crushed by a falling goalpost. From the highest high to the lowest low, emotions plummeted — until Hickman walked through the door moments later, unaware that a eulogy had been given.

Just as encouraging, Stolz and his staff were making major inroads on the recruiting trail, particularly in Michigan, Ohio and Pennsylvania. That's where it all ties together — the 1973 Rose Bowl vote, the upset of a No. 1 team the following year, hyper-aggressive recruiters, overzealous fans, sloppy

HISTORY HELPS SPARTANS WRITE NEW STORY

1988-91
COURTNEY HAWKINS

No. 5 WIDE RECEIVER

On following some of Flint's best receivers to stardom as Spartans:

"I'd already made a verbal commitment to Iowa. But Coach Baggett and I hit it off from Day 1. And Coach Perles reminded me of my high school coach. He was a disciplinarian whose door was always open. It didn't matter that they'd just played in the Rose Bowl. It mattered that Daryl Turner, Mark Ingram and Andre Rison had gone there. The pitch was, 'We send guys from Flint to the pros.' I set a school record with 60 catches. But I broke my collarbone and missed five games as a junior. That was the worst time of my life, I didn't shave or cut my hair. Finally, my mom said. 'Get it together!' When we beat USC for the third straight time, I had two big plays on a jump ball in double coverage and a slant for the go-ahead score."

oversight and a potential threat to the league's top teams.

Before the Spartans went 7-4 in 1975, including a dramatic 10-3 win at Notre Dame, an investigation began. Actually, a couple of them did, searching for improper benefits. Instead of cooperating fully and promptly with NCAA officials, MSU took a combative approach. Big mistake. When the ashes settled the following January, the program had been slapped with a brutal probation — no bowls or TV appearances for the next three seasons, plus scholarship cuts and suspensions. A promising era with Stolz would soon end, as the Board of Trustees chose to clean house.

As was his nature, Hayes told anyone who would listen that he was the one who had put the Spartans on probation by tipping off the investigators. Thirty-six years later, it's more than possible that those tough-guy boasts were bombast and bluster. From a source extremely close to the investigation with no direct ties to MSU, the one who turned Stolz's program in was Schembechler, not Hayes. A payback for the Rose Bowl vote? We'll never know.

A clean sweep of the top three positions in the athletic department brought Joe Kearney in from Washington to be the A.D. The new basketball coach was George M. "Jud" Heathcote from Montana. And taking over the football program, one of the toughest coaching jobs in the country at that time, was Darryl Rogers from San Jose State, moving from one Spartan Stadium to another.

No one did more to bring Big Ten football into the 20th century schematically than Rogers in his four seasons in East Lansing. On the first day of spring practice, he watched his unproven quarterbacks throw for 20 minutes and told little-known sophomore backup Ed Smith that he was the chosen

RED CEDAR REVIVAL

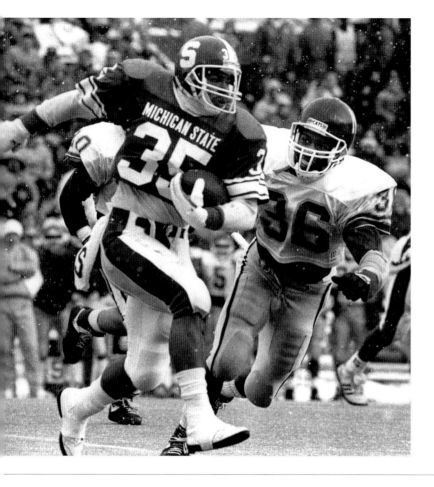

1989-92

TICO DUCKETT

No. 35 Tailback

On beating the nation's top-ranked team and sharing a Big Ten title:

"When we beat Michigan in Ann Arbor during the 1990 season, I scored the game-winning touchdown. That was just a tremendous feeling. Beating Michigan – there's no feeling like it as a Spartan. It's crazy. The celebration starts in the locker room and goes on all through the weekend. There were people back at the Duffy Daugherty Building waiting for us when we got off the bus. It was a non-stop celebration. It feels great to have that victory against your in-state rival. You don't really understand it until you get into the games and see how hard each team is playing. When you're done, it's all about the bragging rights. There's just something about winning a Michigan game that takes it to a different level."

---

one. When he quashed the notion to move stallion-like flanker Kirk Gibson to linebacker, one of the top pass-catch combos in the country was ready to roll.

It didn't hurt that Rogers already had defensive tackle and future conference MVP Larry Bethea on campus or that he took a last-scholarship gamble on an undersized fullback–linebacker from nearby Bath, Dan Bass. From his 32 tackles in Columbus in his first college game to a 99-yard interception return against Wisconsin to his school-record 541 career stops, this Bass was a keeper.

A season of adjustment in 1976 ended with a 4-6-1 mark and nothing close to a marquee win. But a winning attitude took hold the following year, a 7-3-1 campaign. By 1978, the final year of the NCAA slap, the Spartans were ready to do some slapping, too. When that season was over, Rogers' team had earned a share of its first league title in 12 years, beaten Michigan for the first time in nine seasons and broken the record for points in Big Ten play with 41.0 per game.

Smith was a coach on the field and threw as catchable a pass as any player in program history. If teams worried too much about deep balls to Gibson and split end Eugene Byrd, MSU could take smaller bites with throws to tight end Mark Brammer and fullback Alonzo Middleton, as the fifth-ranked Wolverines discovered the hard way before a stunned crowd in Ann Arbor.

On the Spartans' first play from scrimmage, Smith did what was nearly impossible. He overthrew Gibson on a fly pattern, 5 yards behind the last line of defense. Schembechler was apoplectic. After all, that was the one thing he had preached all week: "Don't let 23 get behind you!" If the goal was to keep Michigan honest, the greatest incompletion in MSU history

1993-96

NIGEA CARTER

No. 17/81 WIDE RECEIVER

On coming from Florida to make two of MSU's biggest catches:

"I called Coach Baggett when I got to Detroit and said I wasn't getting on that propeller plane. He drove down and picked me up. Michigan State had never been on my map. But it was what college was in the movies. Plus, my mom had a crush on Coach Baggett. He asked for seconds of whatever she made. It only took me about 10 seconds to go 94 yards with the longest pass in school history. Tony Banks said he was going to throw it to me. And the guy I outran was a 100-meter champ. When I caught the 25-yarder to beat Michigan, it was a dark, snowy night. I've had 255,000 people me they were at that game. But there's no bigger MSU fan than me. I haven't missed a home game since and even left a wedding to get there."

suddenly turned linebackers and safeties into Abraham Lincoln.

Smith surgically attacked the soft underbelly of the defense the rest of the day, as the Spartans rushed for 248 yards and passed for 248 more. The Flying Wallendas never had more balance. Four-time All-Big Ten punter Ray Stachowicz must have felt like the Maytag repairman. And when it was over, a 24-15 upset put them on track for rings, if not the smell of roses. On January 1, 1979, they watched Michigan lose to USC, just as they had done three months earlier.

Rogers has always gotten the credit — or the blame — for interpreting the term "A-squared" differently than most. Actually, he was repeating assistant coach and former captain Dan Underwood's line after the win on October 14 that the Wolverines had "always been arrogant asses and still were arrogant asses," as Henning wrote. But when Rogers used those words at two MSU team banquets, it rekindled the rivalry a bit more.

After an injury-plagued 5-6 season the following year, Rogers wanted to return to the West. The two words he said in his four years in Michigan as often as any but "Thank you" were "It's cold!" And though his departure for sunny Arizona State came on January 18, 1980, three days after Kearney said goodbye, Rogers and Kearney were a package deal, prompting fans to talk about "True Spartans."

On January 20, MSU hired Doug Weaver away from Georgia Tech to be its new athletic director. No one's blood ever ran greener than the former center-linebacker for Munn and assistant coach under Daugherty. Besides his family, the only thing he enjoyed more than hearing the band from his office in Jenison was beating Notre Dame and Michigan. And it took a few years for that to happen again.

Having to act quickly at the

worst possible time for recruiting, Weaver wanted someone who cared about the school half as much as he did. Eventually, he would hire two of them. But on January 29, with most Spartans expecting the return of George Perles, a phenomenally successful assistant with the Pittsburgh Steelers, the school introduced Franklin Dean "Muddy" Waters, better known as "Muddy Who?"

One of the great mistakes or misunderstandings is that Waters was some schlub who should have been coaching high school football. In fact, in the proper setting, he was as good as any coach in the country, as seen by his place in the College Football Hall of Fame for his tremendous success at Hillsdale and building a winning program from scratch at Saginaw Valley. Had he succeeded, Daugherty, which he could have 16 years earlier if Duffy had gone to South Bend, Waters would have done well.

Instead, his hiring made John L. Smith look like a household name and a popular choice 22 years later. The program's funniest coach in the last 45 years always said he had to check his driver's license to make sure his name hadn't been changed to "The 57-year-old" Waters. He didn't help himself by posing for a magazine cover with a clipboard as a shield to deflect flying fruit and rotten vegetables.

But Waters was no rube. He recruited better than most people remember. And his offenses were always entertaining. If the job proved to be more than he could handle, no one ever cared more about his university or would have paid more for the privilege to work there. Was he naïve to the magnitude of big-time football or too loyal to some members of a bickering staff? If so, he was true to himself. The bottom line was a 10-23 record with lots of close losses from 1980-82. His greatest player was probably placekicker Morten Andersen.

The story that says the most about Waters the man was written in the late 1990s, shortly after his successor had been fired and had threatened to sue the school. On a weekend when the players from the 1980s were being recognized, Waters decided not to go down to the field for his introduction and a round of applause. Asked why he wouldn't join the players he loved so much, he said, "If I do that, they'll cheer me and boo George. I'd never do that to him."

The cheers for Perles had been loud and long when he finally rode to the rescue on December 3, 1982. Talking tough and carrying the credibility of four Super Bowl rings, Perles at his best was about as good as it gets. And the Spartans got a lot of that in his first eight seasons, inheriting what was left of a 2-9 team and taking it to six bowls by the end of 1990, including a win in their first trip to Pasadena in 22 years.

Signing a five-year contract that began at $95,000 per season, Perles was smart enough to talk about a five-year plan to reach the Rose Bowl and to deliver on what was interpreted as a promise. He also did more than enough to justify the $175,000 settlement of a suit by the owner of the Philadelphia Stars of the USFL, where Perles' first game as a head coach beyond high school ball was just three months away.

"George Perles is the best thing that has happened to this university in the last 20 years," Breslin said, as the MSU family rallied in a way it hadn't for a decade-and-a-half. "Perles is going to put the MSU football program back on top and keep it there. The greatest thing is that believes everything he says about family, religion and academics being most important. Then, we'll make football players out of them."

Led by holdover linebacker Carl Banks and placekicker-punter Ralf Mojsiejenko, the injury-riddled Spartans showed immediate progress and went 4-6-1 in 1983, including a 28-23 stunner at Notre Dame, where Dave Yarema threw for three TDs. The first sign of what Perles-ball was all about came when noseguard Jim Rinella spotted an Irish blocker 80 pounds on every play and was tougher to budge than a tree stump.

In his first trip to Michigan Stadium as a head coach in 1984, Perles' team beat and beat up the Wolverines 19-7, ending quarterback Jim Harbaugh's season with a broken arm and letting everyone know his year-old challenge that Bo's boys should "pack a lunch and a bring a flashlight" was more than mere bravado. Who can forget Bobby Morse's 87-yard punt return? And in the first Cherry Bowl in the Pontiac Silverdome, a game Waters helped to start, the Spartans lost 10-6 to Army to finish 6-6.

HISTORY HELPS SPARTANS WRITE NEW STORY

1996-99

BILL BURKE

No. 16 Quarterback

On big wins over OSU, Michigan and Florida and a big target:

"Winning in Columbus in '98 was pretty surreal. It was sweet on a couple of levels. No one gave us a sliver of a chance as four-touchdown underdogs. And being from Ohio, I wanted to prove that they should've taken a longer look at me, even if I wasn't a big Ohio State fan. The Citrus Bowl win my last game was great. But the '99 win over Michigan was my favorite. It was at home. We were both undefeated. And the whole time we celebrated, no one left the stands. It didn't seem like I threw for 400 yards. I missed a couple early. We were just focused on getting the win. I never thought about beating Tom Brady. But I had a bigger margin for error. Plaxico Burress was 6-6, 230. I trusted that he could beat any corner."

A 7-5 showing the following year didn't include a marquee win, though MSU scared the corn out of top-ranked Iowa in a 35-31 struggle, as good a game as Perles' teams ever played. The Spartans lost to Georgia Tech 17-14 in the All American Bowl in Birmingham, Ala. But some outstanding recruiting in Michigan and other parts of the country had begun to pay dividends.

Workhorse tailback Lorenzo White, the best thing from Florida since orange juice, set an NCAA rushing record for sophomores, finished with 2,066 yards and wound up fourth in the Heisman race, the same spot he would occupy two years later as a senior. The fact that he hadn't been inducted into the College Football Hall of Fame a quarter-century later could only be considered a gross oversight.

But White had company in the spotlight, as three teammates became two-time All-Americans. Punter Greg Montgomery had at least one 50-yard boot in 33 of 35 games and still holds a Big Ten season record with an average of 49.7 per kick. Offensive tackle Tony Mandarich, a devastating run blocker, once drove a Northwestern defender 20 yards downfield, planted him in the end zone and said, "You stay there!"

And middle linebacker Percy Snow, a heat-seeking missile in the Stunt 4-3 defense, won the Butkus and Lombardi awards as a senior.

In Perles' first six seasons, nine of his players were All-Americans a total of 13 times:

1983 – Banks and Mojsiejenko.

1985 – White.

1986 – Montgomery.

1987 – White, Montgomery and Mandarich.

1988 – Mandarich, Snow and split

49

RED CEDAR REVIVAL

1996-99

AMP CAMPBELL

No. 3 CORNERBACK

On overcoming adversity and finishing with a sixth year of glory:

"I'd never heard of Michigan State. It was always Florida, Florida State, Miami. I didn't want to visit East Lansing. But Coach (Skip) Peete spent four hours at my house when I wasn't even there. I was coming out after '97. But Coach Saban said I'd be a high pick if I came back. When I got hurt at Oregon, I was crushed. There were nights I bawled like a baby, with a metal plate and four screws holding my head. My 2-year-old daughter kept me going. To make it back in '99 and beat Oregon on an 85-yard return brings chills. As I got to the goal line, I said, 'Thank you, Lord!' I almost picked Tom Brady off twice that year. And beating Florida was very important. When Steve Spurrier said I should go to prep school, I always wanted to play them."

end Andre Rison.

1989 — Snow, offensive tackle Bob Kula and defensive back Harlon Barnett.

Yarema, Rison and Mark Ingram provided offensive fireworks in 1986. But with White injured much of the year, the Spartans lost 20-17 to Rose Bowl winner Arizona State and fell to three other teams — Iowa, Indiana and Northwestern — by a field goal. At the time it was a great disappointment, soothed only by a 20-15 win over the Irish. Looking back, it only sharpened the focus for one of greatest years in school history.

The 1987 season began with a breathtaking show on Labor Day evening, "The Great American Football Celebration." It was MSU's first home night game, something other schools wouldn't attempt for many years. And a 27-13 win over USC was the first of two holiday triumphs over the same school, the only time that has happened in NCAA history. White rushed for two TDs, while freshman John Langeloh kicked two field goals — a script to remember.

Any time you give up two safeties and two punt returns for scores in the same half, you're probably not going to win the game, as the Spartans discovered 12 nights later in a 31-8 loss at Notre Dame. The Irish took a 2-0 with no time off the clock, seemingly impossible to do, when Blake Ezor took the opening kickoff at the 1-foot line and kneeled just inside the end zone. Before the end of the quarter, Tim Brown had won the Heisman with 71- and 66-yard runbacks.

The following Saturday, the day after Daugherty's death at age 72, MSU entertained powerhouse Florida State and fell 31-3. About the only highlight was the return to town of Lansing-born, Seminole-schooled Burt Reynolds, better known as Buddy in his playing days. But standing 1-2 with the toughest non-conference schedule in school history, the Spartans wouldn't lose again for 11½ months.

The fun began with the Big Ten opener, a 19-14 comeback win at Iowa. Perles' halftime tirade got everyone's attention. Montgomery's punts, a ferocious defense and a TD toss from Bobby McAllister to tight end Mike Sargent got the job done. MSU passed for only 13 yards, but White rushed for 166 — just the kind of offense its head coach preferred.

Returning home to face Michigan, the Spartans knew they could win games with defense. They didn't know they would need seven interceptions, including four by safety John Miller off color-blind quarterback Demetrius Brown. White rushed for 185 and scored twice in the first half. But it took a pick by Barnett with the Wolverines driving to give MSU its first series victory at home in 18 years.

The first blowout win of the year was a 38-0 suffocation at Northwestern. White outrushed Byron Sanders, Barry's older brother, 187-26. And the game wasn't as close as the score indicated. But the next week's game couldn't have been closer. Illinois spoiled the Spartans' Homecoming and escaped with a 14-all tie, blocking a game-winning field goal.

Two days before the Illini visit, the nation's No. 1 rushing defense got its nickname. That was when "Gang Green" first appeared in the *Lansing State Journal*. And when MSU went to Ohio State as a 1½-point underdog nine days later, Brutus was the only Buckeye who left the stadium smiling. Ohioans Snow and Travis Davis were terrific as the Spartans won the rushing battle 247-2 and the game 13-7. The Buckeyes got 79 yards on the game's first play and just 68 the rest of the day.

When November arrived, the mission was clear: Win out and pack for Pasadena. MSU's stretch run began with a 45-3 pounding of Purdue. Backup tailback Blake Ezor rushed for 151 yards and White 144, setting up a game with Indiana for the Rose Bowl berth. Yes, you read that correctly — the Spartans and Hoosiers, as unlikely a perfecta wager as there was in any conference before the season.

After an emotion-packed memorial service for Daugherty that morning at St. Thomas Aquinas Church, MSU smashed everything in sight. Indiana never had a chance in a 27-3 mismatch. In one of the most heroic efforts in Big Ten history, White carried the ball an astounding 56 times — one shy of the conference record — for 292 yards. It was Toss Right, Toss Left and toss in a 90-yard kickoff return by Ezor to open the second half.

"He's probably not good enough to win the Heisman," Perles said of his brightest star after receiving a bouquet of roses, his voice dripping with sarcasm. "Gaining close to 300 yards isn't enough. Carrying as much as he did isn't enough....But I think it is!"

He hadn't known what to think a few moments earlier when Hoosiers coach Bill Mallory made an unexpected visit to the winners' locker room. In a typically classy gesture after every player dropped to one knee, Mallory delivered as fiery a message as anyone had heard in Spartan Stadium:

"By God, I commend you! We have a lot of respect for you. You're a damn fine football team! Congratulations on winning the title. I'm just going to say this: By God, go out to the Coast and kick their ass, because we're all damn tired ..."

We'll never know how that sentence finished. In less than a second, the locker room erupted. Suddenly, MSU wasn't just playing for itself. It was representing a conference that was 2-16 in its last 18 chances in the Rose Bowl. Despite Perles' protests that the Spartans weren't responsible for those L's, it was up to them to bring home a win. And if the game had started that moment, the margin might have been bigger than it was.

After finishing league play with a 30-9 win at Wisconsin and a 7-0-1 record, MSU finally learned which team it would face on January 1. UCLA was favored to beat USC that afternoon in the Los Angeles Memorial Coliseum. For most of the game, it appeared that would happen. But Rodney Peete got the best of Troy Aikman in the fourth quarter, setting up a Spartans-Trojans rematch.

The team plane left Christmas Day from Capital City Airport and took 187 passengers to LAX, ranging from 1-year-old Nicholas Saban Jr. to 80-year-old Nellie Perles. Buses delivered the official party to the team hotel in Newport Beach, far enough south to avoid most

1998-2001

HERB HAYGOOD

No. 2 WIDE RECEIVER

On four of the sweetest victories any Spartan has ever experienced:

"I hurt my knee in high school, missed three games and came back. On my visit to Michigan State, I learned I had a torn ACL. Coach Saban stuck with me. He never wavered. Winning at Ohio State in '98 was huge. Those were my final two schools. Beating Florida the next year was awesome, being from Sarasota. I knew their guys. So did Amp, Gari Scott and Paul Edinger. And it was Coach Williams' first game. I went 68 yards on fourth down to beat Notre Dame in 2000. When I caught it, all I saw were cheerleaders. I always say I got Bob Davie fired. I was supposed to get it on the last play vs. Michigan my senior year, too. I was all alone before the snap. Their radio guy was screaming, 'Watch Haygood!' That was funny."

distractions while still providing plenty of activities.

Defensive tackle Mark Nichols was the champion eater at the 32nd annual Beef Bowl at Lawry's, downing four 19-ounce portions of prime rib. Bob Hope emceed the Big Ten Dinner of Champions. Magic Johnson entertained nearly 10,000 MSU fans in a packed Century Plaza ballroom. But the highlight of the trip prior to kickoff was the sight of the Spartan Marching Band turning south onto Colorado Boulevard, led by proud former president and professor Walter Adams.

The game saw Perles' players grab a 14-3 halftime lead on White's two TD runs. But despite 17 tackles from Snow, the game's MVP, USC caught fire and tied the game at 17 with 8:33 left. That set up one of the most famous plays in MSU history on third-and-9 at its 30. As McAllister scrambled toward the right sideline and the punt team prepared to take the field, he leaped and floated an adlib toss that Rison snared at the Trojans 36.

Remember the season opener and Langeloh's first two field goals? After hitting from 40 yards early in the fourth quarter, he delivered again from 36 with 4:34 left for a 20-17 lead. But Peete wasn't finished. He led USC on what looked like a game-winning drive until his fumble bounced into Todd Krumm's waiting arms — a ball Perles said that Daugherty had reached down from heaven to knock loose.

At 9-2-1, their best record in 21 years, the Spartans seemed to have everything going. Then, the Green Bay Packers called. A chance to coach one of pro football's most storied franchises was beyond flattering. Twenty years after Vince Lombardi's departure, it was time for someone with some of the same toughness and success in building a championship team. General Manager Ron Wolf had his sights set

1998-2001
JOSH THORNHILL
No. 50 LINEBACKER

On being Charlie Thornhill's son and striving to be all you can be:

"With my dad, I obviously grew up around the Green and White. It was almost a genetic upbringing. I was always around Bubba Smith and Percy Snow and those guys. It was pretty much ingrained in me right from the beginning. Then, I got to Michigan State and learned about being a Spartan from Nick Saban and Ken Mannie. It's just a selfless, team-first mentality. The best quote I saw coming into the program was a sign hanging on Coach Mannie's door. It said 'Tough love – We won't accept you as what you are but as a vision of what you could be.' That sums up my entire time there. With the Michigan State Players Association, we try to keep the Green and White family mentality going beyond four or five years."

on Perles.

Remembering the previous decades, MSU scrambled to keep a coach who had said he "would walk to East Lansing" when he had a contract with Philadelphia. President John DiBiaggio was tied up in Hungary. But with the backing of Breslin, the school countered with a 10-year contract, an annuity and roughly half the income potential Perles would have had with a $450,000-a-year deal in Green Bay. The final arm-twist was a call from Hannah, who said, "George, you're not going anywhere."

Instead, the coach who left that year was Saban, as good a defensive coordinator as there was in college football. He would do all right as a head coach, too. More on that later. But his move to the Houston Oilers was felt as a recruiter, a technician and a teacher. When the Spartans went 0-4-1 to open the 1988 season, Saban's departure was just one of the reasons. The loss of Mandarich for three games for seeking to enter the NFL Draft, then withdrawing that request, didn't help.

Eventually, the Spartans turned it around, won six in a row and met Georgia in the Mazda Gator Bowl on Sunday night, January 1. It was the last game for McAllister and Rison. And when Iowa coach Hayden Fry had said Rison could catch 100 passes a year, he wasn't talking about the NFL. After MSU got behind the Bulldogs, it seemed that Rison might do most of that in one night. He finished with nine catches for 252 yards and nearly brought MSU all the way back in a 34-27 setback.

With Dan Enos taking over at quarterback and Courtney Hawkins filling Rison's role, the Spartans could throw the ball when they had to. But Ezor, Tico Duckett and Hyland Hickson were excellent runners, and the 1989 team finished 8-4, losing close games to Notre Dame,

Miami, Michigan and Illinois and outmuscling everyone else.

Amid allegations of steroid use in a story in *The Detroit News*, Perles' teams preferred what he called "smash-mouth football." Others said MSU would be national champs every year if the game were played in a phone booth. In a 76-14 win over Northwestern, Ezor scored a school-record six touchdowns, though Perles did all that he could to hold that score down on a snowy day. When Wildcats coach Francis Peay said he would pull his team off the field if the student section didn't stop firing snowballs, Perles prayed for one more direct hit.

The Spartans rolled host Hawaii 33-13 in the 1989 Aloha Bowl, as Ezor rushed for 179 yards and three scores. But things had already begun to unravel, with far-reaching ramifications. With Weaver about to step down as A.D., Perles let a disbelieving president know at the team banquet that he wanted to add that job. DiBiaggio, a member of the Knight Commission and a firm believer that those roles were in conflict, said Perles had to choose.

While the team was in Honolulu, new New York Jets G.M. Dick Steinberg called and wanted Perles to become their head coach. Perles preferred to stay in East Lansing but desperately wanted a dual role, even offering to do the A.D.'s job for free. But DiBiaggio held his ground as a power struggle with the Democrats on the Board of Trustees ensued.

When the smoke cleared, Perles was summoned home from New York, where he was about to sign a contract and be presented to a different brand of media. The efforts of trustees Larry Owen, Joel Ferguson and Bob Weiss to secure a fifth and deciding vote had been successful. When Republican Kathy Wilbur agreed, subject to a one-year performance review, it was time to vote.

After an intense period of public comment in Kellogg Center's Lincoln Room, the role-call tally on January 23 became the next day's headline in *The Detroit News*: "PERLES 5, DiBIAGGIO 3." The public reaction to the entire process was overwhelmingly negative. And the wounds took years to heal, lasting until both men left the university.

Against that backdrop, with Perles determined to prove one person could do both jobs and DiBiaggio waiting for his chance to undo the deed, MSU had one of its greatest seasons. Many thought that 8-3-1 team was Perles' best, even better than the Rose Bowl champions. With three losses by a total of eight points, an unforgettable victory over No. 1 Michigan and another bowl win over USC, it was hard to argue with that thinking.

After a 23-all tie at Syracuse, the Spartans lost 20-19 to top-ranked Notre Dame in the final minute on a fluky completion, "The Immaculate Deflection." A 34-10 win over Rutgers in the Meadowlands was marred by Hawkins' broken collarbone, an injury that hurt more the following week in a 12-7 loss at home to Iowa. That outcome sent the Hawkeyes to the Rose Bowl, though they shared the crown with MSU, Michigan and Illinois.

With a 1-2-1 mark when they left for Ann Arbor, the Spartans were given almost no chance of winning. Jay Marriotti's day-before column in *The National* billed the game as "No. 1 vs. no one." Some saw a likely whipping as validation of "The Michigan Way," which only made Perles' players more determined. They were already good enough to win. That day, they deserved to.

Again without Hawkins' services, MSU managed a 7-all tie at halftime, then answered every challenge in the last 30 minutes. Enos, Hickson and Duckett supplied the offense, while Carlos Jenkins and Mike Iaquaniello made big plays on defense. But the Wolverines answered with Derrick Alexander's second TD catch to trail 28-27 with :06 left. Nearly six years before the first overtime period, Michigan coach Gary Moeller had to go for the win.

As the Spartans braced for yet another fade pattern, Desmond Howard broke open inside and was tripped by cornerback Eddie Brown — an obvious foul but a smart decision. While every official missed the call, Howard couldn't hold Elvis Grbac's pass when he hit the ground. As ABC's Keith Jackson said: "HOWARD ... HE DROPPED IT ... He dropped it ... He had it ... and he dropped it."

Instead of getting another chance from the 1-yard line, where they had failed to score in four first-half chances, the Wolverines could only hope for a miracle. And they nearly got one after recovering an onside

HISTORY HELPS SPARTANS WRITE NEW STORY

1999-2001

T.J. DUCKETT

No. 8 RUNNING BACK

On two memorable games long before the 2001 win over Michigan:

"I'd watched a lot of Michigan State games when Tico was there a decade earlier. But I'll never forget my first game as a freshman when we beat Oregon. It was like a kid's dream. You walk out of the tunnel at Spartan Stadium, and the fans go crazy. With that energy, the ghosts of old Spartans, it's a big deal. Then, the last game of that Big Ten season against Penn State, I scored four rushing touchdowns. I'll never forget that T.J. Turner picked off a pass after my fourth score, and we were getting ready to finish off the victory. I'm in my stance at the 20-yard-line, listening to Ryan Van Dyke call the play, and all of a sudden you hear the fans chanting 'T.J. Duck-ett!...T.J. Duck-ett!' I thought that was amazing."

kick. With no time left, Grbac's desperation heave was batted twice and finally grabbed at the 2 by none other than Brown, who had one more catch than Howard in the final three plays.

One year earlier, after a 10-7 win in East Lansing, Schembechler had said crisply, "The better team won." This time, it was Perles' turn, summarizing his biggest road win with a memorable line: "The tougher team won." To a street fighter from Detroit's Vernor Highway, there was no greater compliment.

MSU lost 15-13 on five Illinois field goals the following week, then won five in a row to earn championship rings and a bid to the John Hancock Bowl in El Paso, Texas. With a healthy Hawkins earning MVP honors, the Spartans made it three in a row over USC, 17-16. Finishing his fourth bowl trip the same way as his first, Langeloh's field goal proved to be the difference, this time from 52 yards.

That finish wasn't nearly enough to make DiBiaggio change his mind. He never thought Perles should be coach and A.D. And despite an excellent performance review, the goalposts had moved. DiBiaggio had six trustee votes in his pocket. Thus, Perles never had a chance.

He chose to stay on as head coach. But with a 54-36-4 mark in his first eight seasons, too much damage had been done.

Just as Merrily Dean Baker arrived to take over as A.D., DiBiaggio stunned her and many others by accepting the presidency at Tufts. The school's new president would be MSU alumnus M. Peter McPherson, who had held several high-level positions in the Ford and Reagan administrations and been Bank of America's executive vice president. But Perles was 0-2 in those relationships.

After losing seasons in 1991-92, the Spartans held Rose Bowl hero

RED CEDAR REVIVAL

2003-06

DREW STANTON

No. 5 QUARTERBACK

On a 41-38 win in Evanston, Ill., the greatest rally in NCAA history:

"I think my favorite memory is from our senior year when we came back after being down 35 against Northwestern. I think we just kind of felt the momentum shift. One thing that I've always tried to do in my career is not look at the clock or the score of the game. You just go out there in certain situations and play. You have fun and focus on trying to get first downs. That's really what we said. We just had to move the ball to get the momentum going. When the momentum shifted, you could feel it, and one thing after another happened. The defense stopped them. We got a blocked punt. And offensively, we did what we had to do. It was a complete team victory."

Tyrone Wheatley to 33 rushing yards in a 17-7 triumph over Michigan, Perles' fourth victory in the series. But MSU fell 41-20 to Big Ten champ Wisconsin in the Coca-Cola Bowl in Tokyo, then lost 18-7 to Louisville in the 1993 Liberty Bowl in Memphis, Tenn., to finish 6-6, the program's best record in a four-year span.

It's hard to imagine a more tumultuous season than 1994, lowlighted by allegations of academic shortcuts. The Spartans were 5-6 on the field but forfeited those wins as self-imposed sanctions after a rigorous investigation that prevented further penalties. That four-year probation sealed Perles' fate, though the NCAA didn't hold him accountable. By then, former allies like Ferguson were adversaries. And when Perles was fired in November, no one could have figured he would return as one of the president's bosses on the Board of Trustees.

McPherson's first coaching search wound up with three strong candidates: Penn State assistant Fran Ganter, a breath of stale air, as one trustee put it; Saban, then Bill Belichick's defensive coordinator with the Cleveland Browns, and a secret candidate, Nebraska legend Tom Osborne.

Clearly, Osborne was McPherson's choice. And that hire was closer to happening than anyone knew. Osborne fit the president's profile — a highly successful, proven entity with no ties to Perles or the past. Osborne gave it serious thought less than two months before the Cornhuskers won their first of three national titles in four years. He even presented the option to his coaching staff. But conservative to the core, he finally said no.

The other two choices were thoroughly vetted. Ganter was seen as a possible successor to Joe Paterno, though that job wouldn't open for another 17 years.

HISTORY HELPS SPARTANS WRITE NEW STORY

Eventually, he cooled on MSU as much as it did on him. That left Saban, who wanted the job and was ready to do it. Despite lobbying from many directions, McPherson never saw him as a coach who would go on to win three national titles. Their relationship would never be a plus.

But Saban could make a bad team better and help a good one do amazing things. In five years as MSU's head coach, as long a stop as he has made until his sixth season at Alabama begins, he steered the program through probation to a 34-24-1 mark and four bowl appearances. He also became the school's first coach to win his first game with Michigan, finishing 7-4 against the Wolverines, Irish and Buckeyes.

Saban's first game back with the Spartans was anything but promising. After a 50-10 loss at home to Nebraska, he ripped his players for failing to compete and promised a change before back-to-back visits to Louisville and Purdue. It was a risky move psychologically. But Saban knew the team had talent at the skill positions. It was 4-3-1 and primed for an upset when seventh-ranked Michigan showed up on a snowy November 4.

Lloyd Carr's first team as a collegiate head coach featured the slashing runs of tailback Tim Biakabutuka. MSU never stopped him in a 191-yard rushing day, 122 fewer than he would have three weeks later against Ohio State. But the Spartans had more weapons with the mobility of quarterback Tony Banks, the versatility of runner-receiver Scott Greene and receiver-returner Derrick Mason plus the big-play ability of receivers Muhsin Muhammad and Nigea Carter. They would need every one of them.

After Greene had rushed for two TDs and Mason had scored on a 70-yard punt return, MSU still trailed 25-21 after a Mercury Hayes tally with 3:38 left. That set up as good a drive as any in Big Ten history — 11 plays that gained 103 yards in 2:14. On fourth-and-11 at his 32, Banks hit Mason at the visitors sideline for 11 yards and two centimeters. But during a contentious measurement, the Spartans had a dead-ball personal foul and wound up with first-and-25 back at their 28.

An apparent interception by freshman cornerback Charles Woodson sailed through his hands to a juggling Mason. And when Banks scrambled to his right and found Carter at the goal line for a 25-yard score, the eighth completion for 94 yards on that series, MSU had its third win over the Wolverines in six seasons. Years later, Saban would say that game had given fans an unrealistic view of the gap between the programs.

A 24-20 loss to Penn State in the last minute meant the Spartans were 6-4-1 when they faced Gerry DiNardo's LSU Tigers in the Poulan Weed-Eater Independence Bowl on December 29 in Shreveport, La. MSU lost that track meet 45-26 in Banks' final game. And 1996 was much the same, minus the win over Michigan. A 55-14 whipping at Nebraska and a crushing 32-29 loss in the regular-season finale at Penn State left Saban's program 6-5 before a 38-0 loss to Tyrone Willingham's Stanford Cardinal on December 31 in El Paso.

A 5-0 start in 1997 included a 23-7 win at Notre Dame, the first of five straight triumphs over the Irish. But a bizarre 19-17 loss at two-time defending Big Ten champ Northwestern and a 23-7 defeat by the Wolverines in East Lansing triggered a four-game losing streak, including a 22-21 meltdown at Purdue. It was Michigan's year to earn a piece of its only national crown since 1948 — five fewer than the Spartans' total in that span. But after a stunning 49-14 slam of No. 4 Penn State, a game when Sedrick Irvin and Marc Renaud each rushed for more than 200 yards, MSU lost 51-23 to Washington in the Aloha Bowl on Christmas Day in Honolulu to wind up 7-5.

With recruiting at a critical stage, there were better times for Saban-to-Indianapolis reports to begin. He had talked to Colts President Bill Polian many times, sometimes out of mutual respect and sometimes because Polian's son, Brian, was a graduate assistant for the Spartans. Saban had already been an NFL assistant twice and would later leave LSU to take over the Miami Dolphins. This time, in a hastily called news conference, he said, "I'm committed to the job we have to do here at Michigan State. I've said that before."

That job was never tougher than in 1998, a 6-6 season with no bowl invitation. Sitting home was even harder to swallow after two of the sweetest, most unexpected victories

RED CEDAR REVIVAL

2005-08

JAVON RINGER

No. 39/23   RUNNING BACK

On a mid-career coaching change and an All-American senior year:

"I tore my ACL and couldn't take visits. When I was able to walk again, I made one trip to MSU. I played two years for John L. and two for Coach Dantonio. Coach Smith was awesome. But no one liked his assistants. Players dreaded going to practice. With Coach D., it was completely different. I won't forget losing to Notre Dame in the pouring rain and coming so close twice vs. Michigan. My junior year was the 'Little Brother' comment, which I thought was kind of petty. That set it up for the following year. To finally beat them at their place made us all so happy. It all taught me how to deal with adversity and negative people. I just wish I could go there again now."

in school history. After a 23-16 collapse at home against Colorado State and a 48-14 beating at Oregon, no one could have written the script for a 45-23 rout of No. 10 Notre Dame, an ABC prime-time telecast. Fueled by a Richard Newsome punt block and score and a Julian Peterson interception return, MSU led 42-3 at halftime. And that wasn't the strangest game of the year.

Two weeks after a 19-18 loss at Minnesota, the 4-4 Spartans were almost universally viewed as the next victim of the top-ranked Buckeyes when they left for Columbus. Instead, they came back as the Team of the Week in college football. Trailing 24-9 in the third quarter and punting from the shadow of their goal line, no one could have predicted 19 unanswered points and a 28-24 upset for the ages. But when that short kick bounced off an Ohio State blocker, MSU got the ball near midfield and new momentum.

The passing combination of Bill Burke-to-Plaxico Burress was more than the Buckeyes could handle. And after standout defensive lineman Robaire Smith suffered a broken leg on a cheap shot, Peterson took over and proved to be Joe Germaine's worst nightmare with sacks and takeaways. Ohio State's last chance ended when the Spartans blitzed on four straight plays and iced the win with cornerback Renaldo Hill's interception at the goal line. Suddenly, the hosts' flight and hotel reservations for the Fiesta Bowl and the first BCS Championship were worthless. Not surprisingly, MSU lost 25-24 at home against Purdue the next week.

A 51-28 loss at Penn State was the fourth-straight season-ending blowout. But this one was different. The Spartans had done enough to know they should have been traveling somewhere and realized they could compete with anyone the following year.

HISTORY HELPS SPARTANS WRITE NEW STORY

2006-09

BLAIR WHITE

No. 25 Wide Receiver

On embracing the past and going from a walk-on to the NFL:

"For me, it was about the players who came before me – the All-Americans and All-Big Ten-ers who made this program what it is today and what it can be in the future. I played for them, especially the guy who wasn't the most talented. The guy I suited up for was the special teamer who had to fight to make the team. The trainers won't wrap an ice pack around his knee until they tend to the five-star recruit who wants another bottle of lotion in his locker. My last couple of years, I had the privilege of playing for Coach Dantonio and his staff. One of the great things he did was welcome back the football alumni. I didn't recognize the significance they had in making us Michigan State."

As happened in the winters and springs of 1955, 1965, 1987 and 2010, the disappointment after a non-winning season helped drive the next team to greatness. And 1999 was about as good as it gets.

MSU opened under the lights with a 27-20 payback of Oregon, with the winning TD an 85-yard fumble return by courageous cornerback Amp Campbell, who had suffered a broken neck 12 months earlier in Eugene. Two weeks later, fellow Floridian Gary Scott had the biggest play, an 80-yard catch-and-tightrope sprint to seal a 23-13 win at Notre Dame. But four bigger wins were yet to come in a 10-2 breakthrough, just the second season with double-digit wins in school history.

For the second time in three years, the Wolverines paid a visit in a matchup of 5-0 league leaders. This time, the Spartans got the victory over a third-ranked team in as intense a game as the rivalry has seen. A year earlier, Burress had said going against Michigan's secondary could be like "taking candy from a baby." This time, despite both coaches' best efforts to eliminate bulletin-board material, linebacker Ian Gold said he felt there was only one program in the state – an understandable viewpoint, actually.

But the game was all about deeds, not words. Burke set an MSU record with 400 yards through the air. Burress was brilliant with 10 catches for 255 yards and three scores, plus a memorable pancake block on Wolverines receiver David Terrell, who had been summoned to play defense since no one else could. Morris Watts' play calling was never better, including a flea-flicker to Burress that set the tone in the first quarter. Safety Aric Morris had a key interception of Drew Henson, after Carr chose not to start the third quarter with Tom Brady. And when Brady caught fire, he ran out of time in a 34-31 classic.

Fearing a letdown, the Spartans followed with back-to-back embarrassments on the road, losing 52-28 to Purdue and Drew Brees and 40-10 to Wisconsin and Heisman winner Ron Dayne. Where other teams would have stayed down for the count, MSU regrouped and crushed the Buckeyes 23-7 with second-half domination, then capped its winningest regular season in 34 years with a 35-28 win over Penn State. In a sign of things to come, freshman tailback T.J. Duckett, recruited as a linebacker, rushed for four TDs.

Saban figured that was an appropriate time to inquire about a pay raise. McPherson thought it was time to win a bowl game, something that hadn't happened in nine years. And both men got what they wanted — just not together. When Saban suddenly became a hot candidate to succeed DiNardo at LSU, McPherson wasn't about to beg him to stay. But when Saban flew back to Michigan to try to convince his assistants to join him in Baton Rouge, his staff stuck together and finished the job.

A lot of people know how close the Spartans came to hiring Glen Mason, who had just completed his third year at Minnesota. McPherson thought Mason was the man before negotiations broke down at the 11th hour. But MSU also made another run at Osborne and nearly landed him. The timing was much better between his three national titles and three terms in the U.S. House of Representatives. When it came time to vote, Osborne's family said no.

Foiled in that effort, facing a difficult bowl challenge from No. 10 Florida and fearing the loss of a recruiting class, McPherson went along with Ferguson's plan to promote Assistant Head Coach Bobby Williams, a popular choice with the staff and players. That worked for a while, with Williams going 2-0 against the Irish, 1-1 vs. the Wolverines and 2-0 in bowls, the best postseason record in school history.

That started on January 1, 2000, when the Spartans and Steve Spurrier's Gators exchanged shoves before the Florida Citrus Bowl began. They kept battling for a full four quarters in Orlando, where the 6-foot-6 Burress caught 13 passes for 185 yards in his final collegiate game as a junior. But the hero was the smallest player in uniform, MSU placekicker Paul Edinger. The Florida product began the scoring with a 46-yard field goal, then gave his team a 37-34 triumph by connecting from 39 on the final play.

The drama continued in Williams' first full season, as freshman quarterback Jeff Smoker hit a slanting Herb Haygood on fourth-and-10 for a 68-yard score and a 27-21 win over Notre Dame. As Haygood, a former track sprinter, pulled away from the secondary, he saw himself on the scoreboard and began celebrating. But the Spartans dropped six of their last eight games to finish 5-6. The only other moment of glory was a 30-10 thrashing of Brees and the Rose Bowl-bound Boilermakers.

MSU bounced back in 2001, winning 17-10 in South Bend on Charles Rogers' fourth-quarter catch-and-run. It was 2-2 in the Big Ten and unranked when it hosted No. 6 Michigan in one of the wildest games ever played. Though Rogers and Wolverines receiver Marquise Walker alternated with big catches and inexplicable drops, the dominant force was Duckett, who rushed for 211 yards against a defense that was allowing just 54.4 per game. No. 8 also made every catch he could.

Trailing 24-20, the Spartans took over at the Michigan 44 after a 28-yard punt by Hayden Epstein, less than half the length of his 57-yard, first-quarter field goal. After two of the Wolverines' school-record 12 sacks, the game appeared to be over thanks to a fourth-and-16 incompletion. But MSU got a reprieve on cornerback Jeremy LeSueur's attempted decapitation of Rogers 50 yards away from the ball. And the fun was just beginning.

After a Haygood grab for 17, Michigan came to the rescue again with 12 men on the field, negating a sack. However, the penalty yardage was assessed from the spot of the tackle, not the line of scrimmage. Also, MSU's last timeout to stop the clock wasn't returned when the late-flying flag should have stopped it automatically. So when Duckett split wide-left and caught a 9-yard slant on fourth-and-4, Smoker spiked the ball on first-and-goal at the 3 with :17 left. His second-down scramble to the 2 created a controversy that rages today.

As the seconds ticked away — 5,

4, 3, 2, 1...— the ball was snapped and slammed to the turf. The scoreboard still showed :01 after clock operator "Spartan Bob" Stehlin punched the stop button in the press box. If it seemed like the longest second in history to the Wolverines, Big Ten Coordinator of Officials David Parry later said, "We could find nothing that suggested there had been a mistake made." And seven independent media sources reviewed the play frame-by-frame without finding an error.

The bottom line is that the game was still Michigan's to win. For those who say the Wolverines had already done that if not for an official's ruling, they're right. If not for a pair of silly penalties, MSU never would have had the ball in the red zone. And with one snap remaining, the Spartans still had to gain 2 more yards against a Top 10 team with an analyst screaming, "Watch Haygood!"

Instead, Smoker rolled to his right, got a break when officials missed a hold on defensive end Larry Stevens, then lobbed the ball back across the field into the end zone. As the ball seemed to hang like a balloon, Duckett resisted the temptation to signal for a fair catch. The catch he made a second or two later was fair enough to trigger a wild celebration. The Duckett brothers both had a game-winning TD against Michigan. And Wolverines linebacker Larry Foote had to wait for his helmet to come down after it rebounded high off the turf.

There was no point-after-touchdown attempt, just a 26-24 final that will never be erased despite a lot of whining and the famous broadcast line, "It's criminal!" Just to be sure there was no appearance of impropriety, the Big Ten switched to having the official time kept on the field, a move it had considered for some time. And it wasn't long before the conference became a leader in the development of instant replay. If the developments of November 3, 2001, had anything to do with that, the officials deserved a second chance.

None of that helped the 5-2 Spartans the rest of the way, as their momentum evaporated with consecutive losses to Indiana, Purdue and Penn State. The bleeding stopped with a 55-7 mashing of Missouri in a game rescheduled from the week of September 11. And they finished with a 44-35 win over Fresno State and top overall draft pick David Carr in the Silicon Valley Bowl on December 31 in San Jose, Calif. — in another Spartan Stadium. It was Duckett's last game for MSU and Williams' last triumphant moment.

Almost nothing went right for the 2002 Spartans, who surrendered 42 points or more seven times, including 61 at Penn State, the final chapter in a 4-8 season. After a 49-3 loss in Ann Arbor, Mickey York of Fox Sports Detroit asked Williams, "Bobby, have you lost this football team?" In an honest-but-suicidal response, Williams said, "Don't know." When the plug was pulled two days later, MSU A.D. Ron Mason said, "At that point, I really felt if he wasn't sure, who was?"

Watts took over as head coach for the last three games and went 1-2. But it was time for another coaching search, with Mason zeroing in on Baltimore Ravens defensive coordinator Marvin Lewis. When Lewis made it clear he preferred to coach in the pros, Mason kept his thoughts to himself and a very select group that had to know. That cut down on a lot of the leaks and lobbying with past hires. And only a handful of people had given much thought to Louisville's John L. Smith.

When the story broke the night of the Cardinals' 38-15 loss to Marshall in the GMAC Bowl, the shock in Michigan was matched by the anger in Kentucky. At his introductory press conference in East Lansing, it was clear that Smith had a strong personality and a lot to learn about the culture of the Spartans. Some would question whether he ever did that in a 22-26 stint. Others would point to a lack of acceptance and three giveaways that might have changed everything.

Smith got off to a 7-1 start, losing only to Louisiana Tech, the first sign of trouble. His team still climbed from nowhere to No. 9 in the nation. Then, reality set it. After a 27-20 loss to No. 11 Michigan that wasn't as close as the final score, MSU fell at Ohio State and was blown out at Wisconsin. A 41-10 win over Penn State was the eighth victory of 2003, a record for any first-year coach of the Spartans. But an 8-5 year ended with a 17-3 thumping by Nebraska in the MasterCard Alamo Bowl on December 29 in San Antonio, Texas, the game when quarterback Drew Stanton suffered a serious knee injury covering a punt.

That was the only postseason appearance the Spartans had in Smith's four seasons. His quirky behavior was harder to defend when he went 2-2 against the Irish and 0-4 vs. the Wolverines and Buckeyes. Smith took the stripe off the football helmet, the player's name off the back of the jersey and the fun out of being a Spartan in excruciating losses at Michigan in 2004, at Ohio State in 2005 and against Notre Dame in 2006. After that, he would have had an easier time climbing Mount Kilimanjaro blindfolded.

The defeat in Ann Arbor was difficult to fathom when MSU led 27-10 and DeAndra Cobb was rushing for 205 yards. But when Stanton suffered a separated shoulder on a hit by LaMarr Woodley late in the first half, everything changed. And when the Wolverines remembered that Braylon Edwards was an eligible receiver, the Spartans were in trouble. Failing to recover an onside kick and allowing Edwards to score three late TDs sealed their fate in a 45-37 triple-overtime crusher.

The loss in Columbus will long be remembered for MSU's fast-field-goal futility, when a kick that could have meant a 20-7 halftime lead was returned for a score, shrinking the lead to 17-14. That was when Smith told ABC's Jack Arute on his way to the locker room: "That's a dang coaching mistake! The players are playing their tails off, and the coaches are screwing it up!" After a solid third quarter, the Spartans were slapped 35-24 by the Buckeyes.

And in a second-half monsoon that fans enjoyed a lot more when their team led 37-21, MSU went away from seemingly unstoppable ballcarrier Jehuu Caulcrick and let the Irish escape with a 40-37 win. The Spartans lost eight of their final nine games to wind up 4-8. Their only win was an equally mind-boggling 41-38 turnaround at Northwestern, when 38 straight points created the greatest comeback in NCAA history.

It was great to see Stanton's class and persistence be rewarded with a place in the record book. In terms of fixing persistent problems, it was also postponing the inevitable. A school that had three head football coaches in 40 years from 1933-72 would have a 10th leader in 36 seasons from 1972-2007. But who should get that opportunity?

When then-A.D.-designate Mark Hollis handled the school's most recent search, the goal was to find an established head coach with a championship pedigree and an appreciation for what MSU is about. Instead of hiring the first good candidate, Hollis wanted to wait for a great one. Heading into season No. 6, Dantonio has fit that description about as well as anyone could with one of the best turnaround jobs in Big Ten history.

His credentials in November 2006? For a longtime secondary coach, let's start with a pick-six:

Six years as a trusted assistant in East Lansing and an important role with a 10-2 team.

• • •

Responsibility for a nasty defense that carried Ohio State to the Big Ten's last national title.

• • •

Three years of successful head coaching experience and program building at Cincinnati.

• • •

Support from key allies like basketball coach Tom Izzo and others who could help to unify.

• • •

The values and life priorities that helped assure he would turn corners, not simply cut them.

• • •

A belief that things would change and a commitment to "The Dream, The Dream, The Dream."

Thus, Dantonio was hired as the school's 24th head football coach on November 27, 2006. After assembling his staff, it was assimilation on the run, beginning with recruiting and an appearance at the *Detroit Free Press* All-State Banquet.

The first thing he needed to do was to change the collective mindset. If too many Spartans had suffered from an inferiority complex, as many have suggested, Dantonio made sure everyone knew those days were done. It's one thing to be second on the scoreboard occasionally and something else to be a second-class citizen. That perception had to end.

With a new starting quarterback in Brian Hoyer and a clear No.

HISTORY HELPS SPARTANS WRITE NEW STORY

2007-10

ERIC GORDON

No. 43 LINEBACKER

On picking his dream school and starting more games than any Spartan:

"I fell in love with Michigan State when I was about 12. Grandpa Don had an old ski boat with fat-lipped Sparty on the boat carpet. The rest of my family was all U-M. When I sat in Lloyd Carr's office, he said, 'If I offer you a scholarship, would you go here or Michigan State?' I said, 'Probably Michigan State.' That shocked him. But I didn't get along with some of the old staff. Things were too lenient. When Coach Dantonio put his foot down, it helped a ton. My big regret was the Alabama game. I wound up with my chinstrap over my nose and blood dripping down. But we still won a Big Ten championship. And winning it at Penn State was huge. It was the closest team I've ever been on. I'm just proud to have been a part of it."

1 running back in Javon Ringer, the Spartans went away from the Spread offense and quickly went back to winning. A 31-14 win at Notre Dame gave MSU a 4-0 start in 2007 and as many wins as it had the previous year. But anything easy can't be good, and anything good can't be easy, as the Spartans were about to be reminded.

They were tested and strengthened by five L's in their next six games, none by more than a touchdown. After a 37-34 loss at No. 9 Wisconsin and a 48-41 overtime defeat by Northwestern, the first Homecoming of the Dantonio era was a 52-27 rout of Indiana. But growing pains continued with a 24-17 loss at Ohio State, a 34-27 double-overtime loss at Iowa and especially a 28-24 defeat by No. 15 Michigan, a game MSU dominated for much of the second half and led 24-14 midway through the fourth quarter.

That all changed when quarterback Chad Henne got stepped on by a teammate and had to leave the game for one play. His replacement, Ryan Mallett, promptly fumbled, but the ball bounced straight to running back Mike Hart, who ran for 11 yards and a first down. Henne took care of the rest, hitting nine of 12 passes for 134 yards and two TDs in the span of 5:12.

The last score, his fourth of the game, was a 31-yard lob to wideout Mario Manningham with 2:28 left. Needing six points, the Spartans' couldn't get closer than the Michigan 34.

Actually, the battle was just beginning. Nine weeks earlier, Dantonio had debuted with a 55-18 win over UAB on the same day the Wolverines were stunned 34-32 by Appalachian State, one of the biggest upsets in sports history. When Dantonio was given that score in a postgame radio interview, he asked quietly, "Should we have a moment of silence?" Clearly, that struck a nerve in Ann Arbor. How dare he make a comment like that?

Before, during and after the game in East Lansing, Michigan's players pointed to imaginary watches. And when a smiling Hart was interviewed after the game, he stoked the fire by suggesting his team had been toying with MSU all along, saying, "Sometimes, you get your little brother excited when you're playing basketball — let them get the lead. And then you come back."

When asked about that line and the guests' behavior in general, Dantonio could have brushed that aside at his Monday press conference and looked ahead to the next game. He could have been shy and submissive and let the Wolverines have the last laugh. Instead, he showed the days of bowing down were about to end. Michigan might want to pretend it only has one meaningful rivalry, but that wish will never be granted.

"I find a lot of the things that they do amusing," he said without a smile. "They need to check themselves sometimes. Let's just remember, pride comes before the fall....Pride comes before the fall."

If follow-up questions were salt in an open sore, Dantonio couldn't stop answering them. He didn't feel the need to apologize for a countdown clock or anything his players had done, only that he thought he had let a lot of Spartans down late in the game.

"Can you tell my tone?" he said a bit louder. "This game is an important game! So if they want to mock us, all they want to mock us, I'm telling them, it's not over. They can print all that crap all they want all over their locker room....It's not over. It'll never be over here....It's just starting....Go ahead. Want to talk about Purdue a little bit?"

No one did. They wanted to talk about Hart. And Dantonio gave them what they wanted with a reference to his lack of height and possible confusion about little brothers. Today, he probably wishes he had stayed above the fray in some ways. But on Monday, November 5, 2007, the rivalry intensified and took on new meaning. It was one of Dantonio's best days since taking the job — and there are a lot to choose from in that area.

The impact of his comments was immediate and widespread. Instead of going into the dumper after a devastating defeat as so many MSU teams had done, his players bounced back for a 48-31 win at Purdue and a 35-31 victory over Penn State. "Same Old Spartans?" Not any more. Though they fell 24-21 to No. 14 Boston College and top NFL selection Matt Ryan in the Champs Sports Bowl on December 28 in Orlando, a group that never showed up in the polls did a lot to build the program's base.

That was clear from the first days of winter conditioning in 2008. Seven wins would no longer be good enough. And Dantonio's second MSU team had more than seven victories by November 1. That didn't seem likely after a 38-31 loss at California, a game the Spartans never led. But they recovered to take nine of the next 10, including a 23-7 decision over Notre Dame, a 16-13 escape against Iowa on a fourth-and-1 stop by linebacker Adam Decker and a 25-24 win over Wisconsin on a 44-yard field goal by Brett Swenson with :07 left.

Of course, the signature moment was a 35-21 victory at Michigan, MSU's first win in the series in seven years and its first in Ann Arbor in 18 seasons — as long as some freshmen had been alive. The Spartans opened the scoring on a 61-yard catch-and-run by wideout Blair White, a walk-on who became an Academic All-American and an NFL receiver. And they went ahead on a 64-yard bounce-out by Ringer, who carried 37 times for 194 yards and two scores.

When the Wolverines scored twice to lead 21-14, MSU answered with three TDs in the last 17:27. Tight end Charlie Gantt caught the second biggest pass of his career, a 4-yarder from Hoyer. Ringer put his team on top to stay on a 3-yard run with 6:39 to play. Fullback Josh Rouse iced it on a 7-yard pass from Hoyer, who threw for 282. And the secondary produced four takeaways, two by Marcus Hyde and one each in the fourth quarter by Chris L. Rucker and Jeremy Ware.

With the Paul Bunyan Trophy sitting in the new Skandalaris Football Center for the first time, the Spartans used that emotion a week later for the first of three memorable wins over the Badgers in the last four seasons. Few people remember lopsided loses to Ohio State and Penn State, when MSU hoped to share the league title. And when it lost 24-12 to Georgia and quarterback Matthew Stafford in the Capital One Bowl on January

1 in Orlando, a 9-4 finish was a definite step forward.

That wasn't always evident in 2009, a step backward in the standings to 6-7 and a time for self-examination. But after maddening losses to Central Michigan, Notre Dame and Wisconsin in consecutive weeks, the 1-3 Spartans won their most important game 26-20, knocking Michigan from the ranks of the undefeated as they have in each of the past three seasons.

MSU outrushed the 22nd-ranked Wolverines 197-28 and harassed quarterbacks Tate Forcier and Denard Robinson all day. It was 20-6 with just over 4:00 left when Forcier hit Darryl Stonum for a 60-yard score and engineered a 92-yard drive in the rain, ending with a 2-yard toss to Roy Roundtree with :02 remaining. If Michigan had gone for the win, it seemed to have all the momentum to make one more play. Instead, when Rich Rodriguez chose to take his chances in overtime, the better team took control again.

The Wolverines got the ball first at the north end of Spartan Stadium just as the sun reappeared. But an errant throw by Forcier was tipped by safety Danny Fortener and intercepted by a diving Rucker 4 yards deep in the end zone. That meant the hosts just needed a field goal to win. On third-and-8 at the 23, freshman rushing back Larry Caper did better than that, shedding defensive back Troy Woolfolk like a poncho.

As Wayne Larrivee described it for the Big Ten Network and YouTube followers for generations to come: "Caper…cutting it back…Caper…BREAKS A TACKLE…GOT A FIRST DOWN…TO THE HOUSE…TOUCHDOWN…MICHIGAN STATE HAS WON!…For the first time in 42 years, Michigan State has defeated Michigan two years in a row!"

Think about that for a second – or however long was left on the last play in 2001. The Spartans were 9-31 in the series from 1968-2007. Suddenly, they won two in a row, then three, then four… and now we see the Wolverines have two countdown clocks in Schembechler Hall. Only one has told time correctly.

When MSU plays in Ann Arbor on October 20, 2012, it will have been 1,813 days – 259 weeks – since Michigan's last win in a football series it ruled for four decades. And if the Spartans win for a fifth straight year, their reign will approach 2,200 days by the time the Wolverines visit East Lansing in 2013. That's more than twice as long as the Kennedy presidency.

If the mark of a truly successful program is to have more than a one-game season, MSU has achieved that, too, under Dantonio's leadership. It hasn't been perfect. But it has dealt with its problems, including an ugly altercation on campus that probably cost it a win in the 2009 Valero Alamo Bowl. It definitely cost some players the rest of their Big Ten careers, whether they were removed from the program or just ready to leave it.

A coach never wants to lose a player, whatever the reason. But the school, the program and the team come first. For the first time in memory, it's hard to find someone who wants a coaching change or to have a program like…fill in the blank. Maybe the best way to show that is to see what former players are saying, represented by All-Americans from three decades.

"Mark has laid a great foundation," said Look, a two-sport pro and one of the top game officials in NFL history. "It's not wham-bam-thank you, ma'am. The bad seeds are all gone. No one is perfect. But he wants players who are good citizens to represent the program."

"I'm so proud of everything they're doing," said Lewis, a coach at MSU and in the NFL for 34 years. "The way they're going, they're going to win for a long, long time. And I knew they could. It was just a matter of time with the right people."

"When I look at what has happened the last two years, it's phenomenal," said Gibson, the 2011 National League Manager of the Year with the Arizona Diamondbacks. "It makes us all proud to be Spartans. And it takes so much to make it all happen."

Above all else, it takes leadership and loyalty. Without those qualities? Success is fleeting. With it? A staff like Dantonio's – coordinators Pat Narduzzi and Dan Roushar; position coaches Mark Staten, Dave Warner, Brad Salem, Terrence Samuel, Ted Gill, Mike Tressell and Harlon Barnett, plus strength and conditioning expert Ken Mannie – has a great chance in recruiting and player development.

For MSU to reach its potential, that leadership must start with a Board of Trustees that works together and puts the university first. It has to include a president, in this case Lou Anna Simon, who understands the role and the value of athletics (see: Hannah, John) and is a positive force. And it has to be managed day-to-day by an innovative team player. MSU scored big there by hiring Hollis, the nation's 2012 Athletic Director of the Year.

The loyalty usually translates to dollars. And the response from fans after 22 wins the past two years — as many as Alabama had — resulted in an early suspension of season ticket sales and an acceleration of stadium improvements, including the installation of the Big Ten's biggest video boards. The new board at the south end will be the fifth-largest in the country behind those at Texas, Miami (NFL stadium), Arkansas and USC and roughly 10 times as large as the old display. With twin boards at the north end, no one can say they have a bad seat.

And what will they see? More of what they saw the past two seasons — the pursuit of excellence and the handling of adversity. That's the story of the 2010-11 seasons, presented in the next section through 50 week-by-week looks at the program, good and bad, and with 12 profiles of the key figures and some of the best photography in the country.

Why settle for anything less when the Spartans were the only athletic department in the country in the 2011-12 school year to put teams in postseason play in football, men's and women's basketball, hockey and baseball?

My, how little brother has grown!

A FOOTBALL RENAISSANCE

SPARTANS PERSEVERE AND REACH NEW HEIGHTS

HEART OF A **SPARTAN**

AFTER THE 2009 SEASON, Dantonio's third as the Spartans' head coach, no one outside the Skandalaris Center and the Daugherty Building understood what was about to happen.

But the players and coaches saw the potential and went back to work. After winning 22 games in the previous three seasons, they matched that total in the next two.

With selfless leaders like Greg Jones and Kirk Cousins, MSU embarked on the winningest two-year period in school history and its greatest glory since 1965-66.

We look at back at those 105 weeks with 50 columns, portraits in time, and 12 profiles of people who knew their time to be champions had come.

The columns cover three of MSU's five straight bowl trips and 22 regular-season games in between. They all capture the feelings of the moment. If some of those perspectives seem strange today, so were the events that produced them.

Finally, we take a closer look at a dozen champions: Dantonio, Aaron Bates, Edwin Baker, Jones, B.J. Cunningham, Keshawn Martin, Joel Foreman, Jerel Worthy, Keith Nichol, Cousins, William Gholston and Le'Veon Bell.

The common threads? They all had doubters. They all persevered. And they all have the **HEART OF A SPARTAN.**

A PATH WITH A PURPOSE

MARK DANTONIO WAS MEANT TO BE IN EAST LANSING

HEART OF A SPARTAN

BIGGIE MUNN was larger than life. Duffy Daugherty could charm a corpse.

Mark Dantonio is different that way. He doesn't have to be front and center – as long as his team is there at the end of the season.

With a record 44 wins in his first five years as Michigan State's head football coach, eight more than Munn and 14 more than Daugherty, Dantonio's success in East Lansing is unquestioned.

Yet, in terms of personal exposure, he's a relative unknown. Yes, he's highly regarded by his peers. How could he not be? But his name is still written as D'Antonio, like the professional conga player, and pronounced DanAntonio much too often.

Perhaps that's because of the way he does business. Unlike his close friend (and everyone else's), Tom Izzo, Dantonio isn't an open book. He's more likely to read one than most people in his profession. But he isn't the story, even when he should be.

Like him? Sure. Respect him? Absolutely. But know him? Only as much as he lets you. He's all about the f's: faith and family, then football. And you can skip the f-bombs. In many ways he's a shorter Tom Osborne, minus the triple-option.

So instead of belaboring his accomplishments here, as we've

done before and will do again, let's take the next 2,000 words – more than some fans have ever heard him say – and try to get to know a 56-year-old from Zanesville, Ohio.

Actually, Dantonio was born in El Paso, Texas, where he spent the first year of his life. But after moving to East Central Ohio, closer to Pittsburgh than to Cleveland or Cincinnati, he grew up cheering for the Cowboys, the Steelers, the Astros, the Pirates, the Celtics and, as a devout Catholic, the Fighting Irish.

"Growing up, I spent a lot of time in church," he said of his unshakable faith. "I had a very good foundation. You stray, but you venture back and become stronger. And I always felt better when I prayed."

He felt equally at home on a field, a court or a track. He probably played more basketball than anything else and was a 51-second quarter-miler. But as an all-conference monster back as a junior in the large-school Central Ohio League, Dantonio thought he could play college football.

Few people know that nearly happened at West Point. He had never lifted a weight till his senior year of high school and only weighed 170 after dinner. But Dantonio was always a patriot. And after receiving an appointment, he arrived on the banks of the Hudson in 1974, then called his best audible.

"I was from a relatively small town and didn't go to Army for the right reasons," he said. "I was 18. And I didn't realize what I was getting involved with. I left and enrolled at Muskingum (in nearby New Concord). But I still believe in the premier education and the purpose there."

Dantonio would return to West Point to coach very briefly under Hall of Famer Jim Young 11 years later. But it was his second move as a player, from Muskingum to South Carolina, that put him on a 34-year career path.

"I had to decide whether to try to play big-time college football or not play," he said. "When I transferred, I was on scholarship by the second semester. South Carolina was an independent in those days. But we led Notre Dame at our place, then lost, 13-6. I lettered three years as a fifth defensive back and special teams guy from '76-78."

Dantonio was two years ahead of the greatest Gamecock, Heisman Trophy tailback George Rogers, and a teammate of quarterback Ronnie Bass, "Sunshine" from "Remember the Titans." But the most important relationship Dantonio formed there was with position coach Dale Evans, a strong supporter to this day.

"I thought coaches had a good job," he said. "I had no clue how many hours they worked. But my dad said I'd better get a degree in English or math if I wanted to coach in high school. I got a degree in English education and a job at Westside High in Anderson, the school George Webster attended. I saw his picture every day."

Before his first year ended, Dantonio knew he didn't want to teach English. He left South Carolina and became a grad assistant at Ohio University in Athens – the real "Ohio" – in 1980. He also worked in environmental sciences 20 hours a week, swabbing labs and testing urine samples for radioactivity and checking dorms for fire hazards, all while earning his master's degree.

From there it was on to Purdue, where he served as a graduate assistant in Jim Young's final Big Ten season. That helped Dantonio land his first full-time position as defensive coordinator at Butler Junior College in El Dorado, Kan. His salary in 1982? A whopping $20,000. But when the head coach's job was in jeopardy, he moved back to Ohio.

Dantonio knew a couple of Ohio State assistants, Randy Hart, who had been at Purdue, and Dom Capers, who had grown up 30 miles from Zanesville and had just succeeded Nick Saban as secondary coach. Hart helped Dantonio get a two-year graduate assistant job with Earle Bruce's Buckeyes. Those two teams that would play in the Fiesta Bowl and Rose Bowl. And it was also there that he met a young receivers coach, Jim Tressel.

After just missing several jobs and reuniting with Young for a few weeks, Dantonio got a chance to coach defensive backs at Akron in 1985. Despite an 8-3 record, head coach Jim Dennison was jettisoned to make room for Gerry Faust. But it was there that Dantonio met Saban, a third-year Spartan assistant that season.

Akron was also the site of the most important introduction of his life – to the future Becky Dantonio, an OSU grad. He couldn't have found a better partner, a perfect yin and yang. That courtship proved beyond a doubt that he could land a five-star recruit.

His year with the Zips showed something else, too. Put Dantonio in a tough situation and he'll almost always adapt. He did that when he had to teach bowling at Akron. He had never bowled a day in his life. But he has made up for that by going bowling in 15 of the last 17 seasons, including a record five in a row with MSU.

After leaving Akron, Dantonio still had two more stops to make before arriving in East Lansing as anything more than a Boilermaker or Buckeye graduate assistant. When Tressel left Columbus to be head coach at Youngstown State in 1986, he promptly hired "Dino" as his secondary coach. And as defensive coordinator in 1990, Dantonio helped the Penguins go 11-0 in the regular season and rank second in the nation.

From 1991-94, he assisted another former Buckeye, Glen Mason, at Kansas, where he got to know Bobby Williams. If Dantonio had stayed in Lawrence a little longer, he might have wound up with Mason at Minnesota. Instead, when Saban succeeded George Perles in December of '94, Dantonio swapped his Jayhawk blue for Spartan green.

"I'd met Nick in a social setting," he said. "He was finishing up with the Browns, and he called me about the defensive backs job. I really didn't know him very well. But he knew Jim Bollman, whom I'd worked with at Youngstown. And he knew Dom and Tress. That helped me."

Dantonio helped Saban produce four bowl teams in five tries, capped by a 9-2 regular season in 1999 with wins over Oregon, Notre Dame, Michigan, OSU and Penn State. But before a school-record-tying 10th win against Florida in the Florida Citrus Bowl, Saban bolted for Baton Rouge. With an opportunity to leave for LSU, the entire staff stayed and rallied behind Williams.

Despite being named associate head coach for the 2000 season, Dantonio's first stay in East Lansing was almost done. When Tressel was picked to succeed John Cooper at OSU, he needed a new defensive coordinator. And with the No. 2 scoring defense in the nation, the 2002 Bucks won a lot of close games, including an overtime upset of Miami to earn the Big Ten's lone BCS Championship.

Tressel and Dantonio were a terrific team for three seasons. But as the 2003 season came to a close, it was time for Dantonio to spread his wings and become a head coach. Tressel knew he was ready to do that. But the decision to take over at Cincinnati wasn't easy, just sudden.

"It was a split-second, weekend thing," Dantonio said. "I wanted to raise a family in one place and not be a mover. But I went down there and interviewed at the airport hotel. They took me to the UC campus and to Nippert Stadium. Then, I took a wrong turn getting out and wound up in The Vine, where they'd had riots. I found my way back to I-71 and said, 'Whoa, this isn't Ohio State!'"

If Cincinnati had a choice of whom it should hire, Dantonio had a decision to make, too. The Buckeyes had it rolling. Their head coach was more than a boss. Actually, Tressel was a trusted friend. And Columbus was starting to feel like a place the family could live comfortably for a long time.

"I thought we'd settle in there," Dantonio said. "Then, my wife was reading the Bible, shut it and said the Lord had given her a sign. Sure enough, the A.D., Bob Goin, called and said, 'You'd better decide if you want to be a head coach. I'm going to Florida for Christmas, and I'm going to have a head coach by then.' Dantonio said yes to the offer that followed, then left to go coach in the Fiesta Bowl again."

After a 22-17 turnaround in three seasons in Conference USA and the Big East, including a pair of bowl appearances, it was time for Dantonio to come home to East Lansing. His Bearcats successors, Brian Kelly and Butch Jones, were left an excellent nucleus that went on to bigger things.

"You always want to leave something better than when you got it," Dantonio said. "But I really hadn't talked to anyone here about the job here except Tom Izzo. As a coach you live in a bubble. I had no idea of the state of the program or that they were building a new facility. But Michigan State was a place my kids had grown up for six years. And it was a place that Becky and I believed in."

Their daughters, Kristen and Lauren, remembered the area. It wasn't like they were moving to Mississippi. But there was a chance the Dantonios would miss an opportunity if MSU decided to act expeditiously. The Bearcats had a bowl date with Connecticut. That had to come first.

"Actually, the first call came from a headhunter," Dantonio said. "Then, I talked to Izzo. I knew Mark Hollis. Our children were in pre-school together. And we knew them from St. Martha Parish. But I never crossed the line to talk to Mark. He waited until our season was over. And I think Tom was instrumental in getting them to wait.

"It all happened very fast. I walked in the Saturday after our bowl game and said, 'I'm interviewing tonight at 9:30. Who wants to go?' And eight guys came with me. Dan Enos had worked for me at Cincinnati before coming back here. We retained him for the ninth spot. By Monday afternoon, everyone had signed their papers. By Tuesday, they all had their phones and were out recruiting."

Within a couple of weeks, Dantonio had laid down the gauntlet at the *Free Press* All-State Banquet and let everyone know the days of bowing down to Michigan were over. It took one more defeat, the Spartans' sixth in a row to the Wolverines, before that series dominance flipped, too. "Little Brother" hit a serious growth spurt.

What fans had seen in their wildest dreams, Dantonio envisioned every day on the job. It was just a matter of finding the right people, then developing the attitude to make that rise a reality. After four straight wins over Michigan, Paul Bunyan should have bought property in Mid-Michigan. Previously, he'd only had one-year leases.

But Dantonio has done more than restore the pride in MSU's program with success in "The Backyard Brawl." He has led the Spartans to the first two 11-win seasons in school history, produced the program's first conference title in two decades, become the first coach to win a Big Ten Legends Division title and ended a 10-year drought for postseason wins in the most dramatic of fashions.

"I don't know how long I'll coach – a while longer but not forever," Dantonio said. "Coaching keeps you young. And I probably get along better with young people. But when I'm done, I'll be walking around with a cup of coffee, watching the team practice. I want to keep all my MSU stuff. I don't want to burn it."

If he hadn't been a coach, Dantonio said he would have been a high school principal. Instead, he has laid down the law and made people better. If he was destined to be here, he has made a lot of people see their destiny is well within their control.

That's enough to make him smile and make Spartan fans do backflips. And when MSU finally reaches the Rose Bowl, Munn and Daugherty will have company in Legends Row. That much we know.

Wide receiver Keshawn Martin (82) with the fingertip grab

JANUARY 2, 2010 • SATURDAY

ALMOST HEAVEN (UNLIKE WEST VIRGINIA)

FIVE MINUTES, THREE SECONDS. That's all that stood between Michigan State and a near-perfect day, one of the best in school history.

The Spartans already had won their Big Ten basketball opener at ranked and no-longer-rank Northwestern Saturday evening. That 91-70 triumph was MSU's best game in its first 14 tries this season.

Then, after trailing 17-7, the Spartans found themselves leading Texas Tech 31-27 late in the fourth quarter of the Alamo Bowl in San Antonio, as close to a road game as any team will face in 34 postseason pairings.

Suddenly, the Red Raiders remembered their other significant edge. With the nation's No. 2 air attack going against one of the most vulnerable pass defenses in any country, TTU made a quarterback change, benched a guy who'd thrown for 372 yards and got a game-winning upgrade.

The better team won. It's impossible to ignore the statistical edges: 31-13 in first downs, 460-248 in passing yards and 579-396 in total offense.

The fact is, MSU needed a near-perfect game with a horrible matchup and 12 players suspended, not counting two more who were injured.

Instead, the Spartans got an inspired performance but far too many mistakes to get their first bowl win since 2001, Bobby Williams' second full season as head coach.

Once the decision was made to remove the Rather-nots from any involvement with the bowl, the right decision by head coach Mark Dantonio despite what some apologists believed, an already-immense challenge became a bit more difficult.

They needed a great game from quarterback Kirk Cousins and got 13-for-27 accuracy, including two decisions that led to interceptions.

They needed a consistent running game and got two big runs out of Edwin Baker. They also were credited with 23 rushes of 3 yards or less, not what they hoped to have to hold the ball at least 36 minutes, instead of 28:27.

They needed to be penalty-free and leave all their transgressions at home. Instead, they were flagged five times for 55 yards, 5 yards less than the Red Raiders. Unfortunately, two of those calls were holds that led to a first-quarter punt and a fourth-quarter field goal when a touchdown seemed likely.

They needed to win the kicking game and broke even. Brett Swenson drilled a 44-yard field goal with 8:05 left to give MSU its largest edge. But he had a 52-yarder blocked by penetration up the middle. And the team's regular-season MVP pulled a kickoff out of bounds, allowing TTU to start at its 40.

They needed to find some way to put pressure on Red Raiders passer Taylor Potts and, as it turned out, relief pitcher Steven Sheffield. They got one sack on a blindside blitz by cornerback Jeremy Ware for a loss of 8 yards. It was almost impossible for the front seven to get home before the ball was released, even with wider splits than we saw among Democrats and Republicans in Congress last year.

Thus, it's time to say goodbye to the 2009 Spartans and put a 6-7 season in perspective in two words: Blown Opportunity.

The Spartans aren't that far from reaching their goals and competing for a Big Ten title – in 2011, if not next year.

I said the same thing when MSU won six games in 1986 and 1998. The following years were among the best in school history. It's all up to them.

FEBRUARY 3, 2010 • WEDNESDAY

BACK TO THE FUTURE

NO COACH IN THE COUNTRY has stood up on National Letter-of-Intent Day and said, "I have to apologize to our fans and alumni. We did a lousy job of recruiting this year. I promise we'll try to do better next time."

Mark Dantonio didn't make history that way, either. He addressed the media, then met with boosters and gushed about Michigan State's 21 new players. He stopped just short of retiring numbers.

But in at least a few cases and perhaps more than that, Dantonio could be right this time. He could be onto something if my eyes don't deceive me the way the Fightin' Spartans fooled him.

I know it's risky to make that assumption or give Dantonio credit for anything these days. So what if the program's 22 wins and three bowl bids in his first three seasons are unsurpassed in school history? He clearly forgot how to coach between a 9-4 surprise and a 6-7 pratfall. At least, that's what some fans believe.

I believe MSU's best afternoons of football, at least its best stretch in 44 years, could be just ahead. That doesn't mean the Spartans are headed for a long string of BCS victories. It means the program can become relevant again.

MSU hasn't won more than 16 games in back-to-back seasons since 1965-66. And it only won that many three times: 1989-90 with Dan Enos at quarterback, 1998-99 with Bill Burke under center and 2007-08 with Brian Hoyer at the helm.

Guess what? Based on his performance as a sophomore, Kirk Cousins can be better than any of them. And he has two seasons remaining, including another fall when he won't have to face Ohio State's defense.

Best of all, he should have a better, deeper supporting cast. That's where Wednesday's signatures come in. They represent more than the future of Spartan football. In several cases, they're part of the present.

When Dantonio talks about stacking classes, he's right. And for every freshman who played a significant role on Saturdays last fall, another newbie stood and watched with a redshirt instead of a green one.

This group should give Dantonio the depth we thought he had a year ago. If six or seven players see the field right away, as history suggests, and 12 to 14 of last year's recruits contribute, MSU should have from 18 to 21 players on the field from the youngest groups – the sign of a growing program.

I'm not a big believer in the star system on an individual basis (thanks again, Blair White!). And if you can tell me why the No. 62-ranked left tackle is clearly better than the No. 76 prospect, you're flipping a coin.

Over time, however, the teams with the best personnel usually win, regardless of game-day coaching. Again, that brings us back to the importance of Signing Day and the development years.

Yes, we see exceptions to the rule, including chute-less skydives. For instance, Michigan's last eight classes have been ranked eighth, fifth, second, tied for ninth, 10th, sixth, 14th and ninth in the nation – an average of 7.9.

Iowa's rankings over that span? Try 30, 41, 8, 40, 37, 44, 75 and 43 – an average of 39.5. And I won't even go near Northwestern's numbers. Suffice to say, they shouldn't be beating the Wolverines in football OR basketball.

Neither should the Spartans if the rankings hold Gatorade. Over the past eight years, beginning with John L. Smith's arrival, they've been ranked 96th, 13th (clearly a computer error), 40th, 43rd, 51st, 56th, 37th and 28th – an average of 46.5.

Over the past six seasons, MSU has only had one class ranked among the top 30. That would be this one. And it has only had two groups rated among the top 40. You guessed it! The last two.

So when William Gholston jumps off the screen

HEART OF A SPARTAN

Running back Le'Veon Bell and WKAR Radio's Earle Robinson

when he's sacking a quarterback, I see that as a good thing. The Spartans haven't had a pass rusher off the edge who could carry his chinstrap since Julian Peterson.

When Max Bullough flows sideline-to-sideline like water through a downspout and seems to know an opponent's plays better than its offensive coordinator, that's impressive.

When Mylan Hicks can cover and Isaiah Lewis can deliver a blow better than any corner and safety the Spartans have added since before Nick Saban spoke Creole or wore crimson, that's a major upgrade.

No one should expect those four to perform at an All-Big Ten level this season. But with a little seasoning, Dantonio could have a nucleus of impact players in the back seven, as he could up front with sophomore-to-be Blake Treadwell at tackle.

The offense isn't as pressing a concern, though linemen Travis Jackson and Skyler Schofner should press for playing time before they've declared a major. And that's with some excellent prospects we haven't seen yet due to redshirt years.

Why did they come to East Lansing? The education is good enough. The facilities are new enough. The spotlight is bright enough. And the environment is exciting enough.

But time and again, the No. 1 factor in a prospect's decision is the relationship he has with the coaches and the trust he has that their promises will be kept.

Most of that is simply hard work, as MSU proved again this year. Dantonio's staff – including Enos, a great hire by Central Michigan – went everywhere. And high school coaches, especially a few around Detroit, developed a new respect for the program.

So when Detroit Catholic Central legend Tom Mach, the winner of the 2009 Duffy Daugherty Memorial Award, begins to embrace the program for the first time, when he tells Dantonio he has to take fullback Niko Palazeti, presto, "Nik the Bruiser" becomes a Spartan.

That doesn't mean every signee will make it. Attrition is high in the very best programs. Teams that win less than that need nametags. For years, MSU bought them in bulk.

Still, something tells me this Signing Day was different. Dantonio and his aides identified the players they liked, checked them again and again and built relationships.

Of course, you can scoff at the trust concept and say, "Didn't Dantonio trust Glenn Winston?" And you'd be right – to a degree. But if you talk to any of the new Spartans, you won't get past the fifth sentence before a coach or the entire staff is mentioned. That has to pay off eventually.

I think it's starting to do that, despite the flood of negative stories associated with Rather-gate. I think it was seen in Greg Jones' belief in the staff and decision to stay. And I think it's reflected in zero decommitments and no post-pledge exploratory visits.

It may not be the greatest class in MSU history. But this could be one of the most important ones. With plenty of reasons to doubt the direction, from three straight bowl defeats to a spate of suspensions, the newest Spartans kept the faith.

When Dantonio has back-to-back nine-win seasons, which I believe he will, he'll look back at this group and smile. His Signing Day speech wasn't contrived. It was a peek at a brighter future.

APRIL 17, 2010 • SATURDAY

SPRING FORWARD

*Wide receiver Keith Nichol (7)
and defensive back Dana Dixon (12)*

IT CAN BE THE MOST MISLEADING day of the year. Yet, every year we make the same mistake.

We put waaay too much emphasis on college football's spring games. And we do that at schools big and small, from Seattle, Washington, to Washington, D.C.

We've seen it happen at Michigan State, as recently as last season, in fact. And we'll see it again, perhaps as early as this Saturday afternoon in Spartan Stadium.

But it isn't just an MSU problem. It happens in Ann Arbor, in Mount Pleasant and in places less pleasant than either of those cities.

I remember sitting with Earle Robinson of WKAR Radio, watching a Green-and-White Game in the George Perles era. And I remember us both being duped for the second straight year.

"Man, that's like 12 passes to the fullback!" I said. "Maybe George IS going is let him be more than a third guard in the backfield."

"They keep throwing to the tight end, too," Earle said. "The offense is going to be tougher to stop this year if they keep doing that."

If I recall, the quarterback, a senior with a bowl win under his belt, completed fewer than eight passes a game that season. The new No. 1 tailback averaged nearly 27 carries.

The fullback? He touched the ball a whopping 11 times in 12 games – counting a fumble recovery. And the tight end? He couldn't have been more anonymous in the Federal Witness Protection Program.

That was also the year we kept hearing how an All-America offensive tackle might change positions and revolutionize the art of rushing the passer. He never saw action as a defensive end. Actually, he never saw the field till Game 4, following an NCAA suspension.

Last season's misdirection came with an aerial onslaught never before seen in a spring game. In fact,

HEART OF A SPARTAN

Le'Veon Bell and defensive end Johnathan Strayhorn (57)

Kirk Cousins and Keith Nichol had exactly the same stats that day – 3,011 yards though the air with 22 touchdowns.

Or so it seemed. We spent the next four-and-a-half months debating which passer would be inducted into the College Football Hall of Fame first and whether his first incompletion would come in Game 2 or Game 3.

Instead, Cousins threw two balls to Nichol, a fill-in wide receiver, in the Valero Alamo Bowl. He also threw two passes to the Texas Tech Red Raiders in a 10-point loss that left the Spartans 6-7 for the year.

That's not to demean Cousins' performance as a sophomore. He completed more than 60 percent of his passes, averaged more than 200 yards a game through the air and had more than twice as many touchdowns as interceptions.

It means that whenever the offense looks like the Indianapolis Colts, the defense is usually as inept as the Detroit Lions. And when receivers can fair catch TD tosses, the secondary is fairly awful (see: MSU 2009).

By the loss to Central Michigan last season, Spartan fans – and some slow-reacting members of the media – began to ask the right questions. By a loss at Notre Dame the following week, the answer was obvious.

No, Cousins and Nichol weren't the two best quarterbacks on one team since Joe Montana and Steve Young. They were even the best QBs on the field when Dan LeFevour and Jimmy Clausen faced MSU's secondary.

The same overreaction to spring success occurred last April in Michigan Stadium, when Tate Forcier made his first public appearance and made fans forget about Steven Threet and Nick Sheridan.

Of course, it was hard for Forcier NOT to look

good when one of the worst defenses in college football wasn't even allowed to tap him. Immediately, the nightmare of 2008 was forgotten. Everyone was "All In For Michigan."

So what happened when the Wolverines actually played a game outside Washtenaw County? They lost to the Spartans in overtime and began a two-month conference skid, slipping from 2-6 in the Big Ten to 1-7.

This year's U-M spring game was just as irrelevant. Trust me, I was there for both of them. And the defense again did a football impersonation of the Washington Generals.

In an effort to say something nice about a program that really needs a hug, quarterback Denard Robinson looked very quick and threw the ball better. Also, a lot of money was raised for Mott Children's Hospital.

That's about it. The rest of the game was an exercise in mediocrity. But that didn't stop departing defensive standout Brandon Graham from predicting a 10-win season and others from having football fantasies.

I'm predicting 7-5 for the Wolverines, a definite improvement from a 3-9 record in 2008 and a 5-7 mark last year. But 10 wins? That's more than my Saturday radio partner Tom Crawford would see in a U-M wet dream.

I'm not sure this team could win 10 times in 12 intrasquad games. But I'll give the Wolverines the benefit of the doubt. Seven wins would end a no-bowl streak at two – even it means it's Rich Rodriguez's last season.

In his first season as CMU's football boss, former Spartan quarterback and assistant coach Dan Enos debuted Saturday with a 3-0 thriller. And those last-second points were set up by a controversial penalty.

Does that mean the Chippewas' days of exciting offense under Brian Kelly and Butch Jones are over? Or that Enos is suddenly a defensive wizard? No. And no. It means we shouldn't overreact to anything we've seen.

Four years ago in Kelly/Shorts Stadium, CMU played several QBs in its spring game. Clearly, the worst of that bunch was LeFevour. A few months later he was leading the Chips and beginning a fabulous career.

That brings us back to MSU, where everyone will get a chance to overreact at 1:30 p.m. this Saturday. If one of the Spartans has a big day receiving, that doesn't mean he'll have better numbers than Blair White did.

If freshmen Nick Hill or Le'Veon Bell rush for more yards than Larry Caper and Edwin Baker, that doesn't mean the depth chart will be turned upside down. Experience, even a year of it, still means something.

Here's what you need to know: MSU should be better than it was a year ago. But we won't know HOW MUCH better till September, regardless of how good or bad individuals and units appear this weekend.

The offensive line needs to develop. The defensive front must mount a pass rush. The secondary has to prevent big plays. And the placekicking demands consistency. If three of those four things happen, look out.

Maybe Mark Dantonio had the best idea about spring games, wrap-up scrimmages or any other formats where players are on display. He suggested playing against another team instead of against each other.

Why not make the spring game an exhibition against another program? Because of injuries? That doesn't stop high schools from having four-way scrimmages or NFL teams from playing four preseason games.

It could be a major new revenue stream for athletic departments. It would tell us more about players and teams. And if the student-athletes could benefit some way, it would be a win-win for everyone.

Otherwise, a win in the spring game doesn't mean there won't be lots of losses when it matters.

Middle linebacker Greg Jones prepares to pounce

APRIL 25, 2010 • SUNDAY

NO MORE EXCUSES

NEW PROGRAM? Not with a coaching staff in Year 4.

New quarterback? Not if No. 8 stays healthy.

New running backs? Not unless they're an upgrade.

New success? Not beyond the realm of possibility.

And that's not because of anything we saw in Michigan State's spring football finale.

The 2010 Spartans are positioned to be a major surprise. Expectations are low. And excellence in many areas is well within reach.

How excellent in terms of wins and losses? We'll get there in a few minutes.

First, I have to say I'm not normally this optimistic. I've picked MSU to win the Big Ten football title just twice in 32 seasons in the media – and been wrong both times. I picked Purdue to finish ahead of the Spartans in basketball this season – and still think the Boilermakers, when healthy, were a better team. And I've never picked MSU to win a game in Michigan Stadium, though the Spartans have done that four times in the past 42 years.

It's also important to note that I understand the cynicism of some on this site. When a program is 243-241-9 over the past 43 seasons, nearly the dictionary definition of mediocrity, and hasn't had a winning decade since the 1970s, why should anyone get excited?

From a national standpoint, there's still no reason to do that. But in terms of competing in the Big Ten and building an infrastructure that should produce an average of eight wins a year, those days could be closer than many people think.

We may be on the brink of that breakthrough. In fact, I wouldn't be surprised if MSU is midway through its winningest four-year stretch since its 35 victories from 1950-53, Biggie Munn's last four seasons. If the Spartans can win nine games this season and nine more the next, they'll have 33 W's from 2008-11 (plus January 2012) – two more than George Perles' best teams from 1987-90.

So it shouldn't be a stunner that MSU has had just two 10-win seasons in school history, 1965 and 1999. By comparison, the Iowa Hawkeyes have had four seasons with double-digit wins, including two with 11 victories, in the past eight years. Kirk Ferentz's teams have finished among the nation's top eight teams four times in that span and have won five bowl games since December 2001.

Iowa, Ohio State and Wisconsin, in some order, are supposed to finish first, second and third in the conference again. But the team that's most likely to finish fourth, if not crash the top three teams' party, is MSU.

That's because the Spartans have greater stability and more ability than we're used to seeing in East Lansing. The quarterback could go down as one of the three best in school history. And the receivers and linebackers may be the best in the Big Ten.

They also have a favorable schedule with five of their first seven games in East Lansing, one in Detroit and one in Ann Arbor. Plus, MSU has the Buckeyes right where it wants them – off the schedule.

But let's start with the staff, since Mark Dantonio has more wins in his first three seasons as the Spartans' head coach than anyone since Chester Brewer from 1903-05.

Yes, there's a new running backs coach in Brad Salem, a former MSU grad assistant who returned to Mid-Michigan to replace Dan Enos, CMU's new leader. Nearly everyone else in the Duffy Daugherty Football Building has been on campus longer than Kalin Lucas, Durrell Summers and Chris Allen.

Dantonio is beginning his seventh season as a collegiate head coach, more than enough time to know what he's doing. His recruiting classes continue to get better. And you'll start to see that this fall, if you haven't already.

The only bad news is for Dantonio haters. Unlike

HEART OF A **SPARTAN**

every other fourth-year coach the Spartans have had since Munn's heyday, Dantonio isn't in trouble with his A.D., about to sumo wrestle with his president or looking for a new opportunity.

The opportunity to win a lot of games is there with the return of quarterback Kirk Cousins, almost certainly for two more seasons. Only five players in the past 62 seasons have led MSU in passing three times. And none of them had more completions for more yards as a sophomore than Cousins did last season.

Even with favorite target Blair White the property of the Indianapolis Colts, Cousins has plenty of capable receivers. Veterans Mark Dell and B.J. Cunningham have combined for 171 catches. Gamebreaker Keshawn Martin only needs consistency to be a star. And converted quarterback Keith Nichol has drawn rave reviews in a new role. The tight end position is injury-proof, too, with Charlie Gantt, Brian Linthicum, Garrett Celek and Dion Sims.

The Spartans are just as stacked at linebacker, where All-American Greg Jones has improved his play recognition and pass coverage. With Eric Gordon, Chris Norman, Steve Gardiner, Jon Misch, Denicos Allen and others, the defense should be excellent at the second level. If freshmen Max Bullough and William Gholston contribute and Gholston can supply a pass rush, look out.

Sure, MSU has concerns. The offensive line needs to mesh and open more holes for runners Larry Caper Jr., Edwin Baker, Nick Hill and Le'Veon Bell. If that happens, the Spartans could have the best offense in the Big Ten. If not, they'll struggle near the goal line and at Winning Time again.

The defense still needs to generate a pass rush from the front four. With 2009 freshman All-American Jerel Worthy back in the lineup by September, the line will look better, especially if he quits jumping offside. And with all the depth at linebacker, don't be shocked if Jones or Gholston lines up at end in passing situations to generate pressure.

The secondary, a major disappointment last year, doesn't have much proven depth. Finding a freshman or two to help could be critical by season's end. By the end of the spring game, the corners and safeties had given up more passes of 25-plus yards than a top-three conference team can.

And don't forget the placekicking. Dan Conroy and Kevin Muma will continue to battle for Brett Swenson's job. That graduation could be the biggest loss from last year's team. In one area where Saturday's play was revealing, MSU has to make its 35-yard field goals and get kickoffs inside the 15-yard line to be a factor in the league race.

Despite those deficiencies, the Spartans look

pretty decent and are about to get better. Every program in the conference has questions. MSU could have more answers than it appears.

If eight wins is the new .500 for Dantonio's program, the pendulum of luck is about to swing back in the Spartans favor. MSU wasn't as good as a 9-4 team appeared in 2008 and was better than a 6-7 mark last season.

This year, it looks a lot like a nine-win team. Could the Spartans win 10? If they can finally win a bowl game, absolutely. Next week in this space we'll predict how that happens with game-by-game previews and possible scores.

But it's time to raise the bar a bit. The foundation is built – or should be with Dantonio's four incoming classes. Anything less than an 8-4 regular season will be viewed as a failure here and by one of the most patient fan bases in the nation. Appropriately so.

Placekicker Dan Conroy and Mark Dantonio follow the ball

JUNE 26, 2010 • SATURDAY

CLOSER THAN YOU THINK

CALL THEM THE BIG 10, with or without Nebraska.

The wait is almost over – less than 10 weeks till college football kicks off the 2010 season. It's OK to start tearing those 68 dates off the calendar now.

For Michigan State fans, the dog days between the end of spring football and the beginning of official summer workouts – all conducted under NCAA guidelines – are almost two-thirds over.

And this year, there was other excitement to keep everyone busy. The Tom Izzo/NBA Watch and a "Don't Leave for Cleve!" campaign consumed a couple of weeks in June.

But for the most part, May through July are painfully slow months.

A few recommendations: Invite a few of your friends to join you this Saturday or any weekend in July for pre-preseason tailgating practice, then crank up the Spartan Marching Band CD so loud you'd swear you were all in the north tunnel. Then, try to pick the winners, scores and heroes of all 12 games this season.

If you miss by a total of less than 100 points, congratulations! Report directly to the sports book at The Mirage or Caesars Palace the week after Christmas.

If your guess is off from 101 to 250 points, you're probably smart enough to say, "I nailed that one!" at least three times this year and make people believe it.

If you're wrong by more than 250 points, don't worry. You can always get a job in the media.

In most of the speculation I've read and heard, Spartan fans are cautiously optimistic that this could be Mark Dantonio's best team. Of course, a few Demand Excellencers think MSU will be lucky to win six and won't be happy if it wins 12. And some Sunshine Blowers are already packed for Pasadena, with a stop along the way to watch Kirk Cousins claim the Heisman Trophy and Greg Jones grab the Butkus, Lombardi, Nagurski and True Value hardware.

Both groups are destined for disappointment. But that's part of being a fan. You pick your level of expectation and place it just beyond a reasonable reach. Just watch how a loss in the NCAA Championship Game in Houston next April would leave everyone asking, "Why can't we win the big one?" – a question Izzo fully expects to hear if he doesn't hear "A Second Shining Moment."

Back to Dantonio's guys for a few moments. The Mark of Excellence this season would be winning 10 football games. That has only happened twice in school history, in 1965 and 1999 (plus New Year's), so 10-3 may be too lofty a goal.

That's the key word, however. It's a goal, not an expectation or a demand. A reasonable expectation – and who said fans are supposed to be reasonable? – is probably nine wins (for the second time in three years).

In 2008 it took considerable luck to get there. And last year's team could have done that again if not for self-inflicted wounds. That means eight wins is a minimum standard for acceptable play, with a 7-6 final record a serious letdown, even if it ends with a 30-point bowl win.

Why does 9-4 seem plausible? For lots of reasons, more than the Spartans have had on their midsummer resume under the last three coaches. It isn't asking too much for MSU to be competitive each week and competent enough to make the most of a dream schedule.

Let's start with that lineup, an itinerary that keeps the Spartans in-state till their eighth game of the year, a tricky trip to Evanston for a matchup on October 23. Overall, MSU will leave the state just three times – four if it's safe to assume they won't be bowling and peddling pizza in Ford Field the day after Christmas.

And Dantonio won't have to – or get to, take your pick – face Ohio State, mentor Jim Tressel and

HEART OF A **SPARTAN**

Heisman-hyped quarterback Terrell Pryor till 2011. By then, Pryor should be wearing a headset on an NFL sideline.

But the Spartans have a quarterback, too. Despite his share of first-year mistakes, all Cousins did with an average-at-best running game was complete more passes for more yards last season than any sophomore in school history.

With four-deep quality at wide receiver and the same embarrassing depth at tight end, no passer in MSU annals has had more capable targets, even allowing for occasional drops. Wideouts Keshawn Martin, B.J. Cunningham, Mark Dell and Keith Nichol should all be tough covers for anyone this side of Revis Island in the NFL. And tight ends Charlie Gantt, Brian Linthicum and Dion Sims could all play in the pros eventually.

The running backs have to be better and should be able to run left behind fifth-year tackle D.J. Young and guard Joel Foreman. If Larry Caper and Edwin Baker can't get it done as sophomores, freshmen Nick Hill (a Mike Hart clone with more class) and Le'Veon Bell, a 230-pound bull, were here in the spring and won't be intimidated.

Whenever your defense starts with the league's best linebackers, including a returning All-American in the middle, your team should be a bit stingier than last year. I know, I know. How could it not be?

But the Spartans will be better in the secondary, perhaps even average if they cut the blown coverages in half. If a front four that was fairly solid against the run can generate any kind of pass rush without blitzes, MSU's defense could be respectable or better. And if that doesn't happen, Jones and 6-foot-7 freshman William Gholston can line up wide at end and meet over a sprawled QB.

I know we've heard June rhetoric before. But part of the appeal of picking MSU to finish as high as third in the league is that most people won't do that. I'd be surprised, not stunned but disappointed, if the Spartans aren't 4-0 at the end of September.

They should have enough to beat directional schools Western Michigan and Northern Colorado in East Lansing. Moving the Florida Atlantic game to Detroit can only help. And even with Brian Kelly replacing the not-so-Weis-man, you have to like the Spartans' chances against Notre Dame. It took several breaks for the Fighting Irish to beat the fighting Spartans – and that was in South Bend with Jimmy Clausen and Golden Tate in the lineup.

If MSU has a perfect first month, it'll take a 5-3 conference mark to guarantee nine wins. Even a 4-4 mark could do that if the Spartans produce their first bowl win since 2001, the day Bobby Williams became just the second coach in school history to have two postseason W's.

Anything better than that and the program is in rarified air, provided one of those wins is against Michigan. Who would've guessed two summers ago that a loss in Ann Arbor would ever be embarrassing and unacceptable?

JULY 19, 2010 • MONDAY

MSU'S PICK SIX

IT'S ONE OF THE MOST IMPORTANT seasons in Michigan State football history.

In the past half-century, 2010 ranks with 1965, 1987 and 1999 as a great Green-and-White opportunity.

Duffy Daugherty's '65 Spartans were fresh from a 4-5 disappointment, including a 17-10 loss to Michigan.

They bounced back to go 10-1, dominate the Big Ten and share the national title.

George Perles' '87 contingent was still smarting from a 6-5 no-bowl showing, including a 27-6 whipping in Ann Arbor.

It answered with a 9-2-1 mark, an outright conference title and the school's last Rose Bowl win.

And Nick Saban's '99 players were recovering from a bi-polar, bowl-less 6-6 year, including a 29-17 loss to the Wolverines.

They recovered to go 10-2 and beat Notre Dame, Michigan, Ohio State, Penn State and Florida.

BULLETIN TO THE TERMINALLY CYNICAL: MSU's three redeem teams won a total of 29 games, an average of 9.7 victories.

The three groups before them had won 16 games and been outscored 73-33 by their in-state rival.

What does that have to do with anything we'll see in 2010?

After 22 wins over the past three years, eight more than in the previous three, it's time to see what Mark Dantonio has built.

Though the Spartans are clearly a work in progress, it's time to check the "greenprint".

If MSU sputters or spirals to a so-so season with the most accomplished junior quarterback it has had, a likely Butkus Award winner in the middle of its defense and the league's best receivers and linebackers, something is wrong.

But don't expect to see that, even if past non-performance shouts "Prepare for disappointment!"

This year's Spartans have the personnel and the schedule to win nine games, if not more. Anything less than 8-4 should be seen as a major disappointment after a 6-7 dud.

To go 9-3 in the regular season, MSU will need to win the six games it should and three of the six most difficult matchups.

In order of importance, not degree of difficulty, here are the six Saturdays that will determine a lot of fans' moods and travel plans:

OCTOBER 9 • AT MICHIGAN: The Spartans will try to make it three in a row in the series for the first time since 1965-67. They're 30-67-5 all-time against the Wolverines – 24-34-2 in the last 60 years but just 10-30 in the past four decades.

What happened in those games won't determine how Kirk Cousins and Greg Jones will do in a bigger Big House – better known as "The Stadium on Extenze."

Wide receiver Mark Dell (2) pulls away from Wisconsin

But one factor from the past 40 years is significant and worthy of mention.

MSU has had 10 head coaches in that span, Michigan just four.

Stability matters. And believe it or not, the Spartans are more stable than the Wolverines today. Dantonio has Joe Paterno potential compared to Rich Rodriguez, whose next endorsement could be for Century 21.

Michigan's '09 defense was one of the worst in school history by any objective standard. Without Big Ten Defensive Player of the Year Brandon Graham and No. 1 cornerback Donovan Warren, can it possibly be better?

Not likely. But the Wolverines will want this win more they've wanted any against MSU since 1974, the year after the Spartans were blamed for a scoreboard-ratified Rose Bowl vote.

CHANCE OF AN MSU WIN: 50 percent – 70 percent after a loss to Wisconsin, 30 percent after a victory over the Badgers.

OCTOBER 2 • WISCONSIN: The Badgers are a popular dark-horse pick to win the conference. Bret Bielema's team has enough experience to make that happen.

But the Spartans have beaten better Wisconsin teams than this one in East Lansing. A 49-14 rout of the nation's No. 4 team in 2004 comes to mind.

And the visiting team hasn't won in this series since 2002. That trend should continue if MSU can play decent run defense and locate the Badgers' seemingly invisible tight ends.

The Spartans are underdogs today, two-and-a-half months prior to kickoff. Check back if Dantonio's team is 4-0, as we fully expect it to be.

CHANCE OF AN MSU WIN: 50 percent in the biggest home game of the season. Look for a split in the first two Big Ten outings.

OCTOBER 30 • AT IOWA: Call me a Hawkeye lover, but the best coach in the Big Ten, Kirk Ferentz, has a great chance to have the best team this season, too. In fact, let me be the first to say it: Iowa, not Ohio State, is the team to beat for the conference crown.

The Hawkeyes were No. 4 in the nation, albeit with a lot of good fortune, and were leading Northwestern when quarterback Ricky Stanzi was injured. His team lost that game, then fell to the Buckeyes in Columbus on an overtime field goal – with a backup QB.

All Iowa did was finish 11-2 and dominate favored Georgia Tech in the Orange Bowl.

The Hawkeyes are loaded this season, with defensive end Adrian Clayborn a co-favorite for Big Ten Defensive Player of the Year honors. They also play MSU, OSU, Wisconsin and Penn State in Kinnick Stadium.

CHANCE FOR AN MSU WIN: 20 percent in the most likely loss on the schedule.

NOVEMBER 27 • AT PENN STATE: Could it be JoePa's last game in Happy Valley? Approaching his 84th birthday, any game could be, though he'll probably coach as long as he can.

If this were the first Big Ten game in October instead of the last one in November, I'd like the Spartans' chances better. By Thanksgiving weekend, Paterno will have found a suitable replacement for quarterback Daryll Clark, an MSU assassin in back-to-back seasons.

The Spartans haven't won in Beaver Stadium since a 23-0 thumping in 1965. How long ago was that? Paterno was in his final season as an aide to his Brown and Penn State mentor, Rip Engle.

CHANCE FOR AN MSU WIN: 35 percent – 10 percent if a 45-year run as the Lions' head coach is ending.

SEPTEMBER 18 • NOTRE DAME: Yes, Brian Kelly is an excellent coach. Yes, he'll win big in South Bend. And yes, it'll happen faster than Charlie Weis' first trip through a buffet line.

But are the Fighting Irish ready to win in East Lansing in the third game of the year? Are they good enough without Jimmy Clausen to get that done? Not likely.

If they are, it says two things. Notre Dame is good enough to make Kelly a National Coach of the Year candidate. And the Spartans aren't as far along in Dantonio's fourth year as they should be.

CHANCE FOR AN MSU WIN: 70 percent, regardless of who starts at leprechaun.

OCTOBER 23 • AT NORTHWESTERN: Some would say November 20 against Purdue. Take your pick. But a road game against a bowl team strikes me as tougher.

In the Spartans' first game outside the state of Michigan in 2010, Dantonio will have to have his team ready to play.

It's the week before the trip to Iowa and a trap game for Cousins and Co.

It's also a victory a 9-3 team captures.

CHANCE FOR AN MSU WIN: 70 percent – the same number the Wildcats would put on that game. After all, which school has won three Big Ten titles since 1995 and which one hasn't sniffed a title in two decades? Until that changes, skepticism is justified.

Jon Misch, a leaping Trenton Robinson and Johnathan Strayhorn

JULY 25, 2010 • SUNDAY

1,000 DAYS

THERE'S *A THOUSAND DAYS: JOHN F. KENNEDY IN THE WHITE HOUSE*, Arthur M. Schlesinger Jr.'s moving tale of a Presidential Camelot.

There's Thousand Days, the Boston-based alternative rock band, and "A Thousand Days," the syrupy Clay Aiken song.

There's "Anne of the Thousand Days," a 1969 period piece with Richard Burton and Genevieve Bujold, and *Book of a Thousand Days,* Shannon Hale's 2007 fantasy.

But it's no fantasy, just borderline fantastic, that Michigan State is closing in on 1,000 days since its last loss to Michigan in football or basketball – either gender.

As of 3 p.m. Monday, it'll be 996 days since the Wolverines' 28-24 win on November 3, 2007, in East Lansing, thanks to the most fortunate fumble in series history.

A few minutes later, U-M running-his-mouth Mike Hart made his "little brother" analogy, forgetting how he'd nearly wet himself when MSU rallied for a 24-14 advantage.

Someone from each team should've said thanks – for very different reasons.

The following week, Mark Dantonio threw down the gauntlet and put an institutional inferiority complex in the closet, if not in the trash.

"It's not over," he said with a steely stare. "It'll never be over ... Pride comes before the fall."

Before the teams meet again this fall in Michigan Stadium, it'll be 1,071 days-and-counting since "The Victors" was an appropriate fight song.

The coaches from West Virginia West, Rich Rodriguez and John Beilein, have done what no duo did from 1898-2007.

They're the first pair of coaches to go two full school years without leading the Wolverines to a win over the Spartans in those sports.

Think about that.

And think how many egos could be crushed if U-M misses its chance to beat MSU at the corner of Stadium and Main on October 9.

OK, OK, I can hear some of you screaming.

"Why are you talking about Michigan again?

Because other than the University Research Corridor, anything that's bad for the Wolverines is good for the Spartans.

Because U-M's loss is MSU's gain in appropriations, admissions and statewide attention, like it or not.

Because the Wolverines are temporarily wounded, not permanently toothless, in football – and probably basketball, too.

Because the Spartans have a rare opportunity for long-term parity, a dream just 21 months ago.

And because MSU is doing something it has never done.

The Spartans had never scored more than 58 points in back-to-back football games against U-M – their total from 34-8 and 24-17 wins in 1959-60.

That mark was just erased, while no one seemed to notice.

Dantonio's second and third teams put 61 points on the board with 35-21 and 26-20 triumphs over their archrivals.

He and Charlie Bachman (1933-35) are the only two M.A.C.-MSC-MSU coaches to win two of their first three games against the Wolverines.

And before you say, "Yeah, but look how bad those U-M teams were," consider two things.

It wasn't until his third season and sixth series matchup that Wolverine-hater Tom Izzo broke through and beat the Wolverines.

He'd be the first to tell you U-M opened the door with the Ed Martin scandal in 1996.

Two seasons later, Izzo tore that door off the hinges, one that hasn't been repaired yet.

His teams have won 18 of the last 21 meetings, with no let-up in sight.

Defensive end Colin Neely (89) and Marcus Hyde (HIDDEN) stop Michigan's Tate Forcier

Equally important, Dantonio wants to beat the Wolverines as much as Izzo ever did – and still does, though he downplays that passion these days.

Maybe Dantonio caused the Hart attack with his "moment of silence" comment after U-M's pratfall against Appalachian State.

So be it.

So what if the Wolverines punched back with Hart, Chad Henne and Mario Manningham and left East Lansing with all kinds of punch lines?

He who laughs last – or in this case, laughs second and third – laughs best.

Since 2007, the 10th win in 13 tries for Lloyd Carr against four MSU coaches, the earth has stopped spinning. U-M has gone an unfathomable 3-17 in conference play.

If you think that's no big deal, it took Bo Schembechler nearly 11 seasons to lose 18 games with the Wolverines and almost 16 years to have 17 league losses.

The Wolverines were a whopping 69-8-1 in Big Ten play in the decade from 1969-78.

The Spartans lost seven conference games in 2006 alone.

That happened to be the last season with John L. Smith as head football coach in East Lansing, another wrong-guy-in-the-wrong-place experiment.

But it's amazing what happens when the pieces all fit, as they seem to do today in the Skandalaris Center.

Under Dantonio's leadership, MSU won 22 games from 2007-09 – three more than in the first three years under Biggie Munn, Duffy Daugherty, Denny Stolz, Darryl Rogers or Nick Saban and five more than in the first three seasons with George Perles.

And as maddening as the last three years have been, primarily due to 11 losses by eight points or less, the Spartans have accomplished a few things, too.

Yes, they've lost three straight bowls – all close games against superior teams.

But Saban is the only other MSU coach who began with three straight bowl appearances, losses by a combined 60 points more than Dantonio's three defeats.

And Perles is the only coach who has taken the Spartans to four straight bowls, winning three of those games before it all fell apart.

If Dantonio does what's expected this season, he'll do more than equal that string.

He'll have the winningest first four seasons of any coach in school history.

Going 9-3 would give Dantonio's program 31 wins, one more than Chester Brewer managed from 1903-06, beginning the year after a 119-0 humiliation in Ann Arbor.

Anything less than 9-3 will be a disappointment for the current players and coaches.

It's MSU'S turn to win more than one out of every three close games and time to play 60 minutes, not 45.

It's the Spartans' turn to see how it feels for players to leave without a loss to U-M in football, not just basketball, as Izzo's 2001 and 2002 graduating classes did.

If that happens, if MSU turns two years of unprecedented success against the Wolverines into four, make sure to appreciate how special that run is.

No. 1, it has never happened before.

No. 2, it may never happen again.

But if Dantonio and Izzo can rule this season, the Spartans' two-sport dominance will reach 1,449 days by the 2011 football matchup.

That would be more than a minute of silence.

It would be 2,086,560 of them.

AUGUST 10, 2010 • SUNDAY

STILL UNBEATEN, STILL WINLESS

NO FOOTBALL TEAM HAS EVER WON its first game on Media Day.

None have recorded a big "L" there, either.

Thus, Michigan State is right where it was at 8 a.m. Tuesday – 0-0 overall and 0-0 in the Big Ten.

That's true despite fans' firm belief that they know exactly how the season will go.

The incurable optimists still think the Spartans will win 10 or 11 games and enter the final weekend with championship hopes.

They remember that MSU traveled to Penn State with title aspirations as recently as 2008.

And they're correct about that.

The unyielding pessimists still believe Mark Dantonio's fourth Spartan team won't be any better than his first three.

How could it be? It's Michigan State. That means it's destined to disappoint its followers.

And for the most part, it has.

But there's a third group, the irrepressible realists, who won't be sucked into either trap.

They shake their head at the blind allegiance of the sunshine blowers and roll their eyes at the unfair expectations of the demand-perfection fringe group.

They see an eight- or a nine-win team. That's probably a fair assessment, though no one KNOWS how good the Spartans will be, not to mention their opponents, until they see who's injured and who's in uniform.

Before talking to any of the players or coaches, I thought this could be a 9-3 team, provided ...

It doesn't suffer a major injury at quarterback or middle linebacker – or a rash of problems on the offensive line or in the secondary.

It gets steady, not spectacular, placekicking from one or more of the three new candidates.

And it doesn't fall victim to another off-the-field nightmare like last year's across-the-road trip from Kellogg Center to Rather Hall.

"When negative things happen, there's a chance it can make you more cohesive as a team," Dantonio said of a November incident with more legs than a team huddle.

Cohesion and consistency were lacking last season in a 6-7 pratfall, a three-game slide from 2008.

One of the biggest reasons was a turnover at quarterback and running back. Another was a team that turned on itself.

That shouldn't be a problem this season. The leadership isn't running from expectations or responsibility.

"I expect to win every football game," Dantonio said. "And I'm not ashamed to sit up here and say that."

Talk is cheap on Media Day, where every team worth its hype should think it's going to a big-time bowl.

If athletes can't convince themselves they can win, they won't be able to convince their opponents on Saturday afternoons or evenings.

So it's fair to warn anyone to take press-conference hype with a huge bag of salt, not just a grain of it.

But after talking to a dozen players and three coaches, I'm more convinced than ever this year could be special – just the third 10-win season in East Lansing in 114 tries.

My good friend, Earle Robinson, disagrees. And I have to take note of that.

Earle has been following MSU football since the '60s – the 1960s, in case you were wondering. So I respect his experience, if not his wisdom.

"Why do you think this team is any different?" Earle asked midway through Tuesday's session. "Why should anyone believe it can win nine games?"

"Simple," I said, referring to the answer, not the questioner. "Because this should be one of the best teams MSU has had in 44 years, one that has a fair chance to prove that."

Let me explain with as many facts and as little emotion as possible:

- The Spartans have one of their best schedules in history, a break they may never have again.

- They have nine games in the state of Michigan and no trips elsewhere till an October 23 visit to Northwestern, a matchup that should draw lots of MSU supporters.

- They have an excellent chance to be 4-0 in September, with a home game against Notre Dame the only foreseeable stumble.

- And they don't play Ohio State, the Big Ten champ for five straight years and the No. 2 team in the nation in most preseason polls.

MSU has the second-best quarterback in the conference in Kirk Cousins, regardless of what they say in Iowa City and Madison.

He also has a year of starting experience, setting Spartan sophomore marks for completions and yardage.

If you don't think that matters, check the first- and second-year stats and records for Earl Morrall (1954-55), Charlie Baggett (1973-74), Ed Smith (1976-77), Dan Enos (1989-90), Tony Banks (1994-95), Todd Schultz (1996-97), Bill Burke (1998-99), Jeff Smoker (2000-01), Drew Stanton (2004-05) and Brian Hoyer (2007-08).

MSU also has the best receivers and linebackers in the league – and more depth than it has ever had in those areas.

It has a solid left side of the offensive line and should have a better running game.

It has more maturity on its defensive line and will again have a very good punter.

Another strong incoming class tells us the coaches are working as hard to sell the program as fans are to buy season tickets.

But the best sign, the true indication Dantonio is building a program one small step at a time, is the way the Spartans looked at last season: with determination to do better.

"Last year was a huge disappointment," quarterback-turned-starting wideout Keith Nichol said. "A 6-7 record is NOT acceptable. We had high expectations and didn't fulfill them. But maybe we needed to be punched in the mouth."

Safety Trenton Robinson correctly accessed the secondary play as "awful." And cornerback Chris L. Rucker, my pick as the most improved player in 2010, refused to blame anyone else for what happened.

His position coach, Harlon Barnett, didn't want to replay the past. But he finally accepted the idea his unit's performance was "bad" in a lot of games and many situations. Just the mention of the words "wheel route" was enough to make him cringe for hours.

MSU's players and coaches needed to know a .500 regular season isn't enough.

They needed to understand a win over Michigan isn't a get-out-of-jail-free card.

They needed to see a bowl berth isn't a sign of success if it ends in another eight months of skunk spray.

The Spartans get that now. Their goals have changed. Realistically so.

They can't control what the Buckeyes do. But they can determine whether your bucks and their sweat have been wasted.

Nichol didn't come back from Norman, Okla., to switch positions and be ridiculed as a loser. Fortunately, he didn't see the hate mail when he left.

He returned to East Lansing, the place he always wanted to be, to be known as a winner and to help MSU reach a level it hadn't seen in his lifetime.

The Spartans' only title in that span, a one-fourth share in 1990, was secured just before his second birthday. The program's last Rose Bowl on January 1, 1988, came just before his embryo stage.

No one outside the Skandalaris Center is talking championship now. That's asking a lot in Year 4.

But a championship effort is a great place to start.

Wide receiver Keith Nichol soars to make a circus catch

AUGUST 22, 2010 • SUNDAY

STABILITY + ABILITY = VICTORIES

ANY FOOTBALL TEAM can have a good season.

Some can do a lot better than that.

Some can have a great one.

We've seen that all across the country – even at Michigan State, where the Spartans are a sub-mediocre 243-241-9 over the past 43 years.

Three Big Ten titles, one Rose Bowl and one season with double-digit wins are all MSU can offer in that span.

And since the final gun of the 10-10 tie with Notre Dame on November 19, 1966, the Spartans have never had back-to-back years with more than 16 triumphs.

They had 16 victories in 1989-90, 1998-99 and, yes, 2007-08, as hard as that may be for some to believe.

Sixteen wins is decent when some schools in this state have had 16 losses the past two seasons.

But it isn't good enough to qualify as a good program.

Especially when it backslides from 9-4 to 6-7, as Mark Dantonio's third MSU team did in 2009.

No one cares that another nine-win season would give Dantonio 31 victories in his first four years, the best start and the third-best stretch in school history.

Not with the rancid aftertaste of another loss to Penn State, an embarrassing incident in Rather Hall and a suspension-marred defeat by Texas Tech, making the Spartans 0-4 in bowls since the end of 2001.

The questions today are "Why has success over a four-year span been so difficult to achieve?" and "What does Dantonio need to do to change that?"

The word "jinx" and the lame explanation "Because it's Michigan State" are simply unacceptable.

When Iowa and Wisconsin can bury two and three decades of truly odorous football, MSU can do that, too.

And when Northwestern can win three Big Ten titles in six seasons, "can't" is no longer relevant.

If Michigan is capable of going 3-13 in Big Ten play the past two seasons, the Spartans have a chance to go 13-3 over the next two years.

Five things have to happen to make that kind of run a reality, not just a preseason dream:

ONE • MSU has to commit to a long-term plan and make sure there's a single playbook.

When the Spartans have had 10 head coaches in the past 38 seasons and Joe Paterno is beginning his 45th year as head coach at Penn State, something is wrong.

Perhaps that explains why Paterno has an NCAA-record 24 bowl wins since 1966 and MSU has just seven postseason triumphs since 1896.

And for those who shrug and say, "It has always been that way," the Spartans spanked Paterno's first team, 42-8.

That was before MSU began changing coaches more often than helmet designs. Five of its last nine leaders haven't started year four. Only one stayed here longer than a redshirt-senior.

TWO • The Spartans must continue to recruit with passion and a clear purpose.

They have to hold their own in the state of Michigan, get their fair share of Big Ten players from Ohio and add a few keepers from Illinois, Florida, etc.

They need to be open to the idea that an occasional junior-college player or major-college transfer can help, but only if the fit is right.

Most importantly, given their past transgressions and a fragile state of recovery, they need to comply with every NCAA rule, something I never worry about with Dantonio.

But rules can be broken by other staffers – players and boosters, too, especially when short-term gain is the lone consideration.

THREE • MSU must endure the growing pains that often accompany long-term success.

Granted, that sounds ridiculous after decades of heartbreak. But for the sake of program building, contemporary Spartan history begins in 2007.

That means learning from mistakes, not just repeating them and not breaking in new coordinators or key position coaches without having to do so.

A certain amount of transition is expected. It means assistant coaches are doing a good job. But to keep moving forward, it's best not to have too much turnover.

When a quarterback has the chance to play in 40 games over a three-year span, as Kirk Cousins could, it's a tremendous advantage. So is an accumulation of depth that hasn't been seen at MSU since Duffy Daugherty's heyday.

FOUR • The Spartans need to coach smart and play smarter. Basically, that means getting out of their own way.

It's difficult enough to win in the Big Ten, as MSU has proven with just five seasons above .500 in league play since Penn State's arrival in 1993.

It's almost impossible to win when distractions and self-defeating acts intervene. That includes coaching controversies, substance-abuse issues and off-the-field violence.

The fact is the Spartans aren't good enough to win with blown assignments (see: wheel route, 2009) and ridiculous penalties like a killer offside call against Central Michigan – and won't be good enough to do that for the foreseeable future.

More games are lost than won. Historically, the best teams at MSU and almost every other school have been the smartest ones.

FIVE • The Spartans must learn to build on big victories, not simply to bask in them.

MSU has had a maddening habit of placing too much importance on big victories and assuming the worst after crushing defeats.

It's all about focus. And the Spartans have lost the mental game as often as they've dropped the physical one.

Their fans could pay attention there, too. They've gone back and forth between deliriousness and despair when neither reaction is warranted.

Maybe that's part of being a fan. Maybe it's a normal reaction.

But if MSU goes 4-0 in September, that won't mean it's guaranteed to beat the Badgers in the Big Ten opener on October 2.

It means the Spartans will have three more victories than they did at the end of September last season.

And if they lose to Wisconsin, there's no assurance they'll go into Ann Arbor a week later and leave with their first three-game series win streak since 1965-67.

Likewise, a loss to Notre Dame wouldn't end MSU's hopes to be 9-3. And a stumble vs. the Badgers or even the Wolverines wouldn't end the Spartans' championship hopes.

Stability and ability are still the keys. This year, as much as any season in recent history, MSU is in great position to have both.

Linebacker Eric Gordon (43) provides leadership

SEPTEMBER 4, 2010 • SATURDAY

FOR WHOM THE BELL TOILS

SATURDAY AFTERNOON in East Lansing was a first in many ways.

The first football game for the 2010 Michigan State Spartans.

The first chance to erase the stench of late November 2009.

And the first look at freshman running back Le'Veon Bell.

If you aren't familiar with the name, you'd better learn it.

It has a nice ring to it.

When Bell arrived from Reynoldsburg, Ohio, last January, it didn't take him long to turn a few heads.

He turned the rest in a 38-14 win over Western Michigan in Spartan Stadium.

The 6-foot-2, 230-pounder from Groveport Madison High exceeded all expectations, even Howard Griffith's.

Remember when the Big Ten Network's preseason bus tour arrived in East Lansing a few weeks ago?

Griffith stunned host Dave Revsine and fellow analyst Gerry DiNardo by drooling over No. 24 and saying Bell would win the job outright over sophomore co-starters Larry Caper and Edwin Baker.

Today, the former Illinois star, a player who once scored eight touchdowns in a game, looks like he could be a prophet.

Caper sat out the opener with a fractured hand – a precaution, we were told after the game.

Meanwhile, Baker bounced off defenders and sprinted past them for 117 yards and two TDs on 17 carries, an outstanding effort in any league.

One could argue that Baker, not Bell, was the Spartans' brightest star against the Broncos, given his speed, balance and toughness.

Baker's yards-after-contact showed the importance of physical and mental maturity between his freshman and sophomore years.

The blocking of center John Stipek, guards Joel Foreman and Chris McDonald, tackles D.J. Young and J'Michael Deane and even wideout Keith Nichol was impressive, too.

MSU's net – 297 rushing yards and four scores on just 37 carries, an 8.0 average – was 78 yards better than last season's best showing, also against WMU.

But it was Bell's debut that had everyone smiling Saturday, including an 18-year-old who set school records for a true freshman.

"How you doing?" Bell said with a disarming grin as he began his first postgame Q&A.

"I did a pretty decent job today. It was a great experience to play in front of 75,000 people. I had dreamed of something like this."

So had Mark Dantonio and his staff after struggling to find a tough-yardage back last season, a 6-7 disappointment.

They had to love what they saw when Bell showed the poise, patience and power of a fifth-year senior.

With 141 yards and two TDs on 10 carries, 14.1 per pop, Bell became the first Spartan true freshman to rush for more than 100 – all in the last three quarters.

His 75-yard run was a game-changing play late in the first half, when MSU was sputtering with a 14-7 lead and huddling deep in its end zone.

Bell's other carries were worth noting, too: 9, 15, 5 and 2 yards (TD) in the second quarter, an 18-yard weave for six more points in the third quarter and another 11-yard run in the fourth.

He had 108 yards on six touches before halftime and never lost a yard.

Le'Veon Bell wards off a Western Michigan defender

Running back Edwin Baker celebrates with teammates

"He has great vision and excellent feet," Offensive Coordinator Don Treadwell said. "We think the sky's the limit."

Bell's teammates seemed to share that view and didn't need to share the spotlight.

"He did a phenomenal job," quarterback Kirk Cousins said. "He makes the first guy miss. And that's the mark of a great back."

"Great" is a big word to describe someone who had never carried the ball, much less the load, for a team in need of a breakthrough season.

But Bell gave every indication he could be special. And we didn't get to see his surprisingly soft hands as a receiver or appreciate his advanced level of pass protection.

He and Baker became the first Spartans to rush for 100 yards in the same game since Javon Ringer (156) and Drew Stanton (105) accomplished that in a win at Pittsburgh in 2006.

Bell and Baker gave MSU more triple-digit rushers in one day than it had all last season (Ashton Leggett vs. WMU).

And Bell's yardage was the highest for any Spartan back except Ringer since Jehuu Caulcrick gained 146 against Wisconsin on November 13, 2004.

Caulcrick was a different kind of runner. He sought contact at every opportunity.

Bell can make a tackler lose his footing on one play and lose his breath on the next.

Granted, it's awfully early to start comparing him to NFL backs like Ringer and Caulcrick. Bell has fewer carries at the collegiate level than Ringer had in some drives in 2008.

Let's see what he does against Wisconsin and Iowa before anyone starts projecting career stats.

But Bell's debut symbolized what Dantonio's program is all about. In year four, it's finally time to judge the infrastructure and incoming classes.

Against a mediocre Mid-American Conference team, that evaluation was good, not great.

Let's give it a B-.

The Spartans were much too sloppy for anyone's liking Saturday, with 11 penalties and nine dropped balls – seven on offense and two on defense.

They had 12 men on the field and still couldn't stop the Broncos from scoring. But they did more than enough to match last September's victory total before Labor Day.

In 26 fewer snaps, MSU had 160 more yards than WMU. And that was with no pass play longer than 37 yards and just two longer than 20.

Perfect? No way.

Satisfying? Not really. Not with that many mistakes.

But jumping offside is correctable. Not being able to run the ball is much tougher to change, as 2009 showed.

And for those who think the MSU defense should shut teams down on every possession, it doesn't work that way any more.

High-volume passing attacks are going to gain yards. Remember John L. Smith's team's stats?

The Spartans held the Broncos to 4.5 yards per pass and 3.8 yards per play, then averaged 8.5 and 8.2, respectively, when they got the ball.

In this case, stats were for winners.

Best of all, MSU isn't done winning this month.

Sound the Bell for a 9-3 season.

Keith Nichol with his first big catch against the Broncos

SEPTEMBER 11, 2010 • SATURDAY

TWO OUT OF THREE?

IF IT'S TRUE a team's greatest improvement comes between its first and second games, Michigan State could be in trouble.

Not as much trouble as Florida Atlantic coach Howard Schnellenberger would be in a high school math class, but in jeopardy of serious disappointment.

Yes, the Spartans slashed their penalties from 11 to four and eliminated almost all nine of their dropped passes between a 38-14 win over Western Michigan and a 30-17 win over the Owls.

But a much-maligned defense, the No. 1 reason MSU lost seven games last season, still wasn't good enough to win more than half of the eight Big Ten games it will play in October and November.

It wasn't good enough to beat a decent opponent in a bowl game, something that hasn't happened since 2001.

And it may not have been good enough to beat an unranked Notre Dame team, an opportunity that awaits under the lights in Spartan Stadium.

MSU's defense couldn't get off the field again Saturday, allowing FAU to run 71 plays, 24 more than the Spartans.

After being outsnapped 85-59 by the Broncos, the Spartans had 12 fewer opportunities on offense in Week 2 than Week 1.

That meant their defense has been on the field for 156 snaps and their offense just 106 thus far, hardly the recipe for winning football.

How did that happen? Three ways.

The Owls were 7-for-16 on third down and 2-for-2 on fourth down – 9-for-18 on plays that could have produced a change in possession.

That was better than WMU's combined 10-for-27 success in those situations and much better than MSU's 1-for-7 conversion rate at Ford Field.

The tackling in space was poor too often – a step back from Week 1 when improvement was still needed.

And if the Spartans had been trying to catch Michigan's mercurial Denard Robinson instead of FAU passer Jeff Van Camp or runner Alfred Williams, the Wolverines would have converted a lot of extra-point tries.

That was roughly U-M's effective kicking range in South Bend, but let's solve one team's problems at a time.

MSU had just a single takeaway Saturday, a gift when Van Camp mysteriously lost the handle before a pass rusher reached him.

That was worse than last season's anemic 14 takeaways in 13 games and a major step back from the Spartans' three takeaways against the Broncos.

If a defense can't produce a single interception in 37 throws and can't knock a ball loose in 34 rushes, it has major issues.

Again.

Granted, the yield per play has been impressive – 4.2 yards Saturday after just 3.8 per snap in the opener.

Compared to MSU's offensive numbers – 7.8 yards per play vs. the Owls and a ridiculous 8.0 for the season – the Spartans have been downright stingy.

But no team should be satisfied when its defense has been on the field 22:56 longer than its offense in two games.

FAU had the ball 15:06 longer than MSU, more than an extra quarter of possession time, and could have made things scary in the final 2:50 if Schnellenberger could have multiplied 8 x 2.

Perhaps we need to take the bad with the good. And there were some major positives besides a 2-0 start, something the Spartans hadn't managed the past two years.

Before the season began, we outlined three major concerns for the Spartans to win nine football games, a reasonable expectation given the team's talent and experience.

Ken Mannie, Colin Neely (89), Jerel Worthy (99) and Denzel Drone (52)

HEART OF A **SPARTAN**

Le'Veon Bell steps out of a tackle attempt in Detroit

MSU needed reliable placekicking. Large check mark.

It needed to prove it could run the football. Check mark in ink.

And it needed to show it could stop a decent passing game. Uhhh . . . let's look at the first two areas.

Or as Meatloaf wrote and sang, "Don't be sad. Two out of three ain't bad."

Just not as good as it could be, should be and must be to be a Big Ten title contender.

It could be infinitely worse without the performance of kicker Dan Conroy and runners Edwin Baker and Le'Veon Bell.

Conroy should at least share Big Ten Special Teams Player of the Week honors after drilling field goals from 44, 41 and 51 yards Saturday.

For the year he's 4-for-4 on three-point tries and 8-for-8 on extra-points, a pleasant surprise and a great way to replace Brett Swenson.

Baker has gone from being an unsure freshman to an almost unstoppable sophomore, rushing for 300 yards and three scores on 32 carries.

With excellent speed and balance, "Rock" is no longer a pebble. He's a load for any defender, especially in the open field.

He had 183 yards on 15 carries against the Owls, 12.2 per pop.

Even if you subtracted his 80-yard touchdown run, Baker would have had 83 in 14 tries, nearly 6.0 yards per rush.

His partner in pounding the pigskin, the aforementioned Bell, was impressive again, too.

He carried the ball 10 times for the second straight week and netted 49 yards, 92 less than the week before.

But before Bell lost 12 yards and the football on his final carry on the day, he had 61 yards on nine touches, showing a great blend of power and patience.

He and Baker were impressive enough that projected co-starter Larry Caper was itchier than ever to return to the lineup.

Showing no ill effects from a preseason hand injury, Caper trotted off the field and answered a quick question by shouting, "I'm ready! I'm ready!"

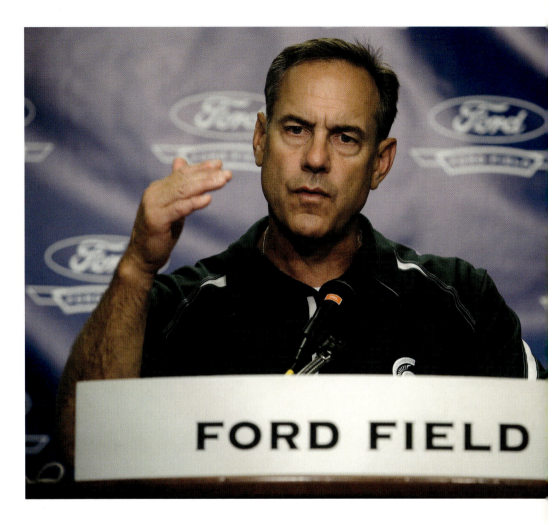

The question is whether his team is ready for the Fighting Irish, a group that couldn't have tackled Gerry DiNardo, much less Denard Robinson, Saturday.

Maybe the bigger question is whether the Spartans are ready to get off the field on defense and get the ball back for an explosive offense, even with quarterback Kirk Cousins struggling a bit.

Cousins has made some errant throws, usually short or behind his targets, and hasn't made the best decisions. But he should. And he will, if he gets enough chances.

If that doesn't happen, MSU will be 2-1 next Sunday morning.

And its fans will be sad.

With the Spartans' September schedule, two out of three is bad.

PUNT, PASS & POISE

AARON BATES GAVE SPARTANS A LEG UP

HE WAS A FIRST-TEAM All-Big Ten punter, a terrific holder for two all-conference kickers and the trigger for two amazing moments as a passer.

But instead of putting a position by his name, he can be described another way, with four simple words:

Aaron Bates ... football player.

No one else has started 52 football games for Michigan State. And when he left with his degree in 2011, no one had appeared in more than his 33 victories with the Green and White.

In a perfect example of right place, right time, Bates and the Spartans were equally fortunate.

The story starts in New Concord, Ohio, a town of just over 2,500 residents off I-70 between Columbus and Wheeling, W.Va., and a community that hadn't produced a Division I player in 10 years.

"There's no fast food in New Concord," Bates said. "A big night would be going to Earl's Pizza. Mostly, we'd be shooting guns, riding four-wheelers, fishing or playing pickup basketball."

Whichever sport Bates picked up, he was easy to pick out – a natural athlete in an area where nature always came first. Yet, he wasn't exactly on the radar for BCS powers.

Division II and III schools were interested in Bates as a quarterback and a baseball pitcher. Purdue offered but was never a serious contender. And if Mark Dantonio hadn't called, he may have wound up at West Virginia, playing for ... yes, Rich Rodriguez.

"Michigan State wasn't in the picture till Coach Dantonio was hired," Bates said of a hastily assembled 2007 class. "But I visited and liked it a lot. It had a little of everything. And I liked Coach D. I really thought I'd succeed anywhere."

All evidence points in that direction. Bates is a born leader, as seen when his peers made him the first non-position player to co-captain the Spartans.

MSU's coaches weren't so sure. It took lobbying by one of the best punters in school history for the program to offer a scholarship.

"You have to credit Craig Jarrett, a graduate assistant at the time," Dantonio said. "We had Aaron in camp, and he didn't punt. All he did was kick. But Craig said, 'Look at his technique and extension. He can be the guy.' The funny thing is that Greg Montgomery had told us exactly the same thing about Craig."

One of the best things about Dantonio is that he doesn't think he invented football. He surrounds himself with good people and lets them do their job. When he listened to Jarrett, who had punted 235 times for the Spartans and 20 more for the Washington Redskins, it was one of his best decisions.

Bates' brainpower has never been in doubt. The three-time Academic All-Big Ten pick was named to the National Football Foundation's Hampshire Honor Society for 2011 with a 3.95 grade-point average in general management.

Long before that, he was smart enough to know the right opportunity to play college football when it arose. And he was sharp enough to recognize a great roommate when Kirk Cousins showed up for the same official visit in January 2007.

"If Ohio State had offered, it would've been hard to turn down," Bates said. "When the Buckeyes won the National Championship with Coach D. as coordinator, I watched that game with my family. But Michigan State IS family. It's what college is supposed to be."

Aaron Bates (18) celebrates with Denicos Allen (28) and Mike Sadler (3)

HEART OF A **SPARTAN**

It's big, even for the Big Ten. And Bates couldn't conceive of seeing more than 43,000 students on campus or several hundred in a lecture class. That cultural adjustment was made easier by a fellow Christian and newfound friend for life.

"It was fate," Bates said. "We hung out together on our visit. And just as I was about to email Kirk, he emailed me. He was a stand-up guy with high moral character. As I saw him speak and saw how much he shared, I tried to do more and got involved with Athletes in Action."

Bates got involved in games long before Cousins did, succeeding Brandon Fields and beating out redshirt-freshman Ed Wagner, who transferred to Delaware. He had never been to a camp until the summer before his senior year of high school. But Jarrett helped Bates change his grip and correct a tendency to pull the ball left.

The Spartans did so well on offense in his first game against UAB that he didn't have to punt until the second half. By the end of his freshman year, however, Bates was one of the best in the Big Ten. And he was well aware of the program's history with Ray Stachowicz, Ralf Mojsiejenko, Montgomery, Jarrett and Fields.

Though his average improved to 45.0 yards per boot as a senior, Bates realized the value of downing balls inside the 10. He experimented until he discovered the nose-down drop that gave his pooch punts backspin. Eventually, he learned to land a high, soft punt the way Phil Mickelson would a 64-degree wedge.

Dantonio credits Bates with setting up the winning touchdown against Purdue in 2010 by pooching the ball to the 3-yard line. Four plays later, Denicos Allen became a human missile and blocked the Boilermakers' punt. And Cousins cashed in with a scramble up the middle to cap a furious comeback.

Bates had his moments with direct snaps, too, beginning with a flip to Charlie Gantt for a first down in the 2009 Alamo Bowl, a play Dantonio dubbed "The Annexation of Puerto Rico." When Keshawn Martin hit Blair White one play later, MSU had a TD with three players completing passes on the same drive.

But that was just a warmup for Bates' 2-for-2 passing in 2010. First, he beat Notre Dame on a fake field goal in overtime with a "Little Giants" adlib, finding Gantt all alone for the win. Then, on a fake punt at Northwestern, he sprung "Mousetrap" and hit Bennie Fowler in a tight window for a first down that helped earn a Big Ten title.

"We had trick plays in every week," Bates said. "And I knew we were going to run 'Little Giants.' When we ran it in practice it worked every time – always to Le'Veon Bell, never to Charlie. But on third down, just before Kirk was sacked, Coach D. asked me, 'Should we run it?' I said, 'I'm not making that call! It's up to you.'"

After the play was called in the huddle, Bell walked to his right wingback spot, turned back to Bates, who was lined up to hold, and said, "Are you serious? We're running it right now?" Perhaps that explains why Bell was jammed on an inside release. But as kicker Dan Conroy flared to the sideline as a safety valve and two Fighting Irish defenders slipped, Bates slid to his right and lofted a perfect 29-yard pass, college football's Play of the Year.

"I'll tell you what, that was tremendous patience by Aaron Bates," Spartan Radio Network analyst Jim Miller said. "He thought about running it. But he held his ground, knowing it was going to come open. He had to trust it. And he trusted it."

Dantonio trusted No. 18, too. Time after time. Not surprisingly, Bates delivered in the biggest moments, drilling a 69-yard punt at Michigan and a 62-yarder against Notre Dame. Let the record show that he helped his team win with his brain, his arm and his instep.

And if the Irish still have nightmares, who can blame them? With a stab in the dark, Spartan Stadium became the Bates Motel just long enough that we can't stop watching it.

Aaron Bates boots the Spartans out of trouble again

SEPTEMBER 19, 2010 • SATURDAY

HOLLYWOOD ENDING, HARROWING END

IT WAS THE SECOND-BEST MOMENT of Mark Dantonio's two stays at Michigan State, followed quickly by the scariest one.

The best news today is that a "minor" heart attack less than an hour after an amazing win over Notre Dame was treated quickly with cardiac catheterization.

Dr. Chris D'Haem inserted a small, metallic stent to open a blocked blood vessel at Sparrow Hospital and said a full recovery is expected.

In the meantime Offensive Coordinator Don Treadwell will manage the day-to-day responsibilities of the head football coach.

Dantonio is still in charge of the program, and the words "acting" and "interim" were never used.

There was no acting involved Saturday night, just high drama and a signature moment in a long, successful coaching career.

From a public perspective, it was better than anything that happened in six seasons as an aide to Nick Saban and Bobby Williams.

Better than any of Dantonio's 24 previous wins in three-plus years as head coach, including an overtime win over Michigan.

And behind only his fiery program-defining response to a 2007 loss to the Wolverines – "It's not over ... It'll never be over!"

If that day made it OK for the Spartans to think like winners again, a 34-31 triumph over ND showed how important it is to act that way.

In a far-from-perfect performance, MSU rallied three times – from 7-0, 28-21 and 31-28 deficits.

With painstaking progress in question and people wondering if Dantonio was the one to get it done, one call said it all.

On fourth-and-14 from the 29-yard line, he said no to a tying 46-yard field goal and yes to a new image and opportunity.

The play's name was "Little Giants," a reference to the 1994 football film with Rick Moranis, Ed O'Neill and John Madden.

If it hadn't have worked, it may have become known as "Dumb and Dumber" or "Titanic" in East Lansing.

Instead, when holder and former high school quarterback Aaron Bates stood up, shuffled to his right and threw a perfect pass to wide-open tight end Charlie Gantt, the luck o' the Irish gave way to the will of the Spartans.

It didn't matter that the snap came after the play clock hit :00, that Gantt wasn't the primary receiver or that two Fighting Irish defenders fell down.

What mattered was that when gifted freshman Le'Veon Bell got knocked off balance as his began his route, a couple of seniors finished the job and triggered a wild celebration.

Suddenly, all was right with the world on the banks of the Red Cedar.

ESPN's Top 10 Play of the Day – perhaps the network's Play of the Week and an early favorite for the Pontiac Game-Changing Play of the Year – changed a lot of impressions.

Dantonio became cool and gutsy again with roughly 50 prospects in attendance and hundreds more watching at home.

His team was seen as a gallant survivor this time, not as the not-ready-for-prime-time players when the game ended at 11:49 p.m.

Shortly after his MSU radio and press trailer appearances, he was suffering disturbing symptoms in the locker room.

With his wife, best friend and chauffeur, Becky, at his side, he quickly made his way to Sparrow, where an EKG produced all the necessary news in a matter of minutes.

It was a time for prayer, but not the first one he had said Saturday night or Sunday morning. He mentioned that when he talked about a play that's still in the headlines.

"All our trick plays are named for movies," Dantonio said a little before 12:30 a.m. "I made the call, 'Little Giants,' said a little prayer and said, 'Let's go!'"

His team went to work. But it has done that every day in some way since its loss to Texas Tech in the Alamo Bowl on January 2.

On a night when the late John Pingel and Brad Van Pelt were honored for their greatness and when injured game captain Josh Rouse tried to run to join his joyous teammates, it was MSU's time to skip the suffering for once.

And if one moment said it all, it was an emotional embrace between Dantonio and Dale Evans, his position coach at South Carolina, seconds after Gantt reached the end zone.

While Joe Montana, a former Fighting Irish QB who'd beaten the Gamecocks with a late rally, watched another team enjoy a win for the ages, Evans couldn't have been happier.

"You talk about a ballsy call!" Evans said. "It takes guts to make a call like that. I'm just so proud of him."

Just one hour earlier, people who should have known better were whining about Dantonio's staff and forgetting all the stuff he inherited in December 2006.

Forty-two games later, with an infrastructure that won't pay all its dividends for several more seasons, the Spartans are in better shape than they've been since the mid-1960s.

Better than they were when Darryl Rogers' teams set Big Ten scoring records and shared a title on probation in 1978.

Better than when George Perles' best team won its second league title in four seasons in 1990 and beat USC for the third straight time.

And better than when MSU beat Florida in the 2002 Florida Citrus Bowl to finish 10-2 under Nick Saban and Bobby Williams.

After decades of sub-mediocrity, the Spartans

Tight end Charlie Gantt finishes off the Fighting Irish

are poised to show long-term progress at long last.

And the poise Dantonio's players displayed on a national stage is proof of that growth.

For the third game in a row, MSU rushed for more than 200 yards and held its opponent to less than 100.

Once again, Bell and sophomore Edwin Baker had big days carrying the ball and broke a long run.

But there were other heroes besides an unlikely passer on the game's final play and an often-forgotten receiver.

Junior wide receiver B.J. Cunningham had seven catches for 101 yards, including a 24-yard score when he stepped out of bounds, came back in and never quit on the play.

Cunningham bailed out struggling quarterback Kirk Cousins on several occasions and combined with Keshawn Martin for 15 grabs and 197 yards.

Much-maligned cornerback Chris L. Rucker had his best game as a Spartan, contributing a game-high 12 tackles, having one of his team's two stops for losses, forcing a fumble and breaking up two passes.

Yes, his receivers caught a few. But Michael Floyd will catch balls against any corner in the country. And his six grabs for 81 yards weren't fatal.

Best of all, Rucker's massive hit on humongous tight end Kyle Rudolph forced Notre Dame to kick a field goal in overtime instead of getting its 29th first down.

And Bates was brilliant long before he became the Big Ten leader in passing efficiency, averaging 45.4 yards on eight punts.

He drilled three kicks of more than 50 yards and placed two inside the Irish 20, with a 49-yard bomb from his 12-yard line – a net shift of 61 yards after a botched return – a key to getting the game to OT.

Dantonio took it from there. And when Gantt found his way to the end zone, not far from where Larry Caper did last year vs. U-M, the party was on.

MSU still needs to tighten things up. It can't have 11 penalties, as it has twice this season. And it needs a junior quarterback to quit taking sacks and throwing to the wrong receiver or behind the right one.

But Dantonio was anything but tight at Winning Time. He made the right call, win or lose, strategically and emotionally.

Even if Dan Conroy had connected from long range on his first pressure kick, a 50-50 proposition, there was no guarantee the Spartans could have won in double-, triple- or quadruple-OT.

There are two guarantees today – that everyone there will remember the night for a long, long time and that MSU has a chance to turn one triumph into a year to remember.

The Spartans' head football coach would expect nothing less.

SEPTEMBER 20, 2010 • MONDAY

YOU'VE GOTTA HAVE HEART

A GREAT NIGHT in Michigan State football history may have become even greater.

If an unforgettable fake field goal and a 34-31 overtime win over Notre Dame weren't sweet enough, Mark Dantonio's postgame chest discomfort may have been the perfect dessert.

Huh? How could a minor heart attack and time away from his team be positive?

The fact is, Dantonio had a blocked blood vessel and was headed down a potentially tragic path.

By sitting down, then heading to Sparrow Hospital with his wife, Becky, before the celebrations stopped, a 54-year-old football coach and family man may have added precious years for both pursuits.

Dantonio was the coolest guy in Spartan Stadium when he went deep in the playbook for "Little Giants," a 29-yard trick play from holder Aaron Bates to tight end Charlie Gantt.

His body fat was extremely low when he climbed a ladder in a crowded tunnel to do a radio interview with Will Tieman, instead of walking up a missing flight of steps.

"Somebody grab the ladder!" Tieman said to those milling around. "We don't want to lose our head coach to a concussion."

Or to anything else. And who could have guessed there was anything wrong in one of the program's finest hours, a trophy-game triumph on the national stage?

Who cares if half the fans on campus Saturday couldn't have identified the Megaphone Trophy or known that only USC has beaten the Irish more than MSU has?

Dantonio knew the series history. So did his players. That helps explain why the Spartans are 5-2 against Notre Dame and Michigan under his leadership.

But he was funny when he met with the media and talked about gutsy moves and movie titles in a triple-wide interview trailer just outside the stadium.

And as he met with recruits and moved toward a scheduled television interview with former MSU quarterback Jim Miller, Dantonio was smart enough to call an audible.

Less than four hours later, he had a small metallic stent implanted in his chest and an excellent long-range prognosis.

Dr. Chris D'Haem, who performed the surgery, made a scary situation sound almost routine. It was certainly much better than the alternative.

Dantonio learned of his problem in time, unlike former Spartan basketball coach John Benington and a couple of Big Ten football leaders, Wisconsin's Dave McClain and Northwestern's Randy Walker.

If Dantonio has to miss a few games or a few more than that, so be it. That's a small price to pay for a clean bill of cardiac health.

Others haven't been nearly as fortunate. But a couple of Big Ten coaching legends did recover to coach another three decades. U-M legend Bo Schembechler suffered a heart attack just before the 1970 Rose Bowl and only learned of his team's 10-3 loss to USC from a nurse in the recovery room.

It was his first season with the Wolverines, and Bo had ballooned from 195 pounds to a pudgy 220, largely by quitting handball and eating too many hamburgers.

Two days before the bowl game, he tried to drink a Coke in his room and couldn't swallow a drop. Then, he felt a pain in his chest and a burning sensation in both arms.

Schembechler's wife, Millie, was a nurse and

HEART OF A **SPARTAN**

B.J. Cunningham (3), Joel Foreman (67), Mark Dantonio and Keith Nichol (7)

immediately called for team physicians Gerald O'Connor and Robert Anderson. The initial diagnosis was a muscle spasm. And an EKG came back OK.

"So what do I do?" Schembechler said in his book, *Man in Motion,* with then-*Detroit Free Press* Sports Editor Joe Falls. "I haven't eaten since noon. So I go back to the room and order up the two biggest hamburgers you ever saw. There I am, eating again."

On New Year's Eve the National Coach of the Year had another warning when he tried to walk about 100 yards up a winding road to a reception with U-M President Robben Fleming.

Schembechler couldn't move and could barely breathe when the same pain hit his chest and his arms. After he finally made it up the hill, sweating and shaking, he introduced Fleming to the audience, then sat down before he collapsed.

At a late meeting with his team, he learned that a player had gotten a girl pregnant. And for the first time in his coaching career, Schembechler couldn't deal with the issue.

He also cut short a final staff meeting, then snored so loud that night that top assistant Jim Young was bothered by the noise in the next room.

When Schembechler woke up with a terrible headache, the doctors were summoned again. A second EKG was ordered while he kept studying the game plan.

Finally, the bad news was delivered. Schembechler knew something was wrong for two days. But at age

40, all he could think about was the game and his team.

"He tells me I have just had a heart attack and must be placed in intensive care," Schembechler said. "I start to cry. No way can I believe it. A heart attack? No game? No Rose Bowl?"

He spent 18 days at St. Luke's Hospital in Pasadena, then returned home to Ann Arbor, where a bed was set up in his living room. Schembechler recruited from there.

Though he was banned from conducting spring practice, he showed up every day and watched from a golf cart. He maneuvered the cart so close to the field that several players ran into it.

But Schembechler listened to his doctors, too. He dropped 45 pounds between January 1 and the first day of practice on August 20. By the season-opener, a 20-9 win over Arizona, he had regained his old fire.

Twenty years later, after another Rose Bowl defeat, he stepped down as the second-winningest coach in Big Ten history. Seventeen years and several careers after that, Schembechler died of a heart attack the day before the 2006 Ohio State showdown.

MSU basketball patriarch Jud Heathcote had a different experience at age 57. It was the summer of 1984, 15 years after Benington's collapse made Gus Ganakas the Spartans' head coach.

The day before Heathcote's heart attack, he had engaged in a spirited discussion – the kind he never lost – with Assistant A.D.-Facilities Gene Kenney. But that in itself was no great shock.

"I'd had a shouting match, if you can believe that," he said 11 years later in his memoir, *JUD: A Magical Journey.* "I don't even remember what it was about. But it was a good one. I was about as mad as I could get without hitting a guy."

Heathcote rushed home from Jenison, mowed the lawn, dashed over to Walnut Hills Country Club for a quick sauna, drove to Flint to see a game, then came back to East Lansing, where he thought he was coming down with a cold.

He got up the next morning, did 20 pushups and had the same feeling. Heathcote was supposed to sit down with A.D. and close friend Doug Weaver at 10 that morning to discuss negative comments about the Big Ten TV schedule and the league office.

Sweating profusely, Heathcote said, "God, I just don't feel very good. I think I'm coming down with a cold."

When Weaver said, "Maybe you're having a heart attack," Jud answered, "I think maybe I am."

After taking a nitroglycerine tablet, Heathcote was driven to Lansing's St. Lawrence Hospital in trainer Clint Thompson's Volkswagen – bumpety, bump, bump!

"God, Clint, can you miss at least a few of the bumps?" Heathcote said. "Geez, this is a long ride!"

When he arrived, his pulse rate was 36. If he gotten there much later ...

"I was in intensive care five days before they moved me," Heathcote said. "I had this cardiology team and got a horrendous bill. But lying in the hospital, my first reaction wasn't, 'Am I going to die?' It was, 'Am I going to coach again?'"

After missing some pre-conference games, he returned to the bench and was the same rompin', stompin' head coach for another 10-and-a-half seasons. The final diagnosis was less than 10-percent damage.

"The doctors gave me all this stuff to read," Heathcote said. "I told my wife, Bev, to read it. I didn't have time. I was working on basketball plays."

At age 83, after joint replacements, open-heart surgeries and the insertion of a pig valve, Heathcote still played golf three times a week and broke 100 until a recent setback.

Dantonio can learn from the past, pay attention to the present and thrive for the foreseeable future. He's young enough, fit enough and smart enough to be around a long time.

And if that happens, if he finishes the job he has started at MSU, he can look back on the night of the Notre Dame game and the morning thereafter and smile.

It was "Victory for MSU!" times two.

MSU's players honored Coach Mark Dantonio with a "D" and injured fullback Josh Rouse with "44"

SEPTEMBER 25, 2010 • SATURDAY

LET THE REAL FUN BEGIN

A 45-7 WIN over Northern Colorado Saturday was a little like doing laundry.

It wasn't the most rewarding experience. But if you didn't do it, you'd stink.

Michigan State did what it had to do in Spartan Stadium to keep its record clean.

And compared to last year's 1-3 start, a 4-0 mark is positively ... positive.

After all, MSU had only been 4-0 four times in 43 seasons – in 1997 and 1999 under Nick Saban, in 2005 under John L. Smith and in 2007 under Mark Dantonio.

You remember Dantonio – the talk of the nation last week after "Little Giants" cut Notre Dame down to size. Seven days later, the Fighting Irish leprechaun was Lilliputian.

Meanwhile, the Spartans played well enough to lead 35-0 and outgain the toothless Bears 387-141 in the first 30 minutes.

Under Don Treadwell's game-day leadership, MSU was businesslike and, apparently, injury-free – as important as any result against an FCS (I-AA) opponent.

Treadwell and the rest of the staff acquitted themselves well this week. And they won't quit working together when Dantonio returns from relatively minor heart surgery – perhaps as early as October 2.

The Spartans worked pretty well all week after last Sunday morning's unexpected visit to Sparrow Hospital. A year ago, that may not have happened.

Maturity matters. So does leadership. And after being seen as a selfish bunch, as 6-7 underachievers, this year's team seems to know what's at stake.

The fact is that MSU is playing for more than its record this season, for much more than its place in the final standings or any statistical areas.

It's trying to change its reputation as a group that's always better from the neck down, as a program that beats itself as often as it's drubbed by a physically superior foe.

"That which doesn't kill us makes us stronger," philosopher Friedrich Nietzsche said in a clairvoyant moment before going insane at age 45.

At age 54, Dantonio is about to become the beneficiary of that adversity training. The "D" on the back of his players' helmets also stood for "determination" Saturday.

Before anyone starts planning for a trip to Pasadena in late December and early January, let's remember three things – direct from the douse-the-euphoria department:

- The Spartans' victim in Week 4 was Northern Colorado, not a Big Ten slayer like Northern Illinois. The Bears were picked to finish seventh in the nine-team Big Sky.

- After nearly a month of the 2010 season, we're still getting to know Dantonio's fourth team – by far his best and deepest one, whatever the final "W" count.

- And MSU still has a lot of work to do to get to 5-0 for the third time since the start of the 1967 season, not to mention a second 6-0 start that's possible.

If the Spartans commit 11 penalties again, as they did against Western Michigan, Notre Dame and Northern Colorado, they'll be headed in the wrong direction – south.

When a team has three times as many penalties as Penn State as this point, the wrench can still be turned a few more times, individually and collectively.

Discipline and focus are still an issue at times for this team, though some would gladly take a penalty or two for the kind of physicality it will take to beat Wisconsin.

I got into an argument about that with an MSU power broker at a wedding Saturday night. Apparently, another 121 yards in walk-offs didn't matter.

"I don't care about penalties," he said, sounding like he was living in the late 1980s. "They don't matter."

If they haven't so far, they will at a most inopportune

HEART OF A SPARTAN

Offensive Coordinator Don Treadwell adds new duties

moment. It's one thing to play with reckless abandon in a blowout and another when that will blow a victory.

And don't try the line about throwaway penalties in the second half with second-stringers. The Spartans had six infractions and 61 yards of walkoffs before halftime.

If that's sniffing a stinky diaper instead of embracing the baby, so be it. If MSU has finally given birth to a beautiful team, it has to become potty-trained at some point.

But most September signs point to exactly what we have said since the end of spring practice. If MSU wins less than nine games, it will be a major disappointment.

After avoiding three banana peels and beating a Notre Dame team that has dropped three straight, the Spartans need only go 5-3 in league play to reach that level.

They can even do that by going 4-4 in the Big Ten and winning a bowl game for the first time in nine years. But why stop there? Why not reach double digits?

MSU is imminently capable of a 10-win season, a feat it has only achieved twice – in 1965 and 1999. Ironically, both of those seasons came after disappointing years.

The big disappointment this time would be for the Spartans to fail to fulfill their potential. They can't control what Ohio State does. They can and must control themselves.

They need to continue to run the ball against the league's best defenses. If they do that, the passing game will flourish this fall.

With Edwin Baker and Le'Veon Bell, plus a healthy Larry Caper, MSU has the backs to do that. With improved blocking up front and from wideouts, it should continue to rush for more than 200 yards most weeks.

It has already matched last year's total for rushing touchdowns. It has done the same for interceptions. Suddenly, linebacker Greg Jones looks like Darrelle Revis.

But we've been down this road before. And MSU hasn't played a real road game. Sorry, Ford Field with 38 opposition fans doesn't qualify.

The Spartans are carrying a B average thus far. They'll need to play a little better to beat the Badgers, much less to remain unbeaten a month from now.

The beauty of this season is that they definitely can. For once, the statement, "MSU can be 8-0," doesn't demand a breathalyzer reading or a drug test.

Yes, Wisconsin is a quality opponent, despite what we saw against Arizona State. That's fine. It's also not fatal.

The big news after four games is a change in the Spartans' 2010 schedule. It's something we haven't seen before. And it can be a beautiful thing.

Next week and for the seven games that follow, MSU has the same opponent.

Itself.

Running back Larry Caper (22) shows soft hands

OCTOBER 2, 2010 • SATURDAY

PROOF IS IN THE POUNDING

IT WAS THE BEST performance of the Mark Dantonio era – a test for his ticker and texting ability.

Michigan State's 34-24 win over Wisconsin Saturday spoke volumes.

Its offense, defense and special teams shouted that the Spartans could become a special team.

They aren't there yet, so don't start packing for Pasadena. The only trip that matters today is the next one, a 63-miler next weekend to Ann Arbor.

But remember the consternation one month ago when some, including yours truly, had the audacity to predict a nine-win season and to suggest that anything less with MSU's schedule and skill set would be a major disappointment?

The Spartans are more than half the way there. And with eight games left, counting a bowl bid, they only need to win half those contests, including visits from Illinois, Minnesota and Purdue, to finish 9-4.

The other five games – at Michigan, at Northwestern, at Iowa, at Penn State and an unknown bowl opportunity – appear considerably tougher. It's possible that MSU could lose them all, though I'd bet my left leg against it.

It's also possible for a fourth-year program to win two of those five and to finish with 10 wins for the third time in school history – or to win three of them and have 11 W's for the first time.

If the Spartans play the way they did against the Badgers, anything is possible. They were that good in the kind of setting where they have often wet themselves.

Let's start with the defense this time, since that's how MSU began the game – with a three-and-out against a team that had scored on every first possession this season. Instead, Wisconsin was forced to punt from its 17, setting up a Dan Conroy field goal.

One week earlier, the Badgers had scored 70 points against poor Austin Peay, even with the visitors' nice payday. In their Big Ten opener, the league's biggest team was held to 292 yards of offense by Pat Narduzzi's troops.

Remember Narduzzi, the No. 1 whipping boy on this website and at countless watering holes where Spartans gather? It's time for a tip of the cap for a job masterfully done.

Playing without two starters on the defensive line, tackle Kevin Pickelman and end Colin Neely, Narduzzi said "Next!" and got Blake Treadwell and Denzel Drone to perform admirably as fill-ins.

Given the circumstances with the D-tackle's dad, we might as well introduce a new word. From this point forward, starting linemen and head coaches don't get "replaced." They get "Treadwelled".

But there were so many heroes, we can't discuss them all and comply with the "24-hour rule," a particularly important concept because the next No. 16 the Spartans will see won't be Scott Tolzien.

Wisconsin's senior quarterback was relatively useless Saturday, completing just 11 of 25 throws for 127 yards and one touchdown – roughly one quarter's production for Indiana's Ben Chappell against Michigan's defense.

Without creating a takeaway and with just one sack, MSU allowed the Badgers to hit just two passes for more than 14 yards – for 28 to Nick Toon and 26 to No. 2 tight end Jacob Pedersen.

Aside from those plays, the Spartans were as good in pass coverage as I can remember in the live-ball era, with corners Chris L. Rucker and Johnny

Eric Gordon stops a Badger receiver in his tracks

HEART OF A SPARTAN

Adams and safeties Trenton Robinson and Marcus Hyde deserving long, loud shout-outs.

The run stoppers were almost as good, aside from losing contain on two bounce-out scores by freshman running back James White, who had four TDs a week earlier.

John Clay, the returning Big Ten Offensive Player of the Year and an automatic 100-yard rusher, was held to 80 on 17 carries, a 4.7 average. And his team managed just 165 on the ground against a swarming defense.

If Tolzien and Clay woke up screaming at 4 a.m. in Madison, they probably saw middle linebacker Greg Jones in mid-nightmare.

Clearly, it helped that Wisconsin had the ball just 23:36. But that's what happens when a defense learns to get off the field and allows just three conversions in 12 tries on third or fourth down.

Meanwhile, MSU was as clutch as it needed to be to beat a team ranked ninth and 11th in the polls and to do it by double digits. It was 11-for-21 on third and fourth down and 2-for-3 on logical gambles that produced 14 points.

There are new graduate-level studies that show most football coaches should go for it more often on fourth down instead of punting or trying field goals, even with an instep as reliable as Conroy's.

But that work is based strictly on numbers. It doesn't include the psychological benefits. Thus, I love the Spartans' mindset this season – and liked the strategy even when Le'Veon Bell was stopped on the 1 – for another reason.

For most of Dantonio's tenure, aside from some soft cushions in pass defense, his teams have attacked. That was true before "Little Giants" made Notre Dame fans swear for hours. And it'll be true whether Treadwell, Narduzzi or their boss is making the calls.

That's the way this "program" – the key word to describe what we see in 2010 – has been built. That's obvious from a positive swagger on the field, not just in dorm fights, this year.

MSU even played with enough poise to have fewer penalties than Wisconsin. After being flagged

a ridiculous 37 times in the first four games, the coaches made that a major point of emphasis and had just four walk-offs. Meanwhile, the Badgers were penalized five times, nearly half their four-game total of 11.

It should be noted that two false starts, credited largely to crowd noise and an extremely active student section, had a major impact.

After a Brad Nortman punt had rolled dead around the Spartan 13, a five-yard penalty made him kick again. And when Keshawn Martin went 74 yards untouched with the re-do, the game was never the same.

The other important moment came on Wisconsin's last possession. After a timeout with 1:17 left, Badgers right tackle Ricky Wagner moved prematurely, forcing a 5-yard walk-off when many still feared a

Denzel Drone (52) and Trenton Robinson close in on John Clay

late TD and an onside-kick attempt. Instead, a fourth-and-17 pass netted 14 yards. Game over.

The Spartans got solid play from quarterback Kirk Cousins, aside from two poorly thrown balls that were intercepted. When he's decisive, when he gets rid of the ball and steps into his throws, he can be an outstanding passer – as good as Tony Banks in the mid-'90s.

His receivers all delivered big-time. Except for a dumb penalty, Mark Dell had a terrific game. Incredibly underrated wideout B.J. Cunningham and big-play tight end Charlie Gantt had TDs, too. And Keith Nichol and Brian Linthicum contributed at just the right times.

Best of all to those who remember last year's one-dimensional attack, MSU outrushed Wisconsin. The offensive line looked every bit the equal of one of the nation's best units.

The Spartans didn't have a 100-yard back for the first time this season. But Edwin Baker had 87. Bell had 75, including 23 on a fourth-down counter-pitch that left a Badger jockstrap near the 40-yard line. And nearly forgotten Larry Caper looked great, averaging 7.3 yards on three late carries and picking up 35 on a near-perfect screen pass.

MSU won't have to be perfect in Game 6, just good enough to do what it should on offense and disciplined enough to keep Denard Robinson from accepting the Heisman Trophy at halftime.

If the Spartans do that, the first half of their season will be a beautiful thing and the best tribute they could ever pay their leader.

Captain Kirk Cousins makes Michigan Stadium his house

OCTOBER 9, 2010 • SATURDAY

STATE-MEANT GAME

THE LINES BELONG in the third film of a Big Ten football trilogy.

"Sp-heart-ans! What is your profession?"

"Win! Win! Win!"

That's exactly what Michigan State has done since 2008 against once-mighty Michigan.

A 34-17 thumping of the Wolverines was the Spartans' second straight win in their new favorite place to visit.

And a combined score of 95-58 in MSU's three-game series streak leaves little doubt, even in minds of doddering, feeble, older siblings, that things have changed – perhaps forever.

We should have seen that coming with the leadership of fourth-year leader Mark Dantonio, who asked the question of the young century in his first season back in East Lansing.

"How long are we going to continue to bow down to the University of Michigan?" he said of the winningest program in collegiate history, ancient historians confirm.

"No longer!" his staff and players have shouted with no need for sobriety tests.

After the wee Wolverine himself, Mike Hart, gave his views on birth order and basketball skill, a strange topic for a Michigan man, Dantonio refused to genuflect.

If "Pride comes before the fall," so do winter, spring and summer, the calendar tells us.

Unless U-M plans to beat MSU in hoops this season, which could happen, it will be four years since the Wolverines have beaten the Spartans in the two major sports when they meet again next October 15 in East Lansing.

Perhaps it's time to change the opening line of U-M's fight song to "Hail to the victims … "

While MSU has matured as an athletic program, not just a sequence of unrelated teams, something much different has happened in Ann Arrogance.

Wolverines, the largest members of the weasel family, are nearing extinction in much of the world and facing extermination as a force in the Big Ten.

They're 4-14 in two-and-a-third seasons of conference play under Rich Rodriguez, who can't shred that ugly statistic.

So when Hart reportedly wrote, "Tomorrow we put little brother in his place," in a note posted near the U-M locker room door, it's time to look at that place, starting with the Big Ten standings.

The Spartans and top-ranked Ohio State are the league's only 2-0 teams. And there's a decent chance MSU could be alone in first place in seven days.

The legal guardians of the Paul Bunyan Trophy will host improving Illinois, 3-2, next Saturday for Homecoming before the Buckeyes play at Wisconsin.

Overall, the Spartans are bowl-eligible for the fourth straight year, matching the longest streak in school history from 1987-90.

And to do that by midseason, when some schools haven't reached six victories in three seasons, is worthy of mention.

So was the absence of warm water in the visitors locker room again Saturday, a fact defensive coordinator Pat Narduzzi pointed out with disappointment.

"Every time we come here, we get a nice, cold shower, too," said one of the heroes of Saturday's game for a plan that worked better than most people imagined. "They spend all that money on 'The Big House' and can't get hot water."

That could be good news for Rodriguez, who had to figure he'd be knee-deep in scalding H2O after falling to 0-3 against the Spartans, one more loss than he has against Illinois, OSU, Penn State and Purdue.

Patience could be in short supply again with the expectations of excellence at U-M and the cost of getting good seats.

Faulty plumbing included, the price for otherwise

HEART OF A **SPARTAN**

Greg Jones and Trenton Robinson enjoy a Dennard sandwich

impressive and much-needed renovations was a whopping $226 million at the corner of Stadium and Main.

But late in the fourth quarter, the project seemed like an addition to the main library if you judged by the silence of Wolverine fans. "That's the best feeling ever," said MSU big-play free safety Trenton Robinson, the best Robinson on the field Saturday afternoon and evening. "To shut up all those people is great. But Coach Narduzzi is a genius."

That label would probably stun some Spartans who think they can do a better job of running the defense. News flash: They can't. And the Spartans responded to Narduzzi's mantra all week: "Make plays on the deep ball," and "Get 16!"

By pinching and pressuring superhero quarterback Denard Robinson and seizing opportunities to make three interceptions, MSU increased its season takeaway total to 14 – the same number it had in 13 games last season.

While we're on the topic of much-maligned assistants, Harlon Barnett's secondary had its seventh, eighth and ninth interceptions, three more than last season and two more than he helped produce in a pick party vs. U-M as a Spartan cornerback in 1987.

Working together and working non-stop, MSU's defensive coaches and players frustrated an early-season Heisman Trophy favorite and made him appear mortal.

Robinson's longest rush Saturday was 16 yards – 71 shorter than his longest sprint at Notre Dame. And the three INTs were triple his total in U-M's five wins.

For once, "Shoelace" was fit to be tied.

He wasn't even the best quarterback on the field, as Kirk Cousins commanded a dominant offense that outgained the Wolverines 536-377 and had the ball 11:50 longer.

"Captain Kirk" completed 72 percent of his passes, hit eight different receivers and netted 284 yards, including one of the prettiest throws in Spartan history: a perfectly placed 41-yard touchdown toss to Mark Dell.

MSU also got a 61-yard run from Edwin Baker, a 41-yard sprint from Le'Veon Bell and 52-yard catch by Keith Nichol on a multi-misdirection pass.

And another quarterback deserves some credit. Freshman wideout Tony Lippett, a high school signal-caller till his senior year, did an amazing impression on the scout team all week and deserves to be called "Denard" till further notice.

One other thing that deserves notice was Dantonio's latest achievement – and it wasn't heading downstairs at halftime without his wife, Becky, knowing that plan.

He became the first MSU coach to start 3-1 against Notre Dame AND U-M. Biggie Munn, Duffy Daugherty, George Perles and Nick Saban couldn't do it.

In fact, no coach since Denny Stolz in 1974 had posted back-to-back wins over ranked teams in consecutive weeks. That happened this month at just the right time.

"Go right through that line of blue!" the Spartans roared in front of their fans and again in a jubilant locker room, where Mr. Bunyan wore a helmet and was draped with a flag.

Long after Rodriguez waved the white flag by punting down 17 points with less than 6 minutes left, MSU waved green ones.

Once again, the Wolverines were hoping a game in this series would end prematurely. Instead, they just got clocked.

William Gholston, John Stipek and Micajah Reynolds parade with Paul Bunyan

ROCK READY TO ROLL?

HARD-HEADED EDWIN BAKER EARNS NICKNAME

Edwin Baker searches for daylight, then cuts upfield

HIS FAVORITE WORD isn't touchdown. It's family – past, present and future.

To know three-year Michigan State running back Edwin Baker is to know his father, Edwin McDonald, and his mother, Dashia Baker.

Their only son is a perfect blend.

His quiet confidence is a gift from his parents. And his nickname, "Rock", reflects that demeanor, along with the fact he's a little hard-headed … OK, maybe a lot.

"I've been 'Rock' ever since I can remember," Baker said. "My dad always told me I was playing on the balcony when I fell backward and hit my head. When I popped up, he said, 'Son, your head is hard as a rock!'"

It took more than one skull session for that moniker to fit as well as his helmet ever could. It took a solid approach to football and a lot of things he has done.

"Maybe it fits my body structure," Baker said. "But when I think of 'Rock', I think of all the hard work I've put in. And I know I'm not going to crumble under pressure. My teammates know that, too."

Growing up, he was so advanced for his age, Baker had to make sure his dad brought his birth certificate to games. After all, who wanted to get steamrolled by a 16-year-old in a 12-and-under league?

A lot of us have seen that kid. He's the one who's bigger, faster, tougher and more intense than anyone else, the guy who has muscles where most boys don't even have places.

"I was always toned up," Baker said. "I ran track, did a lot of pushups and was just more muscular than everyone else. I couldn't help it if other teams said, 'How old is he?' I got that all the time."

He also got a lot of interest from recruiters after eye-popping efforts at Oak Park High. Baker's team didn't win a lot of games. But you don't rush for 462 yards, as he did against Royal Oak, by being an average back.

"I don't know what got into me that day," Baker said. "I just wasn't going to be tackled. I got hit out of bounds and horse-collared and just kept going."

He averaged 11.2 yards per carry as a senior, down from 11.5 per pop as a junior. And missing four games his final season didn't stop Baker from being ranked as high as the second in the state and 31st in the country.

"I wanted to get recruiting out of the way," he said of an early commitment to Mark Dantonio. "Michigan State felt like home to me. And my family could see me play. I had letters from Texas and Tennessee. Then, Michigan tried to get in after I committed. I really had no interest. They weren't my type of people. I'd been there for track meets and seen how they carried themselves. That just wasn't for me."

Arriving in East Lansing

HEART OF A **SPARTAN**

in 2009, two years after Kirk Cousins but at the same time as Battle Creek Central star Larry Caper, no one realized how two heralded backs would take turns in the spotlight, then be passed by lightly recruited Le'Veon Bell.

"I was supposed to redshirt," Baker said. "I'd never sat a minute in my life and was a little down when they told me. But I knew Coach D. had his reasons. I trusted him. And he helped me develop. Then, Glenn Winston got hurt at midseason. They pulled my redshirt for the Northwestern game."

As freshmen, Caper rushed for 468 yards and Baker 427. By the end of the year, the roommates were splitting carries and finishing each other's sentences, though Baker rushed for 97 yards in the Alamo Bowl to Caper's 25 and had a 5.0-3.9 season edge in yards per carry.

But the play everyone remembered was Caper's tackle-shedding, 23-yard sweep that gave the Spartans a 26-20 overtime win over the Wolverines – one of the most famous runs in school history. Baker would have to wait for his big day and big play.

It didn't take long. When Caper broke his hand in August 2010 and missed the season's first two games, Baker responded and carried 32 times for 300 yards and three TDs. That included a career-long 80-yard dash against Florida Atlantic at Ford Field.

Without Baker's 56-yard score the following game against Notre Dame, there never would've been a "Little Giants" miracle in East Lansing. Three weeks later, he ran wild in Ann Arbor, rushing 22 times for 147 yards, including a 61-yard score with a taunting penalty.

"The Michigan game was kind of personal for me," he said of his first statement in the series. "That was all I'd heard about, 'Michigan, Michigan, Michigan.' But the 'Shhh!' thing when I scored was just spur-of-the-moment. I said, 'What can I do to make a statement after the 'Little Brother' stuff.' I didn't know I'd get a penalty. If I had, I probably still would've done it."

Baker rushed for 179 yards and four TDs against Minnesota a month later, then helped clinch a share of the Big Ten title, MSU's first in two decades, with 118 yards on the ground at Penn State.

His 1,201-yard season total was the 13th best in school history. And with a 5.8-yard average, Baker was a first-team All-Big Ten selection as a sophomore, joining Levi Jackson, Lorenzo White and Tico Duckett in that elite club.

Ranked among the top 20 Heisman Trophy candidates and viewed as a serious contender for the Doak Walker Award in 2011, Baker set some lofty personal goals. But when people heard him say he'd rush for 2,000 yards and 21 scores, they wondered how.

The Spartans netted just 1,931 yards and 21 TDs on the ground in 14 games, with Baker dropping to 665 yards and a 3.9 average. Counting a terrific catch in the end zone at Iowa, he finished with six scores. He also had a couple of potentially costly fumbles and saw Bell start the last six games.

But when MSU needed him to play big against Michigan, Baker stood much taller than 5-foot-9. He was a giant with 167 yards and a TD on 26 carries. On a day when the Spartans threw for just 120 yards and netted 333, No. 4 had more than half his team's offense.

After rushing six times for 10 yards against Georgia, 16 fewer touches than Bell had in a two-TD day, Baker decided it was time for a new challenge – pro football. With 462 carries in three seasons, only 72 more than Javon Ringer had as a senior, he figured he'd leave while he knew he was healthy.

Near the end of a three-day wait, Baker was the 250th pick in the draft, a seventh-round choice of the San Diego Chargers. He wasn't the high selection he hoped to be. But he earned another chance. And if that road is a little . . . rocky, he'll be ready.

"I decided the day after the bowl game," Baker said after performing better at MSU's Pro Day than at the Combine in Indy. "I think I'm a great candidate for the NFL. I don't have a lot of wear and tear on my body. And it was the right thing to do in my heart."

When he puts his whole heart into it, we know he can go a long, long way. Though he never played baseball for the Spartans, "Home Run" Baker can touch 'em all.

OCTOBER 16, 2010 • SATURDAY

SE-HEAVEN-AND-O

THEY HAD THREE PENALTIES for 40 yards in the first quarter – including two for 25 on the same play.

They gave up a go-ahead field goal just before halftime when Keshawn Martin fumbled a fair catch he never should've been back to attempt.

They were held to 93 rushing yards, 132 less than their season average.

And their longest run was just 15 yards – 2 more than Le'Veon Bell netted all day and 6 fewer than he and his teammates lost in 31 carries.

So why was Michigan State's 26-6 win over Illinois every bit as big as it was boring in stretches?

Because the Spartans weren't half-bad.

In fact, they were outstanding in the last two periods, outscoring Illinois 23-0 Saturday afternoon.

If they hadn't woken up against a surprisingly good team, one that has lost three times to programs with a combined 19-1 mark, MSU could've joined some other upset victims.

We'd seen that before against the Fighting Illini, who'd spoiled the Spartans' championship bids in 1956, 1963, 1974 and 1989, provided their only Big Ten blemish in 1987 and prevented an outright title and a Rose Bowl berth in 1990.

But on the 100th anniversary of the first Homecoming weekend – ironically in Champaign, Ill. – MSU buried the "Same Old Spartans" tag – possibly forever.

With Leonidas himself, movie mega-star Gerard Butler, loving every minute of his visit, 55 players performed like 300.

And after a game many past squads would've found a way to squander, MSU found a way to stay perfect (cue the "Theme from *The Magnificent Seven*").

After 44 seasons of fits and starts, the Spartans are 7-0 for the first time since their last undefeated season – a year that also featured an unforgettable 60-minute tie with Notre Dame.

Why did this MSU team step on the Ur-banana peel and avoid a classic pratfall?

Because Mark Dantonio's fourth Spartan team – and yes, it's still very much his team, whether he watches from the press box, the sideline or outer space – is more talented and more mature than any we've seen in a generation.

You have to go back to 1990 to find an MSU group with a similar ability to persevere. That team finished 8-3-1 but overcame key injuries for an upset win in Ann Arbor, a piece of the Big Ten crown and a character-revealing bowl win – the program's third straight triumph over USC.

This year's Spartans haven't lost a lot of players to injury. But they did work without their head coach for a while – a traumatic event that only brought them closer.

They also won Saturday without a key performer, senior cornerback Chris L. Rucker, who was serving a minimum one-game suspension for silly, senseless, selfish behavior in East Lansing after last weekend's win over Michigan.

When secondary coach Harlon Barnett said "Next!" true freshman Darqueze Dennard responded and played like an experienced upperclassman.

But MSU has been lucky – knock on red cedar – with injuries thus far.

And aside from the Rucker situation, MSU has lived up to its 2010 motto.

"Humble and Hungry."

The Spartans haven't lost focus with a sudden outpouring of love. And they haven't stopped fighting the foes and forces that keep good teams from being great.

Eight weeks ago in this space, we talked about whether my 9-3 projection was drinking the green Kool-Aid. A lot of understandably jaded fans believed it was wishful thinking.

Now, MSU would have to go 2-4 the rest of the way

A swarming defense holds Illinois without a touchdown

to finish with that record, a minimum expectation for a team with rare depth.

The Spartans have a better chance of playing for the BCS Championship than they do of finishing with four losses.

Think about that. A team that failed to receive a single vote in the preseason Associated Press writers poll and the *USA Today* coaches poll is one of the best stories of the college football season.

And the best is yet to come if you listen to anyone in the Skandalaris Center.

MSU isn't pinching itself in disbelief. It's pinching ballcarriers, punching balls free and putting a versatile offense in position to deliver victories.

Four more takeaways against Illinois gave the Spartans a 7-1 turnover edge the last two weekends. After proving they could win despite turnovers against Wisconsin, they showed it's not always better to give than to receive.

Pat Narduzzi's oft-maligned defense, one of the top three in the Big Ten this year, already has 18 takeaways in seven games – four more than it produced last season in 13 matchups.

Included in that total are 12 interceptions, double last season's total. And if you don't think that's important, you didn't watch MSU get almost as many yards on pass-thefts as running plays against the Illini.

Yes, Greg Jones & Co. could do a better job of getting off the field on third down. But after holding

HEART OF A SPARTAN

the Badgers, Wolverines and Illini to a combined 47 points and 1.024 yards, that's a little like complaining that Salma Hayak can't do roofing.

The Spartans are all alone in first place in the conference – a half-game ahead of Iowa and Purdue and a game up on OSU and Wisconsin.

The Hawkeyes host the Badgers next week before they welcome MSU. And I'm not convinced that the Buckeyes are done losing.

What does that mean? That the Spartans are in complete control of their own destiny in the Big Ten. They don't need any more help to claim an undisputed conference championship, their first in 23 years.

All their preseason questions have been answered except one: Can they finish the job?

After spring ball, no one knew that placekicker Dan Conroy, kickoff specialist Kevin Muma, holder-passer-punter Aaron Bates and long-snapper Alex Shackleton would be the best collection of specialists in the nation.

Conroy is 13-for-13 on three-point attempts and 28-for-28 on PATs. Muma has gotten much better on kickoffs. Bates should be a 10-year pro. And Shackleton, a third-generation Spartan, has maintained his anonymity -- job one for any player who looks backward between his legs before he triggers the scoring.

Without a productive offense, Conroy never sets foot on the field.

Without a destructive defense, the offense's job is infinitely more difficult.

If MSU hasn't always made it look easy this season, it has always made the past seven Saturdays fun.

Magnificent, indeed.

May the ride continue and head west-southeast – all the way to California or, dare we say, Arizona?

Saddle up for adventure, folks, starting with stops in Evanston and Iowa City. And with all that's at stake, if there aren't 20,000 Spartans at Ryan Field next Saturday, a lot of fans should ask themselves, "What is your obsession?"

William Gholston is grabbed again in pursuit of the passer

OCTOBER 23, 2010 • SATURDAY

EIGHT ISN'T ENOUGH

AH, THE COLORS OF AUTUMN!

The back of Colin Neely's No. 89 white jersey was basted with purple Saturday afternoon.

It was that kind of day in Evanston, Ill.

Ryan Field was nearly half-green when the guests finally ruined Northwestern's Homecoming.

It has been that kind of season for Michigan State.

Rallying from a 17-0 deficit and putting "Same Old Spartans" in the rearview mirror, Mark Dantonio's team had the mark of a champion.

With five touchdowns and terrific plays on defense and special teams in the final 32:50, MSU heard the snooze alarm just in time.

And with former NU and Notre Dame legend Ara Parseghian on hand to see it, the Spartans woke up the echoes of their greatest comebacks.

Today, they sit alone atop the Big Ten – the only unbeaten team in league play at 4-0, halfway there with more than a prayer.

With Oklahoma and LSU losing, MSU should rank fifth in the second BCS Championship standings at 8-0, an amazing start for a program that's just starting.

The best part of the latest triumph was the way everyone pulled together and picked each other up when lesser teams would've said, "We'll do better next week."

Oh, the Spartans said that, too. They know they'll have to play better football to survive next Saturday in Iowa City.

But every player, coach and long-suffering fan knows MSU has the ability to do that without major gifts from the disappointing Hawkeyes, 2-1 and 5-2.

A favorable schedule won't matter this time. And the game won't be decided by officials. Like a pass to B.J. Cunningham, it's all in the Spartans' hands.

They decided long ago that's fine with them, as they proved again in their first game outside the state of Michigan.

As predicted by anyone with a clue, the Wildcats were tough to tame. For more than 59 minutes, they scratched and clawed the way a Pat Fitzgerald team usually does.

Despite some ignorant comments in the media that MSU could win with 10 players, it needed 55 to survive as tough a test as recent history had promised.

The Spartans overcame a litany of errors:

- The loss of 32 yards with a hold by offensive tackle J'Michael Deane on the first play from scrimmage.

- A rare misplay of the ball by cornerback Johnny Adams on a 44-yard pickup that set up the first TD.

- A fumble by running back Edwin Baker near midfield and two failures to convert on third down by Le'Veon Bell.

- And a bubble-screen lateral and slotback pass that sucked in freshman corner Darqueze Dennard for a 28-yard gain.

That was only the first quarter, when the Wildcats had a 158-64 edge in total offense and should've had more than a 7-0 lead.

It got worse for MSU before it got better. It could've been 24-0 if not for defensive end Tyler Hoover's goal-line strip and Adams being Johnny-on-the-spot.

That was the first sign of life for a team that refused to join the ranks of the once-beaten, despite the heroics of NU quarterback Dan Persa.

"I played against Persa in high school, and he did the same things to us then," Neely said. "We just needed to wake up. Being down 17 will do that to you."

So what if placekicker Dan Conroy finally missed a field goal after 14 makes, 13 this year?

So what if receiver/return ace Keshawn Martin was sidelined with an ankle injury and the defensive front had a few new faces?

HEART OF A **SPARTAN**

Johnny Adams (5) is Johnny-on-the-spot with a big hit

Receiver Bennie Fowler and defensive end-turned-tackle Johnathan Strayhorn seized their opportunities with a 22-yard reverse for a score, a 23-yard catch of Aaron Bates' latest surprise toss and two critical sacks.

That gadget play saved the Spartans, just when everyone was wondering if Dantonio had gone daft. Instead, it may have been his shrewdest call of the season, certainly the equal of "Little Giants."

Trailing 24-14 with 13:56 left, MSU faced a fourth-and-6 at the Wildcats 31 and couldn't kick a field goal into a strong wind. After a timeout, Dantonio sent the punt team on and ordered a deliberate delay-of-game penalty to set the "Mousetrap".

"We had to get them to take the cheese," he said of another superior head-fake.

After Bates boosted his off-the-charts passing efficiency, roommate Kirk Cousins took full advantage of that reprieve and led the Spartans to three fourth-quarter scores.

"Captain Kirk" finished 29-for-43 for 329 yards and three TDs, with no interceptions.

"You want to know how you go 8-0?" Dantonio said. "You go 8-0 with players who can lead. There's a ripple effect."

On the snap after Bates found Fowler, a gunner who appeared to be covering a punt, Cousin hit wideout Mark Dell with a 13-yard pass to cut the deficit to 24-21.

After an NU field goal made it a six-point game and Bates shanked a 22-yard punt to midfield, MSU still had plenty of work left.

The fun was just beginning.

A three-and-out by the defense gave the offense another shot from its 12, the same spot where the Spartans began game-winning drives to beat No. 1 Ohio State in 1974 and Michigan in 1995.

Overcoming 15 yards in losses from two sacks and a fumble that was pounced on by guard Joel Foreman, another soon-to-be-forgotten game-saver, Cousins was 7-for-8 for 98 yards on the march.

He hit Dell, a determined Keith Nichol and future MSU career receiving king Cunningham for three 18-yard completions.

"We weren't running the ball the way we have," Nichol said. "As wide receivers, I think we all said, 'OK, we're going to have to go win this game.'"

On third-and-15, Cousins found Nichol again in traffic for 14, then coolly rolled left and connected with tight end Charlie Gantt for 8 yards on fourth-and-1.

A flip to Baker netted 13 more before Cunningham's acrobatic grab in the back of the end zone finished an 11-play Drive of the Year.

"I always knew I'd catch it," Cunningham said. "I'm left-handed. All I had to do was bring it in."

It was time to bring in Conroy, who was still kicking himself after the game for being human. His extra-point gave the Spartans a 28-27 lead. But a lot happened in the last two minutes.

After a four-and-out stand when a 60-yard field was feasible, MSU needed one first down and a couple of kneel-downs to leave with a win. But when Baker broke free, he didn't stop running. A 25-yard score meant Persa & Co. had another shot to tie.

"We'll keep teaching," Dantonio said of a spread-beating burst. "I'm sure Vegas loved it."

Outside linebacker Eric Gordon finally ended the drama with his team's lone interception, though even he forgot to stop running.

"That's a hard thing to do," he said. "I thought I was a running back again for a second. But the best part was looking up in the stands and seeing all that green. Our fan support all year has been tremendous."

So has their support for each other, though Cunningham and middle linebacker Greg Jones had a serious disagreement after the game.

They each insisted they were Fowler's roommate and had more involvement with a breakout performer. And while Cunningham was his roomie on the road trip, Jones has had that privilege more often.

"I've never seen a guy work so hard," Jones said with a smile, then a serious look that would end a lot of arguments. "B.J. was his roommate this weekend. But I LIVE with Bennie! I see him every day!"

We all saw him Saturday. We saw something else, too.

The heart of a Spartan and a togetherness no budget can buy.

There was nothing fake about it.

OCTOBER 30, 2010 • SATURDAY

JEKYLL & HYDES

IT WASN'T HALF-BAD. It was half-horrible Saturday.

The Michigan State Spartans laid a collective dodo egg in their best chance for national relevance in college football since November 19, 1966.

Making nearly every mistake imaginable in the first two quarters, they were crushed by the Big Ten's biggest underachievers, the Iowa Hawkeyes, 37-6.

It wasn't a shock that MSU lost. The oddsmakers knew it. Most analysts predicted it. And for the first time this season, I had to spend most of the previous week explaining why I thought the Spartans would stumble.

I just didn't think they would soil themselves for 40 minutes – on an afternoon that seemed to last four hours – in sun-drenched Kinnick Stadium.

Just as no one saw MSU as the No. 5 team in the nation two months ago, no one saw this total collapse coming. Not Mark Dantonio, not Kirk Ferentz and not a nation that overreacts to every development every day.

But when a visitor rushes for just 31 yards on 20 carries and surrenders 122 yards and a touchdown on three interception returns, that's what happens.

When it telegraphs three picks, never produces a takeaway and commits more than twice as many penalties as its host, it's a green-print for implosion.

So what do we think we know after nine weeks of play this season? Just this:

- Teams are almost never as good as they look after eight straight wins and seldom as bad as they seem after a 31-point loss.

- The Big Ten won't be represented by the 8-1 Spartans or anyone else in the 2011 BCS Championship in Glendale, Ariz.

- MSU will share the conference title for the first time in 20 years if it wins at home against Minnesota and Purdue and prevails at Penn State for the first time since 1965.

- The Spartans will play in the Rose Bowl for the first time in 23 years if they win their last three games, if Wisconsin wins its last four, as it should, and if Ohio State loses, as it certainly could in Iowa City.

We know the 2010 Spartans aren't perfect. Neither are any of us. But they can't worry about that today or spend 30 seconds scoreboard watching. All they can do is keep their eyes on the prize.

If a trip to Pasadena isn't enough inspiration for MSU's players and coaches, they have bigger problems than the butt-whipping they just endured.

If that isn't enough for Spartan fans, they need to get a grip on reality. Their favorite program has shown progress in so many ways this season. The fact that it won't have a 13-0 season is disappointing, not devastating.

What was tough to take was MSU's third terrible start in 15 days. This time, it wasn't against Illinois or Northwestern. And it led to an avalanche of 37 straight points.

Maybe the Spartans need to scrimmage for a quarter before the opening kickoff. For some reason they've been late to the party. By the time they arrived this time, the Hawkeyes had eaten the food and emptied the beer.

Iowa went 80 yards in 12 plays on the game's first possession to take a 7-0 lead, settled for a field goal on its second series and made it 17-0 on a nifty pick-and-lateral in the first quarter.

The Hawkeyes swiped another horrendous throw by Kirk Cousins and built their lead to 23-0, then drove 70 yards in four plays to make it 30-0 when the half mercifully ended.

At that point I began to get a string of merciless text messages from Tom Crawford, my Spartan-hating co-host on "The Jack and Tom Show" Saturday mornings on 1320 WILS. And why not? MSU's first loss was clearly the highlight of Michigan's last three seasons.

Three Spartans combine to stop Iowa running back Marcus Coker

Indeed, in Iowa's first five possessions (one without the offense setting foot on the field), there were five scores – four TDs and a field goal. And after its first punt of the day early in the third quarter, another six-play, 61-yard march ended any thought of a comeback.

The Spartans couldn't tackle or cover. That included all-everything middle linebacker Greg Jones. They made Adam Robinson look like Emmitt Smith. And they made Stanzi-to-Marvin McNutt a winning combination for the second straight year.

This wasn't about Chris L. Rucker, a non-factor in his first game back in a green-and-white uniform. With two-game starter Darqueze Dennard out since Tuesday, he was pressed into service and didn't make a major impression.

Rucker wasn't made available to talk and wasn't talked about by Dantonio. A couple of questions were shed a lot easier than MSU shed Iowa blocks.

But as badly as the defense played – and it allowed 6.1 yards per snap without intercepting a pass or recovering a fumble – that wasn't what got the Spartans beat.

MSU was ready for a running clock with 22:35 left because its offense was truly offensive. It had eight possessions of 1:45 or less. And whenever you have as many punts as points, it's going to be a long day.

Ironically, our media party of five spent Friday night in Morris, Ill., the hometown of ex-Spartan quarterback Todd Schultz. When we ran into old No. 9 at a restaurant, we had no idea that Cousins would nearly match Schultz's worst moment, a five-pick performance against Michigan in 1997.

All that was missing was Charles Woodson, though Iowa cornerback Micah Hyde did a decent impression with a breathtaking, 66-yard dash-and-dive after a pitch from seemingly invisible safety Tyler Sash.

Meanwhile, Marcus Hyde, Micah's brother, had a day he'd like to forget. His 15-yard late hit after a 26-yard Stanzi scramble set up a score, as did his whiff on a probable pick that became a 56-yard pickup for backup tight end Brad Marcus.

The bottom line was that MSU needed to pack its A game to have much of a chance against a team still stinging from a 31-30 giveaway to the Badgers seven days earlier. Instead, it deserved its F.

But if F stands for futile, it doesn't have to mean fatal. It didn't the last time the Spartans saw a memorable streak end.

After a 6-0 start in 1999, including a win over No. 3 Michigan, MSU hit the road and the skids with a 52-28 loss to Purdue and Drew Brees, and a 40-10 defeat by Wisconsin and Ron Dayne.

Instead of staying down, the Spartans regrouped, won four in a row against the likes of Ohio State, Penn State and Florida and finished with 10 wins for the second and last time.

This year's team can do even better. But will it?

Dantonio said he'll learn a lot about his team next weekend. That's probably true for the entire month of November, when the Halloween costumes come off.

That's what's really at stake today, once MSU removes the stake from its heart. Is it a championship team or just one that looked that way before it got punched in the mouth?

The last four rounds are all the judges need to see.

NOVEMBER 7, 2010 • SUNDAY

DAYLIGHT SAVORING TIME

TIMES CHANGE. And not just when we turn the clocks back an hour one Sunday each autumn.

They change for every football team – some sooner and some more often than others. But change they must. And change they have in the Big Ten Conference.

Nowhere is that reversal of fortune more evident than in the state of Michigan. Suddenly, Michigan State is Michigan – atop the standings and grumbling with justification about a 23-point triumph. And the Wolverines are what the Spartans were – dysfunctional, delusional and defenseless.

Let's start at the top, with Mark Dantonio's 9-1 team, a whole that's stronger than the sum of its parts in a season that has been a whole lot of fun to watch.

As we first pointed out last spring, Dantonio came into this season needing nine victories for the winningest first four years of any coach in the program's history. Saturday's 31-8 win over Minnesota gave him 31 wins since inheriting a group of seniors that had won just 14 times from 2004-06 under John L. Smith.

After leaving Chester L. Brewer (1903-06) in his rearview mirror, Dantonio won't settle for becoming the first MSU leader with two nine-win seasons in his first gubernatorial term.

If the Spartans play the way they can, better than they did Saturday afternoon, he can end Year 4 with 34 wins. It's way too early to predict bowl outcomes when we don't know the matchups. But whether MSU meets Boise State or Stanford in the Rose Bowl or faces Florida or South Carolina in the Capital One Bowl, anything less than 33 wins the evening of January 1 would be a disappointment for Dantonio.

Think about that. Brewer began with 30 wins in four years. Biggie Munn and Duffy Daugherty each had 27 W's in that span. Nick Saban had 25, Darryl Rogers 24, "Sleepy Jim" Crowley, Charlie Bachman and the aforementioned Smith 22 and George Perles just 21.

Yet, even with longer seasons and more opportunities, we expect more victories in the 21st century, as well we should. There's no reason the Spartans can't post 8.5 victories per season. With the kind of infrastructure Dantonio is building, a 9.5-win average is within the realm of possibility.

For a school that has yet to experience 11-win excellence and has only seen 10 W's twice, with the 1965 and '99 teams, it's strange to think that a near-shutout of a team that had won the previous three series matchups wouldn't be enough.

Changed times, indeed.

But that's where we are in early November 2010, 19 years after Earvin Johnson told the world he was HIV-positive. The only thing positive today is that Magic, Tom Izzo and the MSU basketball family are having more fun watching football than they've had in a long, long time.

Their favorite team stands all alone in first place in the league, a half-game ahead of Iowa, Ohio State and Wisconsin. And if you want to dismiss that as a scheduling quirk, since the Spartans will be the last of those teams to get a much-needed bye, don't lose sight of three irrefutable facts:

- MSU is guaranteed no worse than a share of its first Big Ten championship in 20 years if it beats Purdue on November 20 in East Lansing and defeats Penn State in Delirious Valley on November 27.

  That's true regardless of whether it's Joe Paterno's last home game or just another chance

HEART OF A **SPARTAN**

for the Spartans to win in State College for the first time since 1965, the last season that JoePa was the top assistant for Rip Engle.

- MSU will play in the Rose Bowl if takes care of its business this month, if Wisconsin finishes 3-0 with wins over Indiana and Northwestern in Madison, sandwiching a trip to Ann Arbor, and if the Buckeyes lose to the Nittany Lions, Hawkeyes or Wolverines.

  The Spartans are that close to Pasadena, Calif., and a big party at Magic's place. They haven't been to the Rose Bowl in 23 seasons, since a 20-17 win over USC on January 1, 1988 – their second of three straight wins over the Trojans in a season with no setbacks after September.

- MSU has a lot of work to do while it's resting and rehabbing over the next 13 days. Dantonio wasn't playing mind games when he expressed his dissatisfaction with what he and 71,127 others saw Saturday in Spartan Stadium.

His attack netted just 320 yards against a team that was ravaged the week before at home by OSU. Aside from the heroics of runner Edwin "Rock" Baker and some solid blocking up front, it was a sluggish show that somehow produced close to a point for every 10 yards of total offense.

Kirk Cousins was mediocre seven days after the worst game of his college career – 9-for-20 through the air for just 131 yards and no touchdowns, snapping a string of 16 games with at least one scoring toss. Unable to plant and shift, he threw another interception and launched more balls off his back foot.

If Cousins plays well the rest of the way, his team will be smiling all winter. If not, it won't have enough to finish the job. No. 8 doesn't have to be great. But he can't be less than good.

Some teams can win committing five turnovers. Some can allow eight touchdowns, three field goals and a two-point conversion and be the toast of Washtenaw County, where a head coach was one deflected pass from being toast.

But that's what U-M did Saturday in a mind-

Edwin Baker steps away from the Golden Gophers

HEART OF A SPARTAN

numbing 67-65 win over Illinois. And that's what Rich Rodriguez did in securing the 14th win in his last three seasons (see: Smith, John L.).

A tip of the cap to an offense that scored nine TDs against a previously solid defense, the only unit in the league that hadn't allowed 30 points in a game this year (26 vs. MSU, 24 vs. OSU and 23 vs. Missouri, all once-beaten teams).

But if the Wolverines made Barnum & Bailey look boring, they also defied their history, as they have since RichRod arrived in Ann Arbor. Whatever defensive coordinator Greg Robinson is making, he ought to give two-thirds of his salary – OK, 75% – to the offensive staff.

The big debate after yesterday's game was whether John Beilein's basketball team has any chance to score 67 points against the Fighting Illini this winter. I say it's a 50-50 bet, but only if the teams meet a second time in the Big Ten Tournament. That would be an average of 33.5 points per game.

It was all part of a big weekend for the Wolverines. They got slapped with an extra year of NCAA probation but got RichRod's failure to foster an air of compliance dropped from the list of major violations. Still, they're the only group in NCAA history with major violations in separate cases for football, basketball and baseball.

Some call that "The Michigan Difference."

But it's all part of the scene in 2010. Times change. So have the standings.

Greg Jones adds to his impressive tackle totals

NOVEMBER 13, 2010 • SATURDAY

THERE FOR THE TAKING

MAYBE IT ISN'T THE 1966-67 school year – or 1978-79 or '99-2000, for that matter.

Maybe it's better.

But you have to go back 44 seasons to find a time when Michigan State was a bigger name athletically.

That was the year the Spartans won back-to-back Big Ten titles in football, hosted Notre Dame in "The Game of the Century," finished 9-0-1 in their last undefeated season and earned a sliver of their last national title, provided the NFL's No. 1 draft pick and four of the first eight selections, shared the conference basketball crown with Indiana, finished third in the nation in hockey and won their only NCAA wrestling championship.

You have to go back 32 seasons to find similar success for MSU in more than two sports.

That was the year the Spartans stunned mighty Michigan in football in Ann Arbor, shared the Big Ten title and would've played in the Rose Bowl if not for a crushing probation, tied for the conference championship and captured the national crown in a Magical hoops run and ruled the league in baseball – just the fifth time a school had won trophies in all three sports.

And you have to go back 11 seasons to find MSU's last 10-win season in football and its most recent NCAA title in basketball.

That was the year the Spartans earned their fourth and final January bowl triumph and made their lone appearance as the stars of "One Shining Moment."

MSU's next moment is now.

All the Spartans need to do to be assured of a share of their first Big Ten football championship in two decades and win 11 games for the first time in history is to beat Purdue next Saturday in East Lansing, then edge Penn State Thanksgiving weekend in Happy Valley.

Yes, we know MSU hasn't won there since 1965 – the last year that Joe Paterno was a Nittany Lions assistant. But this is a different Spartan team. Or at least it has been thus far.

It would be the shock of the season if Mark Dantonio's fourth MSU team doesn't blast the battered Boilermakers and get to double-digit wins for just the third time since the school began playing football 114 years ago.

Purdue has one amazing performer – defensive end Ryan Kerrigan, my choice for Big Ten Player of the Year. He can wreak havoc with any offense, sack and sideline quarterbacks and force game-changing turnovers if he isn't neutralized to some degree.

But it doesn't take an advanced degree in football theory to see the differences in speed, strength, skill, depth, experience and motivation between the Spartans and Boilers.

After a much-needed bye week, MSU should be ready for whatever Danny Hope's program can muster. And if Purdue couldn't produce an offensive touchdown in a 27-16 loss to Michigan Saturday in West Lafayette, it's not going to beat the Spartans if they're focused on the task at hand.

The big question about next week's Senior Day farewell to Dantonio's first incoming class, a group that's about to play in its fourth bowl game, is whether Spartan fans will respond appropriately.

That means a full house. And I don't care if the weather is rotten – I know, an easy thing to say for someone who sits in the press box.

In many ways, MSU fans have shown amazing loyalty through more than four decades of sub-mediocrity. They've paid championship-level prices through a seemingly endless string of disappointments and have seen just one 10-win season in 45 years.

But this year's players and coaches can't be blamed for past frustrations. They can't be held accountable for a steady stream of teasing triumphs and deflating letdowns.

Thus, it's time for Spartan fans to salute this team

for what it has done, not to punish it for previous years' pratfalls.

It's time to celebrate the successes of the last four seasons, the best start for any football coaching staff on the banks of the Red Cedar.

And it's time to change the culture, as MSU finally did in basketball in 1998. Before that, except in the two Magic years, Jenison Field House and Breslin Center often had thousands of empty seats. When Indiana visited Breslin early in Izzo's tenure, those holes were filled with Hoosier fans, prompting a pre-game rant I can't repeat.

Eventually, the gaps were filled with green – long after Johnny and a decade before Draymond. Whether that show of support came after consistent success or helped produce it is open to debate. The effect is has had on outcomes is irrefutable.

Now, there's a chance to show the same love in Spartan Stadium. I don't care about deer season, a dramatic dip in temperature or other games on TV next Saturday. The only excused absences for MSU fans next week are for illness, serious family issues or supporting their sons in state football semifinals.

Otherwise, the Spartans' best fans will be in their seats 10 minutes before kickoff and will probably watch players sing the "MSU Fight Song" two minutes after the game ends.

Why students can't get to the game by noon and why anyone without a medical alert has to leave early in the fourth quarter is beyond me. For some, the need for one last drink or post game libations must be dangerously strong. For others, the answer to traffic snarls is as simple as a little pre-planning.

Why does that steady stream of late arrivals and early departures diminish the day? Because it never happens at Iowa or Wisconsin and seldom occurs with wins at U-M, Ohio State or PSU.

If the Spartans do their part on the field and complete an undefeated home season, their fans should show up, stay in their seats and salute that surprising progress.

They should also become the biggest Iowa Hawkeye fans east of the Mississippi River. "Go Hawkeyes!" signs and shouts should show what MSU thinks about OSU's visit to Kinnick Stadium next Saturday.

If Iowa beats the Buckeyes, MSU can go to Pasadena by going 3-0 in November and 7-1 in a two-month span. If OSU is out of the equation, the Spartans would play in the Rose Bowl regardless of how many points the Badgers score against the Wolverines and the Northwestern Wildcats.

I've always wondered how U-M can put 110,000 fans in its football stadium at premium prices and can't give away enough tickets to get 10,000 to show up for basketball games. The Wolverines couldn't fill Crisler Arena when they were cheating and winning – and not against Upstate, the only State team they can beat these days.

It's time for MSU to answer the same question about late-season football in its home finale. There's a Big Ten championship to finish chasing. And there's a program-turning senior class to salute.

Success is there for the taking – and for the sharing.

NOVEMBER 20, 2010 • SATURDAY

SECOND CHANCES... FIRST PLACE

THE TEARS BEGAN FLOWING before the opening kickoff. They were still being shed four hours later – by both teams.

That's what Senior Day triumphs are all about.

Michigan State's sweet sendoff, a 35-31 surge past Purdue, proved that and upheld another football truth.

If it's better to be lucky than good, it's best to be both.

And the resilient, resourceful Spartans were just good enough at just the right times Saturday afternoon.

Trailing 28-13 with less than 11 minutes left, they scored three touchdowns and a two-point conversion to leave with a four-point win.

A group that trailed Notre Dame in overtime, Northwestern in the fourth quarter, Illinois in the third quarter and Wisconsin and Michigan in the second quarter rallied again to beat the Boilermakers.

That explained the tears of joy from Mark Dantonio's players and the sniffles and sobs from Danny Hope's.

One team was tied for the Big Ten lead – one win away from its first league title in two decades. The other saw a bowl bid disappear faster than Edwin Baker.

"I always dreamed about doing this," MSU safety Marcus Hyde said, unable to hide his emotions just after the game ended. "But we're not done."

Hyde and his fellow seniors are finally done playing in Spartan Stadium. Most will take positive memories with them, even allowing for past tribulations.

"I almost feel we deserve this," MSU linebacker Jon Misch said, returning to the field to cherish the moment. "I know most people were kind of worried."

Not kind of. Extremely. And with good reason.

After taking a 7-0 lead on their first possession, refuting the idea they came out flat, the Spartans took a long snooze.

For more than 43 minutes, MSU made nearly every error imaginable:

- It allowed an 80-yard run up the middle – untouched.

- It telegraphed a pick-six to the left side (see: Iowa).

- It clanged an extra-point off the right upright.

- It dropped a perfect shotgun snap.

- And it was flagged for silly penalties.

"We heard a few boos," quarterback Kirk Cousins said. "But this is Division I football. It's a big business with big expectations."

Based on the first three quarters, no one could've expected Cousins to account for five TDs and a two-point conversion, including a game-winning 3-yard scramble.

But after hobbling off the field to get shots in his sore shoulder and sprained ankle, "Captain Kirk" gave himself a second chance.

"I was very close to pulling myself out of the game," Cousins said of a team-first decision. "I have a footwork problem. I can't plant and pivot without excruciating pain."

Not any more painful than the way Purdue's cornerbacks felt after surrendering 14 catches for 159 yards, three TDs and a two-point play to MSU wideouts Mark Dell and B.J. Cunningham.

Both players learned a lesson from the infamous Rather Hall incident 12 months ago and made the most of a second opportunity.

"Mark Dell is a special receiver and a special talent," Cousins said of a senior who caught eight balls for 108 yards and 14 points. "He came in as a big-time talent. And some wondered when he'd show it."

Many wondered if senior cornerback Chris L. Rucker would even get the message. After four years of peaks and valleys, he nearly fair-caught an ill-conceived lob that gave MSU new life with 12:12 to play.

"I was thinking turnover the whole second half," said Rucker, whose indiscretions landed him in jail this fall. "When that ball was in the air, I thought of my drop at Notre Dame last year. I told myself, 'Whatever you do, don't drop this one!'"

Rucker's redemption and a spectacular blocked punt by human missile Denicos Allen were two of the season's most important moments.

I'd rank Allen's snuff as one of the three most important blocked punts in school history, along with a key play in the '54 Rose Bowl and a rout-starter in the '98 Notre Dame game.

But it wasn't Allen's day to savor. That outpouring of sentiment came from a group that has won nearly twice as often as it has lost.

After helping to limit defensive end Ryan Kerrigan, arguably the league's best player, to four tackles and one 8-yard sack, senior offensive tackle D.J. Young put a wild ride in perspective.

"It has been three short, long years," said a walk-on who transferred from Bowling Green with no guarantees, much like this year's team. "And we're not done yet!"

Not if the Spartans' second chances keep setting up a series of firsts.

The most important is a share of first place in the conference with one game to play – one very tough game, history tells us.

MSU hasn't won in Beaver Stadium since 1965, Joe Paterno's final season as Rip Engle's top assistant at Penn State.

In fairness, the Spartans went 29 years without a return visit to State College, Pa. But they are 0-8 there since the Nittany Lions began Big Ten play in 1993.

At 6-1 in the conference, MSU needs a victory next Saturday and a Michigan win at Ohio State – OK, you can stop laughing – to earn a trip to the Rose Bowl.

If that doesn't happen, a 10-1 Spartan team would almost surely wind up in Florida, probably in the Capital One Bowl on January 1 in Orlando.

Dantonio's teams have played in the shadow of Disney World before. But in a year of do-overs, this group will probably get a chance to do it right.

It's the first time MSU has had 10 wins before the final regular-season game and just the third time that has happened, bowl wins included.

It's also the first time the Spartans have had a senior class with 32 Ws in a four-year span. And whatever their final record may be, it could be broken by a group with no better than an 8-5 record in the 2011 season.

Another first this year is a 7-0 record at home. MSU had never won more than six games in Spartan Stadium. And it's a record 9-0 in games in the state of Michigan.

Now, the challenge is to do what others haven't been able to do. But there's a reason for that. Six of the eight MSU teams that lost in Happy Valley didn't make a bowl game.

This one has. It's one win away from the first 11-win season in school history. With subtle variations, it's also in position to follow the Tom Izzo flight path: NIT, NIT, Sweet 16, Final Four.

I'd equate the losses to Boston College in Orlando and Texas Tech in San Antonio to NIT appearances and view the loss to once-No. 1 Georgia in the Capital One Bowl as a Sweet 16 season.

With a share of the Big Ten title and 11 or 12 wins, this year could be seen as the football version of a Final Four.

The real fun in hoops was what happened in Year Five. And next year could be similarly exciting in football. But we're getting way ahead of ourselves.

As several Spartans said repeatedly, "We're not done yet."

Even if they were almost done as title contenders. Let's hear it for second chances.

Chris L. Rucker (29) and Eric Gordon unload on a Purdue receiver

NOVEMBER 27, 2010 • SATURDAY

ELEVEN IS HEAVEN

MARK DANTONIO didn't jump for joy. Instead, he recalled a leap of faith.

It was an August day when he told his Michigan State football players, "We WILL BE Big Ten Champions."

Three months later, after Saturday's school-record 11th win, he can change "will be" to "are".

It said as much – and much, much more – on the sweet-looking hats that Dantonio, a devoted staff and 69 devout believers in uniform wore after a 28-22 win at Penn State.

Nothing can ever take that away – not the cynics who searched for lingering traces of "Same Old Spartans" DNA and not the BCS or its independent selection committees.

The only similarity was the scary way Game 12 ended. But this time, MSU made the plays. It ran the ball when it wanted to run. It even recovered an onside kick.

And it finished the job at Beaver Stadium, a house of horrors for MSU that went from awful to half-full in three-and-a-half quarters.

The Spartans hadn't won in Sad Valley since Duffy Daugherty got the best of Rip Engle, 23-0 in 1965 – 10 helmet changes ago.

They'd lost eight straight times in State College, starting in 1994 and continuing in every year with a Congressional election.

It had been longer than that – 20 years, to be exact – since MSU had won a Big Ten football title. Only Indiana and Minnesota had seen longer droughts.

But they don't elect or anoint the league's best. They add up the victories. And the Spartans will match resumes with Wisconsin, Ohio State or any other one-loss team.

"We're one of the top eight or nine teams in the nation," Dantonio said. "We're the only team that has beaten Wisconsin. And we beat them convincingly … I'll say it twice. We beat them convincingly."

If having the ball 14 minutes longer and gaining 152 more yards than an opponent count, Dantonio is right. If those stats don't matter, two numbers on the scoreboard do.

A 34-24 win on October 2 would've broken a two-way tie and sent MSU to the Rose Bowl if Iowa could've held on last week against Ohio State.

The Buckeyes' blasting of mistake-a-minute Michigan Saturday and the Badgers' biting of never-in-it Northwestern created a three-way tie at the top at 7-1, 11-1.

Despite being 1-0 against the other champs, compared to 1-1 for Wisconsin and 0-1 for OSU, the Spartans won't be able to vault those teams and play in Pasadena.

It doesn't matter that Dantonio's team played the toughest schedule of the league champs, including eight teams that were bowl-eligible when Saturday's games began.

And it doesn't matter that the computers like his team better than Jim Tressel's, not when the *USA Today* and Harris polls comprise two-thirds of the BCS rankings.

There was a time when ties were broken in favor of the team that had been away from the Rose Bowl the longest. Victory for MSU.

There was a period well into the '70s when the league had a no-repeat rule. Bye-bye, Buckeyes. See: Wisconsin at MSU on October 2.

And there were years when the conference A.D.s met in Chicago the day after the regular-season ended to vote for the Big Ten representative.

Mark Hollis could get there today, if necessary. His case for the Spartans is tough to refute.

"We're very deserving of a long look," he said, practicing his pitch to the BCS games. "We were ranked seventh in the league going in. And we came out as champions. We endured a lot. We had signature moments. And we led the Big Ten in TV rankings."

Tremendous blocking springs Edwin Baker at Penn State

MSU-PSU wasn't the marquee matchup on the networks. Michigan-OSU and Northwestern-Wisconsin had more sizzle, supposedly. They also proved to be duds.

But unless Oregon State stuns No. 1 Oregon in Eugene or South Carolina beats No. 2 Auburn in the SEC Championship Game, look for the Badgers to play TCU in the Rose Bowl.

Expect the Buckeyes to get the Big Ten's second BCS invite, probably from the Orange or the Sugar, and the Spartans to wind up playing the SEC's third selection – Alabama, Arkansas, LSU or South Carolina – in the Capital One Bowl.

MSU has been to Orlando before. But it has never gone there or anywhere else with 11 notches on its belt. It has finished the regular season with 10 wins just once – before its loss to UCLA in the 1966 Rose Bowl.

After "Little Giants," a head coach's heart attack and subsequent blood clot, "Mousetrap" and one game when the Spartans forgot to show up, they went 3-0 in November.

Trailing Purdue 28-13 last week, MSU recovered with a 22-3 fourth-quarter surge for a four-point win on Senior Day.

And before an announced crowd of 103,649, at least 10,000 of whom came dressed as empty seats, the Spartans struck early and just often enough.

They didn't do it with takeaways, just physical plays and more discipline than anyone expected. The Big Ten's most penalized team had just three

HEART OF A **SPARTAN**

United they stand at Penn State before winning a Big Ten title

infractions. The least penalized program had six.

But when safety Trenton Robinson tried to take an interception out of the end zone and fumbled in the final two minutes, Penn State had another chance. It got the TD but not the last possession it needed.

"It's funny," said Brian Linthicum, who teamed with fellow tight end Charlie Gantt for eight catches and a touchdown, then made the biggest grab of the day on an onside kick. "We've practiced that play several hundred times. And I've never had the ball come to me – not once!"

Two Kirk Cousins kneel-downs later, the party was on at JoePa's house – by invitation only.

An omnipresent Penn State chant should've been changed to "WE ARE ... NOT HERE" – or loaned to the visitors, as Greg Jones suggested in the final seconds: "WE ARE ... LEAGUE CHAMPS."

A moment later, Dantonio was doused with a Globetrotter-esque bucket of confetti, while the real ice bath landed on stunned defensive tackle Kevin Pickelman.

After a group prayer at midfield, led – of course – by a kneeling Cousins, the unsung hero of the day spoke more and smiled more than anyone expected.

"I talked to the guys before the game," said defensive end Colin Neely, a Bethlehem, Pa., native. "I told them, 'Don't be scared to be No. 1!' And I knew if I was going to say that, I had to back it up."

Neely couldn't sleep and was waking up friends with messages before 7 a.m. Saturday. Less than seven hours later, he'd already made three big plays.

He stopped a misdirection play for a 9-yard loss on third-and-1, forced passer Matt McGloin to step forward into the waiting arms of tackle Jerel Worthy and maintained leverage on a sweep until the Nittany Lions had no choice but to hold him.

About an hour later, they were holding each other – and not just to stay warm on a near-freezing day. It was the embrace at the end of the race.

"We're Big Ten Champions," Cousins said. "No one can ever take that away from us. It's going on the wall in Spartan Stadium."

Why not? They finally climbed Mount Nittany. And they stand with company on the Big Ten mountaintop.

"ACTION!" ATTRACTION

GREG JONES DIRECTS DEFENSE & MORE

HE'D LOVE TO DIRECT hit movies some day. Until then, Greg Jones will have to settle for direct hits on ballcarriers and one of the better highlight films in football.

As a Michigan State middle linebacker and two-year captain, Jones wrote his own story, a Hollywood script.

As a New York Giants rookie, the next unforgettable scene was a Super Bowl celebration – and a postgame marriage proposal to ex-Spartan basketball player Mandy Piechowski.

Jones' path to East Lansing and his choice to finish what he started was fact, not fiction. One of the leading men in MSU's turnaround was the director himself.

"Leadership is sacrifice, commitment, responsibility and trust," he said. "It's all of those things. And a leader does that all of the time, not some of the time."

Besides leading the Spartans in tackles three years in a row, Jones led by example and helped his team mature. The Cincinnati native was a good player at Archbishop Moeller High. But no one knew he'd develop into a two-time All-American.

"When we were coaching at Cincinnati, he was at our camp playing defensive end," MSU defensive line coach Ted Gill said. "It was a pleasant surprise to see him progress each year. He has really developed into not only a fine player but a fine young man."

That's what often happens in fine families. And when it comes to teaching life's lessons, few can keep up with the Joneses.

Greg's dad, a bartender at a country club, set a great example by working, not whining. When it was time to pay his son's participation fees at Moeller, he made weekly stops at the school to drop off his tip money.

"I remember meeting his dad more than Greg," said Bob Crable, Jones' high school coach and a star linebacker at Notre Dame in the late 1970s. "His dad had very good questions and wasn't focused on football. He wanted to know how Moeller would benefit his son."

It helped in many ways. Yet, Jones wasn't a can't-miss prospect. And his choice to attend MSU was as complicated as comical.

"He was always fast," Crable said. "But his upper body wasn't developed. We didn't know if he'd be a running back, a defensive back or what. He played defensive end for a couple of years. Then, we looked at changing the defense for him."

Crable was a big fan of Mark Dantonio, then the head coach at UC. It was Crable who told Dantonio just how good Jones could be with the Bearcats.

That was never a viable option for a player who wanted to play in the Big Ten. In fact, he committed to Minnesota and would have been a Golden Gopher if Glen Mason hadn't been fired after his team blew a 38-7 lead over Texas Tech in the 2006 Insight Bowl.

Suddenly, Jones' mind was filled with uncertainty. And his voicemail was filled with messages.

"The defensive coordinator at Minnesota, Greg Hudson, was a Moeller grad, too," Crable said. "Greg really liked him a lot. But I sat Greg down and told him he could de-commit and go somewhere else."

One of the first calls came from East Lansing. Dantonio's staff had a second chance with a new destination and overcame one of strangest recruiting roadblocks

HEART OF A **SPARTAN**

in history.

"I couldn't get through to him," Dantonio said. "Finally, I asked what Minnesota had to offer that we didn't. He said, 'Coach! ... The Mall of America!' I couldn't believe it. I told him, 'Greg, we have malls in Michigan, too!'"

They also had more than their fair share of problems in a program that had gone 14-21 from 2004-06 in its last three seasons under John L. Smith.

No one could have known that Dantonio's first incoming class would go 6-2 against the Fighting Irish and Wolverines, compete for two Big Ten titles and play in four warm-weather bowl games.

"We have a lot of stepping up to do if we really want to prove ourselves," Jones said in 2010, his final year in East Lansing. "That's everybody, not just the seniors. And it's my job to help those guys out."

First, he had to help himself. Despite earning National Linebacker of the Year honors in 2009, Jones knew he had to get bigger to get better and added 15 well-packed pounds.

We heard "Tackle by No. 53, Jones" so often, it was no surprise he became a leading candidate for the Butkus Award as the country's top linebacker with a sprint-and-strip against Western Michigan, two sweet interceptions against Northern Colorado and a near-theft of a handoff to Wisconsin running back John Clay.

"My junior year hurt so much," Jones said of a 6-7 finish. "We never had a losing season like that. Yeah, we made it to a bowl game. But we needed to win it. And that did influence my decision to come back a little bit."

When many thought he'd be an NFL rookie, Jones sat down with his family and stayed grounded. A media arts and technology major, he chose to pursue a degree and the football. He wasn't done pounding the books or Big Ten ballcarriers.

"I wasn't as big as I needed to be," Jones said. "And it was a family decision. We all thought it would be better if I came back, finished my senior year and got my degree. I had unfinished business."

So did his teammates – at least those who returned. An ugly incident in Rather Hall the day after the 2009 regular season ended made Jones shake his head.

"That whole thing was one bad decision after another," he said. "They weren't all bad guys. But everybody makes mistakes. We have to make better decisions when times get tough. I wish someone would've told me about that so I could've stopped it."

Jones stopped enough runners and sacked enough quarterbacks to rank third on MSU's career tackles list behind four-year phenom Dan Bass and Butkus and Lombardi award recipient Percy Snow.

"I looked at their pictures every day," Jones said. "You always wonder, 'Who's the top dog? Who's the best?' And I actually got to meet Percy a couple of years ago. It was tremendous. I was star-struck. Then, there's Dan Bass, who did about everything you could. Just to be mentioned with those guys is truly amazing."

Jones didn't have 32 tackles against Ohio State in his first game as a freshman or a 99-yard interception return against Wisconsin, as Bass did. But he did something no other Spartan has done. He surprised his dad on a campus visit with the unveiling of his All-America plaque.

"That meant a lot," the son said of a smiling father. "I always felt that he did so much for me, to see his face made it all worthwhile. His face got red in a way I don't normally see. He's usually laughing at me or just laughing, period. But he couldn't get any words out at first. Then, he thanked me and told me he loved me."

Jones already knew that. So did anyone else who'd watched the family interact. And that was clear before the move from Moeller to MSU.

"Mr. Jones never, ever, ever complained," Crable remembered. "That was a message he left with his son. When players leave Moeller, they can purchase their helmet. I think it costs about $200. But I recommended that they give Greg's helmet to his dad as a gift."

When Jones left the Spartans, he didn't sit and watch his favorite film, "Ferris Bueller's Day Off." Instead, he went from Big Ten to World Champion – one sweet sequel.

Jesse Johnson (26) likes the confetti look for Mark Dantonio

DECEMBER 11, 2010 • SATURDAY

A LITTLE CREDIT, PLEASE

MARK HOLLIS SAID he wouldn't rest till the Spartans have the paint of roses on their cleats.

This New Year's Day, they'll have to settle for credit card codes.

That doesn't make the Capital One Bowl a postseason football scam.

A matchup with defending national champ Alabama in Orlando is a near-perfect opportunity, albeit an awesome challenge.

If Michigan State plays as well as it can, it'll show the nation just how far a long-forgotten program has come.

If the Spartans play the way they did for most of this season, not just in a convincing win over Wisconsin, they'll represent the Big Ten well.

If not, perhaps they don't deserve all the BCS angst and lobbying a flawed system demands.

The fact is, Wisconsin, Ohio State and MSU all finished 7-1 in the Big Ten and 11-1 in the regular season.

With a limit of two BCS bids per conference, one of the league's three champions was destined for disappointment.

All we all know which group that is today – the one in green.

The Badgers are bound for Pasadena and a Rose Bowl matchup with TCU, while the Buckeyes earned a trip to New Orleans and a Sugar Bowl date with Arkansas.

Under previous guidelines, the Spartans would be headed to Pasadena. After all, they're 1-0 vs. the other two champs, while Wisconsin is 1-1 and OSU 0-1 in head-to-head matchups.

If you look at the longest-time-away tiebreaker, MSU would be No. 1 there, too. The Spartans haven't been to the Rose Bowl since January 1, 1988. Bucky won three times there, in 1994, 1999 and 2000. And Brutus beat Oregon there last season.

But that's not the way it's done these days in the Big Ten. With expansion just ahead, those factors will never be relevant again.

And who knows what will happen with the Buckeyes and an investigation into NCAA irregularities?

For now, it's a string of rumors and denials involving a Columbus tattoo parlor and impermissible benefits.

What if it all happens to be true? What if it turns out that Jim Tressel or his assistants knew what was happening and failed to report the problem for whatever reason, including eligibility issues?

If that's the case, shouldn't those players be ineligible now? Shouldn't that be factored into OSU's eligibility for a BCS opportunity in the Sugar Bowl?

Maybe another year. Maybe with other players – or even another coach.

For now, a letter this week from the U.S. attorney's office seeking information about the transfer of trinkets, trophies, rings and signed jerseys and cleats for tats and cash is just that, an inquiry.

Don't expect any sanctions from Tressel, the school, the conference or the NCAA till we know a lot more – certainly not while one of the league's cash cows cashes in with a trip to New Orleans and a winnable game against the Hogs.

If the Buckeyes weren't part of the equation this year, there would be a two-way tie at the top and a simple solution.

It was MSU 34, Wisconsin 24 on October 2 in East Lansing. End of debate.

But with OSU still in the picture, one with the clarity of bad body art, the tie was broken by the BCS standings, a benchmark with all the validity of standardized testing.

Pick your poison – the *USA Today* Coaches Poll, with ballots from laser-focused leaders or designated underlings who seldom see 90 percent of the teams; the Harris Interactive Poll, a slight improvement but still an odd cross-section of voters, or a hodgepodge of computer rankings with different views and garbage-in, garbage-out nonsense.

Kevin Pickelman, Greg Jones, Jerel Worthy, Tyler Hoover and Eric Gordon

In each evaluation, the Spartans began the season with a distinct handicap. A 6-7 showing last season, capped by a third straight bowl loss, left MSU off the radar screen and with as much chance of making a BCS game as Boise State had.

They had to be perfect, as it turned out. An 11-1 record wasn't quite good enough for either team – and wouldn't have been in any format where marketing mattered more than on-the-field outcomes.

Thus, the Spartans were prisoners of the system, one where coaches vote with ignorance and self-interest and computers spit out numbers that don't agree, let alone make sense.

MSU sits seventh in the *USA Today* and Harris polls and 11th in the average of six computer rankings – not quite good enough in a year when the top three teams didn't play.

But what if the Spartans had faced South Florida instead of Florida International? What if they'd hosted Colorado instead of Northern Colorado?

Would their record have been any different? No.

Would they have been a better team? No.

Would their poll and computer numbers have risen? Probably.

But they didn't. As a result, some voters didn't know how much stock to put in "Little Giants" and how much in "Field of Nightmares," a.k.a. Kinnick Stadium.

Dantonio ranked MSU fourth, as you might expect. Illinois coach Ron Zook had the Spartans fifth. In a surprise to some, Wisconsin's Bret Bielema had them sixth. So did the Crimson Tide's Nick Saban, who was only voting in his best interests, as it turned out.

Others weren't nearly as kind.

Stanford's Jim Harbaugh, a "Michigan Man," ranked MSU 10th, seven spots below one-loss Stanford.

Mississippi State's Dan Mullen also had the Spartans 10th, seven places below Wisconsin and just six ahead of four-loss Mississippi State.

Nebraska's Bo Pelini put MSU 11th, three notches below three-loss Nebraska.

And so it goes – or in this case, doesn't go to a BCS bowl.

Instead, it's back to Florida for the third time in Dantonio's four seasons, this time to face a team with five projected No. 1 draft picks next April and plenty to prove after three largely inexplicable losses.

How good is Alabama? Just the best team the Spartans have played since a 38-7 loss to the visiting Buckeyes in 2006, John L. Smith's last uphill climb.

If MSU doesn't come to play, the score could be embarrassing again. Bama is finally healthy. It knows a blowout is the best deodorant after blowing a 24-0 lead over archrival Auburn. And it doesn't plan to take prisoners in its last game – at least for this season – as National Champions.

What can the Spartans do about that? Maybe a lot. Maybe not.

They have to want to win more than the Tide, which won't be easy. They need to play mistake-free football against a bigger, faster team. And they need a superior effort on the offensive and defensive lines, where the game could be lost before it can be won.

After an appropriate period of mourning, MSU will realize three things:

Life isn't always fair.

Neither are bowl matchups.

All a team can do is try to prove that and, eventually, improve its image.

JANUARY 1, 2011 • SATURDAY

TIDE ROLLS, SCORE SNOWBALLS

SOMETIMES AN OPPONENT IS JUST BETTER.

Bigger, stronger, faster, more skillful.

Healthier and more experienced, too.

If the teams played a best-of-seven series, it would almost certainly be a sweep – as long as the superior team cared.

Alabama cared Saturday afternoon.

And Michigan State was careless at the worst possible time.

The result was a Crimson Tide tsunami.

The score of the 2011 Capital One Bowl was 49-7 – and could've been 70-0 if Nick Saban had kept the pedal to Bama's mettle.

"We were outcoached, outplayed and out-physicaled," MSU coach Mark Dantonio said. "There's no way to sugarcoat this one."

There wasn't much Dantonio and his staff could do to prevent the biggest bowl loss in school history and the worst by a Top 10 team in two decades.

It was a team most thought would play for a second-straight BCS Championship vs. one few thought could contend for, let alone win, a Big Ten title.

And that's the way it looked when the teams collided like a bug and a windshield.

The Tide rushed for 275 yards. The Spartans had minus 48, just 3 yards better than Michigan's -51 output on the ground against MSU in 1965.

Continuing in the misery-loves-company

Greg Jones stops Heisman Trophy winner Mark Ingram

department, the Big Ten went 0-5 on New Year's Day – the first time the league has lost more than three bowls on one day.

The Wolverines and Spartans allowed 101 points. With Northwestern and Penn State factored in, the total yield was 183 points – 45.8 per game.

So MSU wasn't alone. It was just the most disappointed and humbled.

It leaves Orlando with two unanswered questions: Where was the team that won 11 games? And how did Bama ever lose three of them?

That doesn't absolve the Spartans of a litany of errors, including incredibly poor execution in a 28-0 first half.

It's one thing that Bama scored on every possession when it tried in the first two quarters and something else that MSU was an enabler.

The Spartans got to the Tide 24- and 3-yard lines on their first two drives, then lost 43 yards on penalties and sacks before throwing an interception and punting.

Slow-developing runs had no chance. And MSU couldn't have protected quarterbacks Kirk Cousins, Andrew Maxwell and Keith Nichols with 12 players in the huddle.

Actually, the Spartans tried that once. It was one of their four pre-snap penalties on offense in the first two quarters. On defense, two offside infractions didn't help.

Neither did shoddy tackling that made Mark Ingram look like a Heisman Trophy winner, which he was a year ago, and Julio Jones look like a cross between Calvin Johnson and DeSean Jackson.

Two MSU players with SEC athleticism, wideout B.J. Cunningham and pass rusher William Gholston, were injured and couldn't play.

They were joined by a steady stream of Spartan teammates as the game-long carnage continued.

It was the worst physical pounding I've seen MSU take since a 48-14 loss at Oregon in September 1998, a game that was 48-0 till the Ducks quit caring.

And for quarterback damage, it ranked with a 20-10 loss to Big Ten champ Illinois in 1983, the league's only team to win nine conference games.

There was another similarity in those mismatches. Any time your Most Valuable selections come down to two trainers and two doctors, you have problems.

But a full complement of players, including Lorenzo White and Percy Snow, wouldn't have changed the outcome by more than a touchdown or two.

As Duffy Daugherty might've said, "Blaming injuries for this loss is like blaming the Johnstown Flood on a leaky toilet in Altoona."

Indeed, it looked like the Tide wore track shoes and the Spartans were in snowshoes for most of a sun-drenched day.

The Bama that led Auburn 24-0 on November 26 arrived before kickoff. The team that somehow lost to Cam Newton & Co. 28-27 never made it to Florida.

That was obvious from the opening possession, with help from one MSU gift. A needless pass-interference call on Chris L. Rucker nullified a third-down incompletion and prevented a Tide punt.

Rucker had asked for the assignment of shadowing Jones, instead of just covering him half the time. But a Bama adjustment put Jones in the slot much of the game.

A reverse and fullback-like block by quarterback Greg McElroy put Jones in the end zone.

It was painful to watch and more painful to play as the game developed. Cousins' contusions aside, wideout Mark Dell and linebacker Eric Gordon deserved better endings to their college careers.

The only reasons the score wasn't bigger were a replay overturn of a fumble-recovery score and Saban's decision to play everyone who wasn't wearing a hounds-tooth hat.

Some will question his choice to call a running play on fourth-and-2 at the MSU 27 with a 35-0 lead. What was he supposed to do? Kick a field goal? Take a knee? Practice the pooch punt?

When Bama scored for the final time with a fourth-team running back, Saban seemed visibly disturbed. Believe it or not, he wanted to beat the Spartans, not punish them.

Bottom line, the Tide had more sacks than a bagger at Meijer and more yards-after-contact than a foreclosure company.

Johnathan Strayhorn zeroes in on his Crimson Tide target

HEART OF A SPARTAN

Yes, Brian Linthicum had a "SportsCenter" snare, Bennie Fowler had a shutout-spoiling catch and Aaron Bates did his usual fine punting.

That's about it. Any time a punt is a highlight, it's a very short tape. And when fans cheer a fumble recovery by a center for a 30-yard loss, it's a very long day.

Edwin Baker, an All-Big Ten runner, had more room to move on the team plane. And when his team allows as many touchdowns as it posts points, it isn't going to be a happy trip home.

So Bama heads home with its NCAA-record 33rd bowl win. The Spartans come back with $420 of free loot from Best Buy and a fifth straight postseason loss.

As in more respectable setbacks against Boston College (Matt Ryan), Georgia (Matthew Stafford) and Texas Tech (a full roster), MSU was facing a decidedly better team.

The last fact shouldn't change the goal to do that again and produce a different outcome. That's how champions are built.

For the record, TCU ended a storybook season last January with a loss to Boise State in the Fiesta Bowl. And Oregon closed with a crushing loss against Ohio State in the Rose Bowl. The Frogs and the Ducks have done all right since then.

It's up to the Spartans whether that cleansing occurs. No one can take away what they've accomplished – just as no one can make them feel better today.

They still set MSU season and four-year victory marks, won their third straight game over U-M and claimed the first league crown in many of their lifetimes.

The fact is, across the country, they'll be remembered for Saturday's whipping more than all their other successes. Impressions aren't fair. They also aren't final.

Being the most improved team in the Big Ten again is a worthy goal. Anything less might not be enough.

Max Bullough (40) with his own version of the Flex defense

APRIL 16, 2011 • SATURDAY

BEWARE OF FALSE STARTS

IT HAS BEEN MORE THAN 15 WEEKS since Michigan State played a football game – and that's being kind, given the outcome.

It has been more than 20 weeks since the Spartans won one.

So it's only natural that players, coaches and fans would want to erase the memory of a 49-7 nuking by Alabama last January 1 as soon as possible.

The problem is that they won't be able to do that this spring, regardless of whether the Green beats the White or vice versa on April 30 in Spartan Stadium.

There's nothing that will happen in spring ball that can accurately predict how Mark Dantonio's team will do in Year 5, following an 11-2 breakthrough.

At best, the defending Big Ten tri-champs will have to wait till September 3, when Youngstown State visits East Lansing.

And if the threat of an Appalachian State-style stunner doesn't do it, MSU won't be able to prove its worth to the nation till it plays at Notre Dame two weeks later.

The Fighting Irish ... you remember them.

When last seen in Ingham County, they were trying to figure out how Aaron Bates became Aaron Rodgers and Charlie Gantt turned into Charlie Sanders on the most famous fake field goal of the 21st century.

But Brian Kelly's program ended its season with a second straight bowl win, something the Spartans haven't done since 1989-90.

Following Saturday's annual Blue-Gold game in Notre Dame Stadium, Kelly used the word "confident" to describe certain aspects of his team.

What's he supposed to say, that the Irish will be 0-for-the-state of Michigan again?

The first coach who says, "I really don't like these guys, and we'll be lucky to win as many as we did last season," gets a steak or lobster dinner at the restaurant of his choice.

Besides a chance for skill development and experimentation, that's what spring practice and spring cleansing is: the second of three opportunities to start anew.

There's Signing Day in February, where every incoming class is seen as a successful shopping trip.

There's the Color-vs.-Color game in April, where hope springs eternal.

And there's Media Day in August, where everyone comes together for the first time with a zero to the right of the hyphen in the team's record.

Perhaps the least illuminating of those days comes right before or after Easter most years.

At least Signing Day shows where a program hopes to be in three years, while Media Day lets us see who's in shape and committed to win.

Spring games, usually just glorified scrimmages, have little relevance to what happens in September, let alone in conference play.

Coaches take depleted rosters, split them in half and play with extra precautions.

Last year's seniors are either standing on the sidelines or a long way from campus, pursuing their dreams of a pro opportunity.

Their eventual replacements, the freshmen and junior-college transfers who are supposed to be better than the guys who just left, are very seldom in uniform yet.

Many of the returning players are in street clothes, recovering from surgeries or nursing injuries they'd try to play over in rivalry games.

Quarterbacks are in red or yellow jerseys, wisely protected from the kinds of hits that can ruin or redefine a season.

Kick returners, who can turn a game or a championship chase in a matter of seconds, are non-factors in spring showcases.

And regardless of the roster formulation and rules, there's never enough talent on the field long enough to show how a team will fare in the fourth quarter.

Whether it's offense vs. defense, 1s vs. 2s or a supposedly even game with assigned parity, it's hard to tell who's good and who's not.

We saw that Saturday at Michigan Stadium, where The Brady Bunch did everything it could to put the Rich Rodriguez Era in mothballs.

When Denard Robinson and Michael Cox broke free on long runs, did it mean that U-M had more than one ballcarrier in 2011?

Or was it further evidence that Jordan Kovacs and some other DBs had no idea of how to make an open-field tackle?

When Robinson and Devin Gardner made throws that weren't dropped, were they any better than the overthrows and telegraphed interceptions?

Whatever the season holds for a team with its first five games and its last two at home, one thing was clear under the cloudiest skies.

You'd have had better luck finding Final Four banners from the early '90s than fans of RichRod's 3-3-5 defense among 25,000 True Blues.

Actually, that crowd would've fit in one end zone of Bryant-Denny Stadium in Tuscaloosa, where a record 92,000 crazies came to worship the Crimson Tide.

Believe it or not, that was more people than Bama had on the field on defense against the Spartans on New Year's Day.

And they came to salute the SEC team from their state that didn't win a national title – at least, as of April 17.

They came to see the new statue of a clapping Nick Saban and to see the Tide's next group of future first-round draft picks, not that the NFL matters down there.

When MSU fans get their chance to dream big at the end of this month, they won't see a statue of Dantonio, despite the best four-year start for any Spartan coach.

They won't see whether Kirk Cousins and Andrew Maxwell can stay composed after sacks or whether Keshawn Martin has regained his kick-return jet gear.

They'll see what they want to see and say what they want to say, regardless of how the Spartans stack up in seven games that could go either way.

If they're glass-is-half-full, green-glasses types, they'll see pressure on the quarterbacks as proof that ends Tyler Hoover and William Gholston will be brilliant.

If they can't stand imperfections in any lives other than their own, they'll probably see a retooled, injury-depleted offensive line as proof of future disappointments.

Both groups could be right with their theories. But we won't know that this month or next month or the month after that.

What will we learn from the Green-White Game? Not nearly as much as we think or as much as the coaches want.

Perhaps the biggest eye-opener, the most revealing aspect, will come well before the players take the field.

When two groups of seniors take turns drafting underclassmen, it'll tell us just how the veterans look at some guys we know the least about as potential contributors.

We saw that three years ago when Cousins was picked well ahead of hyped redshirt-freshman Nick Foles, now the marquee player at Arizona.

And we may get an indication of how sophomore and junior running backs and linebackers are viewed by their peers in 11 days.

If that doesn't tell us enough, it'll have to do for now, until the Spartans start playing people they don't know with plays they haven't practiced for weeks.

We'll have to wait till Labor Day weekend or a few weeks beyond that to know how much we don't know about this team.

And that wait will be half the fun.

APRIL 30, 2011 • SATURDAY

PROGRESS COMES BEFORE THE FALL

IT WAS AS PROMISING a Green-White Game as we've seen in a long time. I say that having watched 42 in a row.

Yes, we've witnessed more fireworks in a Michigan State spring football finale. But after quarterbacks Kirk Cousins and Keith Nichol resembled Tom Brady and Aaron Rodgers, respectively, in 2009, we saw that team go 6-7.

Likewise, we've seen groups that loved to hit more than Manny Pacquiao. But most hit a wall at some point when the offense couldn't do enough with the defense's hard work.

That's the toughest part of analyzing spring practice as a predictor for fall performance. Is a big gain a sign of offensive strength or a defensive deficiency? And is a negative play proof of an improved defense or a sign the offense stinks?

In the Green team's 24-10 win over the White squad Saturday in Spartan Stadium, there were many more pluses than minuses on both sides of the ball – enough to suggest an 11-win season wasn't a one-year wonder.

Let's take a look at 12 of those areas, one for each game in the regular season or one for each team in a bigger Big Ten. Take your choice. Just don't ask that we divide them into Legends and Leaders.

UNCOMMON DEPTH • In Year 5 under Mark Dantonio, we see the importance of infrastructure and the difference between a team and a program. You'd have to go back to the mid-1960s to find comparable 2s and 3s on the depth chart.

If MSU is a long way from being injury-proof, it has proven to be a legitimate option for 247Sports' three- and four-star recruits. If it isn't always the school of choice, a tendency that takes decades to become DNA, it's in the discussion in 2011.

While some other schools have more tradition, especially over the past 45 years, that didn't prevent a Big Ten co-championship breakthrough. And it won't have anything to do with a bid for back-to-back ring presentations.

A VETERAN QB'S VALUE • The Spartans have shown major improvement or won Big Ten titles with seniors Earl Morrall, Steve Juday, Ed Smith, Dan Enos, Jim Miller, Bill Burke, Jeff Smoker and Brian Hoyer under center.

They could do that again with Cousins, who starred Saturday afternoon and was ranked as ESPN's No. 3 senior passing prospect for the 2012 NFL Draft, a mile behind Stanford standout Andrew Luck and a hair behind Arizona's Nick Foles.

If you've forgotten, Foles began his career in East Lansing and was a much more heralded signee than Cousins. He was also the first challenger Cousins dispatched on his way to become a three-year starter and captain.

ANOTHER TARGET CENTER • When MSU said goodbye to wide receiver Mark Dell and tight end Charlie Gantt, some wondered how those departures would affect a productive but still stoppable passing game. They can stop wondering.

With B.J. Cunningham and Keshawn Martin healthy, Nichol better in his second year as a wideout, Bennie Fowler set to blossom and Tony Lippett too talented to keep off the field, new receivers coach Terrence Samuel should smile

And with Dion Sims back in the lineup (no jokes,

Kirk Cousins and Edwin Baker work on timing and technique

please), the Spartans are three deep at tight end. He has Charmin-soft hands for a 277-pounder and two position peers, Garrett Celek and Brian Linthicum, who'd start for most teams.

A WISHBONE BACKFIELD • Edwin Baker has made no bones about wanting to rush for 2,000 yards and 21 touchdowns this season. Himself. In 13 games last season, 12 MSU ballcarriers netted 1,978 yards.

If Baker had an injury-free year and a workload worthy of Lorenzo White or Javon Ringer, I suppose anything is possible. But there's only one football. And less is more when a team has an excellent passing attack and five legit running backs.

Le'Veon Bell's shoulders are pain-free. Larry Caper can also catch and run. Nick Hill, who makes look-alike, play-alike pal Mike Hart seem big in more areas than his mouth, was a star this spring. And Jeremy Langford is equally explosive.

A SET-FOR-ASSEMBLY O-LINE • The Spartans have had bigger stars at center, guard and tackle than you'll see this year, though spring no-shirt Joel Foreman has a chance to be very good this fall.

The best news is the development of depth in the trenches, with assistant coach Mark Staten predicting an eight-man rotation. In an ideal world, five excellent players would be preferable to eight possible contributors. Timing is everything.

But if new tackles Dan France, Skyler Schofner and Fou Fonoti approach their potential, guards Foreman and Chris McDonald improve at all and centers Travis Jackson and Blake Treadwell are OK, 2,000 rushing yards may not be enough.

COORDINATION NATION • It isn't how good five blockers can be, it's how often they can be good together. A line, like a nation, is only as strong as its weakest link. And MSU has a chance to have a unit, not a collection of individuals.

We didn't see that this spring due to injuries. But with competition preventing complacency, the Spartans should get nothing but better up front. Foreman and utility man Jare McGaha are the group's only seniors.

Don't be overly concerned with the team's 12 penalties for 73 yards Saturday, with many coming from overanxious blockers. That's what spring football is for. Most players will get better and more consistent. So will the refs.

WELL WORTH THE GAMBLE • Dantonio was Ohio State's defensive coordinator when two-way contributor Chris Gamble helped the Buckeyes win a national title. Redshirt-freshman Tony Lippett could be just as good.

We saw him catch a deep ball down the left sideline for a 57-yard pickup and chase down speedy Keshawn Martin on a reverse. And if Martin got revenge on a 38-yard TD, it was a senior's moment.

Look for Lippett to help on offense and defense this year. Howard Griffith of the Big Ten Network already named last year's best Denard Robinson impersonator this season's Top Newcomer.

"MR. SPRING" READY FOR FALL • We've seen this movie before. Diminutive Chris D. Rucker did his thing again Saturday and made a couple of big catches in the Green-White Game.

But instead of dropping balls when it counts and disappearing from the depth chart before Labor Day, the only Rucker remaining on the roster may be relevant in his fifth go-round.

As Cousins explained about Rucker, it's all a matter of confidence. If he can finally use his superior speed, the Spartans will be a better team. And other forgotten players may say, "Hey, I can do that, too!"

GO GREEN, GO WHITE • While Draymond Green's cameo appearance for the White team and quote of the spring – "I just don't want to be tackled" – drew a lot of attention, Anthony Rashad White's play for the Green was more significant.

The junior defensive tackle could be MSU's MIP. He was a force all spring and could team with Jerel Worthy to give the Spartans their best inside tandem since Mark Nichols and Travis Davis wreaked havoc in 1987.

Best of all, by pushing the pocket, White, Worthy and returning starter Kevin Pickelman could make 6-foot-7 bookends Tyler Hoover and William Gholston even more imposing on the outside.

TAKE 5 AT YOUR OWN RISK • Junior cornerback Johnny Adams may never be President like namesakes John and John Quincy, but he's the leading performer in the secondary, joining fiery free safety Trenton Robinson.

Adams' technique is much improved, though he'll have to find a new way to cover 6-7 basketball players. He was the first overall pick in the underclassman player draft. And we saw his terrific speed vs. the run and the pass Saturday.

If you recall his leaping, game-changing pick vs. Notre Dame and his instant-reflex goal-line swipe at Michigan, get used to those kinds of plays. Adams and the Spartans' family of DBs could be better than we think.

HOLES TO FILL, NOT CRATERS • Congratulations to departing middle linebacker Greg Jones, who went to the New York Giants, and to cornerback Chris L. Rucker, who became an Indianapolis Colt, three picks apart in Round 6.

A jubilant Jerel Worthy has plenty of reasons to smile

HEART OF A **SPARTAN**

Gantt, Dell and punter Aaron Bates should also get free-agent opportunities. And you'd have hoped all five would've gone a bit higher or been drafted somewhere, a key selling point with top prospects.

But when a team has more than five times as many wins as draft picks, it's doing a lot of things right. And when its NFL selections are the 22nd and 23rd of the 29 from its league, a lot of teams are suffering greater attrition.

FIFTH-YEAR, GOALS-TO-GO • One of the biggest problems for MSU and programs a lot like it has been sustaining the level of play and commitment it has taken to reach the top.

If the Spartans lose twice as often this season, complacency shouldn't be the reason. There's a horrible memory from New Year's Day to erase, a record to chase for career wins by seniors and a new Big Ten title format as motivation.

There will only be one first winner of the Big Ten Championship Game, just as there were only three final co-champs. And though most people think Nebraska will rule the Legends, a team that lost three of its last four games is no sure thing.

If that sounds like a lot of sunshine on a cloudy day, it isn't a recipe for football perfection. In fact, there are many more treacherous rocks to climb on the way up a higher mountain.

That will become clearer next week, as we celebrate Mother's Day with our annual post-spring, game-by game forecast – as usual, not as good as most fans want but much better than many of them fear.

Edwin Bakes picks his way on a well-blocked play

JUNE 11, 2011 • SATURDAY

ONE TITLE, NO ENTITLEMENT

NORMALLY, when a team is 7-1 in league play and a school-record 11-2 overall, it tends to feel pretty good about itself.

When it shares the Big Ten crown with two Top 10 teams and gets its first championship rings in 20 years, it's understandably happy.

And when it has a third-year starting quarterback who's projected to be a second-round NFL draft pick, the league's best depth at running back and receiver, a defense with at least two future pros and an all-conference kicker who made 14 of 15 field goals, it often starts thinking about postseason matchups.

If the Michigan State Spartans do that for more than a split-second this summer, they're asking for serious trouble.

They won't have to ask twice.

While it's perfectly fair to expect a nine-win season and hope for more in 2011, the difference between seven and 11 triumphs is smaller than Nick Hill next to Antonio Jeremiah.

That was obvious last year when MSU won all five of its close games – almost the complete opposite of 2009's disappointments, except for a win against Michigan in overtime.

Though it deserved each dramatic victory it earned in Year 4, Mark Dantonio's program easily could have had back-to-back 6-7 seasons.

You can imagine the hostile reaction on this site and elsewhere if that six-play collapse had occurred.

Instead of wondering if Dantonio might leave for Columbus, Ohio, fans would've been lined up like cabbies at closing time, waiting to drive him to the airport.

For the first time in 11 years, the Spartans responded in every winnable situation, edging Notre Dame 34-31 on a fake field goal in OT, beating Wisconsin 34-24 with help from a late, fourth-down gamble, topping Northwestern 35-27 and Purdue 35-31 with furious, fourth-quarter rallies and holding off Penn State 28-22 despite a brief death wish in the closing moments.

In MSU's wins, it averaged 33.6 points and never put up less than 26. In the Spartans' losses, they were outscored 86-13 and never posted more than a touchdown.

So it wasn't that MSU was a dominant team, just a resourceful, resilient one that sang the fight song more often than tailgaters at night games.

The question is, what does that mean for this year's Spartans, a group with excellence and experience on both sides of the ball?

It means there's a fine, fine line between love and a waste of time, as a favorite song from Broadway's "Avenue Q" tells us.

That was as true last September, October and November as it's liable to be this fall in East Lansing and the five cities MSU visits – OK, in seven if things go well enough to include Indianapolis and Pasadena.

Or as the reigning Big Ten Coach of the Year once warned in his finest moment on the job, "Pride comes before the fall."

That's a fact for everyone in every line of work, not just a delusional few with doctorates in football arrogance.

Let's take a look at one quarter late last season, the last one that most Spartan fans saw in person, when a Senior Day salute turned sour for nearly 48 minutes.

That game against the Boilermakers was on the Big Ten Network late Saturday night or early Sunday

HEART OF A **SPARTAN**

Jerel Worthy takes the high road against the Boilermakers

morning, take your choice, so it's fresh enough and important enough to serve as a point of reference.

Purdue, my pick as the league's biggest surprise this season, nearly got an early start on canceling scheduled coronations last November 20.

The visitors tried to keep Hope alive all year and led MSU 28-13 early in the fourth quarter before they fell apart like an Indy car that slams into Turn 4.

The trouble began when fill-in quarterback Rob Henry panicked and lobbed a deep ball, an intended throwaway, that MSU cornerback Chris L. Rucker nearly fair caught and returned 20 yards into scoring position.

After the Spartans' fourth false start of the day, they got another unexpected break – an offside call on All-America defensive end Ryan Kerrigan that turned a fourth-and-10 field goal try into a third-and-5 mulligan.

To MSU's credit, it took full advantage. B.J. Cunningham came back to the ball on the right sideline and grabbed Kirk Cousins' pass in the end zone to cut the deficit to 28-20.

The Boilermakers promptly answered when the Spartans had an awful breakdown in kickoff coverage, allowing Purdue to start in MSU territory.

When the possession stalled, lead-footed kicker Carson Wiggs drilled a 52-yard field goal – 15 yards shorter than his ICBM in this spring's finale – and put the Boilers up 31-20 with 8:42 to play.

After patient completions to tight ends Charlie Gantt and Brian Linthicum for first downs, another Cousins-to-Cunningham strike took the ball to the Purdue 9 just when most MSU teams would've said, "Well, it has been a good season."

A challenge on a possible TD catch by Cunningham correctly went in the Boilers' favor, costing the Spartans a timeout and making a lot of media members start reminiscing about other blown opportunities.

Suddenly, Mark Dell caught an isolation slant for his second TD of the day, then made a fingertip grab for the two-point conversion that made it a three-point game with 6:54 left.

With the crowd roaring for every step, MSU came up with big stops on defense and a mammoth play on special teams, the types of efforts that usually differentiate winners from whiners.

But Purdue had something to do with that, too, committing its fifth false start and inexplicably drawing a delay-of-game penalty that forced a third-and-21 situation.

Seconds later, the Boilers blew a simple assignment in punt protection and allowed Denicos Allen an all-out rush and an uninterrupted path to the ball – a kick that left an outline on his stomach where it hit him and seemed to vanish.

Even then, the Spartans needed plenty of good fortune. Cousins barely got to the goal line before fumbling on a go-ahead scramble, a ball Purdue had every chance to pounce on before guard Joel Foreman did.

But the visitors had one more shot and nearly made the most of it, converting a fourth-and-6 scramble with a 14-yard strike to the tight end, then getting a break when Trenton Robinson was flagged for a late hit on Henry at the MSU sideline.

It would've been a painful-but-appropriate lesson for a team that ranked last in the league in penalties if the Boilers had scored to win in the last minute.

Instead, on fourth-and-8 at the 10, Henry was flushed from the pocket and was planted like a seedling by middle linebacker Greg Jones. When a desperation heave was intercepted by outside backer Chris Norman with :43 left, the Spartans had their fourth of five escapes.

Normally, people will say, "Forget last season!" But that's not the best way to handle success, as Cousins knows.

The trick is to remember how those games were won, applying the lessons from a lot of close calls and blending confidence with a real concern that dodging bullets for a living usually leads to an early funeral.

With that, MSU should know that it's entitled to only one thing – its opponents' best efforts against a team they expect to topple.

And its supporters should understand, though a repeat title or more is possible, the only guarantee is another series of Maalox moments.

"WHO'S HE?"
A BIG KEY

KESHAWN MARTIN'S HEART SIZE MATTERS MOST

IF KESHAWN MARTIN could be anyone for a day, he'd be the President of the United States.

Martin would probably make it mandatory for all Americans to spend their weekends watching college and professional football during his first day on the job. Before he gets to the Oval Office, however, he'll try to impress the coaching staff of the Houston Texans.

"Whichever team I'm on, I'm able to help it win in a lot of ways," said Martin, a versatile fourth-round draft pick. "But I'd definitely like to be a wide receiver in the NFL."

He was a quarterback, defensive back and wide receiver at Westland John Glenn High. Martin also played basketball and ran track in hopes that one of those sports would allow him to play at the next level.

Michigan State soon came calling. But the coaches didn't know how to classify Martin's unique set of skills. He was recruited simply as an "athlete".

Offense, defense, passing, catching, intercepting, returning – you name it, Martin could do it. When he became a Spartan, Martin chose to receive. But his heart was under center.

"I liked playing quarterback best," Martin explained. "Just knowing that basically you're the head of the team, you can win the game or lose it at any moment. The ball is always in your hands. I liked that."

Instead, the quarterback position would end up in the hands of someone named Kirk Cousins. Martin was perfectly fine with that, though. Having experience as a quarterback actually helped him become a more effective pass catcher.

"I believe that my game transitioned well from playing quarterback to playing wide receiver in college, then hopefully moving on to the NFL," Martin said. "I think I know what a quarterback is expecting out of his wide receivers."

Everyone got more than they were expecting from Martin. He was listed as a wide receiver, but it was always a guessing game to see where 82 would be when the ball was snapped.

His versatility allowed him to score five different ways in his MSU career: rushing, receiving, passing, punt returns and kick returns. And if he'd played cornerback for a half-season, chances are he would've had six.

Martin didn't care how he made it into the end zone or how far he had to travel. He took his 17 career touchdowns any way he could get them. Still, he had his favorites.

"I think my favorite would probably be a punt or kickoff return," Martin said. "It really gets the fans going, especially if you're at home and have the fans on your side. It's great to know that you have the ability to catch punts and make guys miss. But when I'm back there I really don't think about that. I think about catching the ball first and getting up field and whoever is in the way try to get past those guys so I can get a touchdown."

He scored quite a few, as he dodged, dipped, ducked and dove his way through defenders en route to the goal line. Martin will leave MSU ranked second in punt return yards and is one of just three Spartans to return two

Keshawn Martin takes flight to score against Michigan

punts for touchdowns.

Not bad for someone who wasn't highly recruited.

"I really didn't have that many offers coming out of high school, and Michigan State found me," Martin explained. "It means a lot, proving people wrong when they say that you can't do something that you know you can do. Michigan State gave me a great opportunity. And every Saturday for four years, I just went out and played my hardest for my school and myself."

The Spartan family will miss Martin's talents on the field, but he made sure to leave his legacy as a utility player in the mind of one underclassman. Sophomore Tony Lippett is as versatile as Martin and will be transitioning from defense to offense this season.

"We both played quarterback in high school," Lippett said. "So as far as being a utility player, I learned just being quick, getting in and out of breaks, making people miss, that aspect of his skill."

While Martin had a positive effect on the development of younger players, the experience he had on and off the field in East Lansing impacted him as well.

"It definitely shaped me in a good way," Martin said. "Michigan State is all about toughness. I really feel like that helped me out a lot, learning a whole lot of stuff from the coaches that I never knew or just working hard because I wanted to succeed. I feel like I learned all that at Michigan State."

He'll take much of what he learned, and the memories, with him to the next stage of his football career.

Oh, the memories. There are a lot of them.

The 84-yard run from scrimmage and 93-yard kickoff return at Minnesota in 2009, when he was the only player in the nation with 80-yard plays three different ways.

The two TD receptions in the 2011 Michigan game, a 14-point win for the Spartans, when he accounted for two-thirds of his team's offensive scores.

The 57-yard punt return for a TD against Northwestern this season that helped MSU win the first outright Big Ten Legends Division title.

The memorable Senior Day against Indiana when he had 182 total yards – 99 on eight catches, 64 on punt returns and the remaining 19 on a reverse.

The 35-yard gain at Penn State in 2010 that set up MSU's second score and helped the Spartans to their first Big Ten crown since 1990.

That doesn't begin to describe the devastation he inflicted on Wisconsin. As a sophomore he had a 91-yard TD reception. As a junior Martin had 190 all-purpose yards, including a 74-yard punt return, and averaged 27.1 yards per touch. As a senior he scored on a 34-yard reverse and a 15-yard pass. And he nearly rescued MSU in the first Big Ten Championship Game. After grabbing nine passes for 115 yards, a punt return that could've made the difference was negated by a running-into-the-kicker penalty.

His favorite moments?

"I would definitely say winning a Big Ten Championship and being runners-up the following year," Martin said. "Those are great accomplishments, not just for me but for Michigan State University. It means with the right players and good coaching you can become an elite team. That's what Michigan State has become. It means a lot to have done that."

There's no question that Martin was a key ingredient to his school's recent success on the field. But he'll miss much more than the game of college football when he leaves East Lansing.

"My teammates," Martin said in a nostalgic tone. "Hanging out with them on and off the field, having that team bond that we had in our locker room, that is probably the one thing I will miss the most. It was a journey."

It's a journey that comes to an end for every athlete. But for Martin it's also an opportunity to pursue his dream of playing in the NFL. The tough, hard-working attitude he learned as a Spartan fostered his college success and will continue long after leaving MSU.

Whether that success is on the field or in the White House, only time will tell. Either way, Martin will be ready for his moment in the spotlight and his chance to shine.

Kirk Cousins puts in the time to have the time of his life

JUNE 18, 2011 • SATURDAY

LOOKS A LITTLE BIT LIKE...

IT'S ONE OF THE THINGS coaches hate – understandably so.

But it's something the media often asks and fans always wonder.

"Who does Willie B. Goode play like?" is the way it's often phrased with prospects.

And "Which former player is most like Kerry DeLode?" goes the question with current athletes.

We need to rank and compare players and teams to put their performances in perspective.

We can't just say, "He's good."

We have to know, "How good?"

And eventually, "As good as ... ?"

The best way to do that is to have a frame of reference – at Michigan State and every other school in the country.

So let's compare some 2011 Spartans to past stars in the program and, in many cases, in pro football.

No one is saying the current players have accomplished as much as their Green and White predecessors in three or four seasons.

In many cases, they will. In some, they won't.

The idea is to look at size, skills and intangibles and project what their careers might be.

So take a trip to fantasyland and see if you see the similarities:

KIRK COUSINS (8) **vs. JIM MILLER** (16)

Miller was more heralded than Cousins when he arrived on campus. But both had to wait their turn, then win the job over higher-profile competition – Miller over Bret Johnson and Mill Coleman, Cousins over Nick Foles.

Both have been high-percentage passers and reluctant runners. And both have been outgoing, outspoken leaders – to the point some members of the media have rolled their eyes at never-ending optimism.

Miller appeared in 37 NFL games over 11 seasons, started for the Bears through a 13-3 regular season and earned a Super Bowl ring as a backup with the Patriots. Cousins is projected as a second-round draft pick and should have a great chance to start eventually.

Today, Miller is an NFL analyst for Sirius radio and the Spartan Radio Network. Cousins is destined for a career in television and can match Miller word-for-word, not to mention throw-for-throw.

EDWIN BAKER (4) **vs. BLAKE EZOR** (26)

When George Perles preached, "Pound, Green, Pound," no one other than Lorenzo White pounded the rock more often than Ezor. "Rock" Baker doesn't carry it as often but, pound for pound, is just as tough.

Ezor was even faster than Baker, who's plenty fast enough. But Baker is thicker and a bit shiftier. Neither player has ever enjoyed falling backward, as several stunned linebackers can attest.

The other similarity is their confidence. Ezor was a banty rooster who thought he could run through a wall – brick or concrete. He scored six TDs in a rout of Northwestern and four more in a bowl win over Hawaii. Baker has set a goal of 2,000 rushing yards this season.

B.J. CUNNINGHAM (3) **vs. MUHSIN MUHAMMAD** (1)

Both came in under the radar in terms of national profile. But everyone knew Muhammad's name – his last one anyway – by the time he left. And Cunningham should become MSU's career leader in receptions by mid-September.

Muhammad was as physical as any wide receiver since Kirk Gibson and made more than his share of acrobatic catches. Cunningham also has size on his side and can make all the leaping, juggling grabs you need.

Like Muhammad, Cunningham had his brush with the law. And like "Moose", Cunningham has learned from that experience. If he becomes half the man Muhammad did, some NFL community, not just a franchise, will be very fortunate.

Muhammad ranks 16th in NFL history with 860 regular-season catches, not counting Super Bowl TDs with the Panthers and Bears. And don't be shocked if Cunningham is one of the big surprises in the 2012 draft.

BRIAN LINTHICUM (88) vs. MARK BRAMMER (91)

Neither has a reputation as a big, bruising blocker. Brammer was a complete tight end and drove secondaries nuts as a primary target, especially when teams were preoccupied with Gibson. Linthicum also has Velcro hands and can catch any ball, including onside kicks.

The big difference is that Brammer started his first game on campus in 1976. Linthicum took a circuitous route to East Lansing. And the transfer from Clemson still has to share the position and get on a waiting list for catches.

Brammer played five seasons with the Bills. Linthicum has the tools to last at least that long if he continues to develop as a fifth-year senior.

KESHAWN MARTIN (82)
vs. DERRICK MASON (80)

Mason was one of the best all-purpose players in MSU history. When healthy, Martin has similar game-breaking skills as a wide receiver, kick returner and threat on reverses.

Remember Mason's punt return for a score against Michigan in 1995? Martin's game-changing runback vs. Wisconsin last year was just as big. But Martin, a converted quarterback, still has to become the kind of receiver who can scald a young Charles Woodson, as Mason did.

Mason holds the NFL season record for all-purpose yards with 2,659. With 924 catches, he's 12th on the all-time receptions list and has a chance to crack the top 10 this season. Martin is long way from Canton. First, let's see him excel in Indianapolis. But he can.

MAX BULLOUGH (40) vs. JIM MORRISSEY (40)

The number is the same. So is the game. When Morrissey was an excellent middle linebacker in the early 1980s, he teamed with Bullough's father, Shane, to stop Chuck Long's deciding two-point try in Iowa City.

Morrissey was tall, instinctive and rangy. Bullough appears to be all those things and should be much more physical. If he leads the same way Morrissey did when MSU reached a bowl game for the first time in 19 seasons, look out.

A 10-year pro and a "Super Bowl Shuffle" Pip as a backup backer with the Bears, Morrissey was the last player to wear No. 51 for Chicago. But Max is the one who can pad his family's tackles lead over the Butkuses.

WILLIAM GHOLSTON (2) vs. BUBBA SMITH (95)

A lot of these comparisons require a leap of faith. Again, this doesn't mean Gholston is as good as a College Football Hall of Famer and MSU's No. 2 Big Ten Icon. It suggests where there's a Will, where's a way.

"Kill, Bubba, Kill!" was more than a catchy chant in the mid-'60s. It was a legitimate concern for the parents of quarterbacks and halfbacks. Even at 6-foot-7 and filling out in all the right places, Gholston won't be as intimidating as Smith, the No. 1 pick in the '67 NFL Draft.

But Gholston insists he can dunk on a 12-foot basket and could be the toughest Spartan to throw over in 45 years. If he uses his amazing gifts to reach a potential he hasn't touched, he'll have a longer pro career than Smith did.

A lot of obvious players have yet to be paired. I decided to stick to those who've enrolled. But if you want to compare Taiwan Jones' video to Carl Banks or Julian Peterson, have at it.

Let your imagination go like a hungry Greg Jones on a blitz.

And let the debates begin.

JULY 30, 2011 • SATURDAY

QUITE THE EXPERIENCE

IT'S BEING HEARD all across the country, not just in Washtenaw County. And that's a good thing, as annoying as the comments can be.

Until Paul Bunyan began paying property tax in East Lansing, as announcer Sean McDonough joked, a lot of people nationally thought Michigan State wore winged helmets, too. It did – before Michigan did and as recently as 65 years ago.

Today, most casual fans know the difference between the state of Michigan's bitter rivals. You know, the ones with dueling countdown clocks? And they care enough to ask two questions:

"Will MSU ever win a big game/bowl game?"

"And was last year's Big Ten title a fluke?"

The answers: "Yes" and "No," respectively.

If the visiting Spartans could beat top-ranked Ohio State in 1998, when Mark Dantonio was an aide to Nick Saban, there's no reason to dread a trip to play the suspension-riddled Buckeyes on October 1.

If MSU can win a record six straight times at Notre Dame, as it did from 1997-2007, there's no reason it can't start a new string in the shadow of "Touchdown Jesus" with a victory in 2011 – a tossup game.

And if Dantonio's players can win three in a row over Michigan, including a pair in Ann Arrogance, there's no reason they can't do well at Nebraska, 1-3 in its last four games, or at Iowa, where last year's 30-0 halftime deficit won't carry over in the rematch.

Does that mean the Spartans will win all four of those difficult road games – five if you count a regular-season finale at Northwestern, a team that thinks it should've won the matchup last year?

No. But it means they can win any of those games. If they can win any of them, there's a chance they can

Chris Norman, Darqueze Denard and Trenton Robinson sandwich Michigan's Roy Roundtree

HEART OF A SPARTAN

win most of them. And if they can win most of them, there's a shot to win ...

Let's not get ahead of ourselves. Cautious optimism is still the best road to happiness. I said MSU would be 9-3 heading into a school-record fifth straight bowl appearance, and I'm not ready to change that prediction. But the Spartans can do better the same way they can do worse – by fooling us on the field.

Yes, this schedule is the toughest a Dantonio team has faced or will face in the foreseeable future. A better team than last season's 11-win squad may not be able to match that record. I also wouldn't be shocked if MSU played 14 games for the first time – one the first Saturday in December and one the first Monday in January.

Why now? Why when the offensive line lost three of five starters plus its tight end, when the defense lost two leaders at linebacker and two all-league types in the secondary and when the special teams lost the best combination punter-holder-passer the program has known?

Because the Spartans have the perfect blend of experience – the knowledge they can go where no group has gone before, something the 2010 team did, and the awareness they have to get better, lots better than in a couple of epic failures – to realize their dreams.

The beauty is, they can. Dantonio's players have everything they need to qualify for and actually win the first Big Ten Championship Game. They can become Legends AND Leaders. They'll also have no one to blame but themselves if they're out of the running by Halloween.

Fifth-year quarterback Kirk Cousins and fourth-year free safety Trenton Robinson have been around long enough to know that. Along with third-year running back Edwin Baker, they represented MSU extremely well at the Big Ten Kickoff Meetings in Chicago.

Cousins' speech at the Kickoff Luncheon, on behalf of all the assembled players from the conference, drew a standing ovation of nearly a minute – almost as long as the longest gap between Brady Hoke's chants of "We're Michigan!"

If you haven't seen Cousins' talk in its entirety, take

7:54 and watch it now. It'll make you feel great. And it'll make you feel privileged to have a future governor or senator under center for one more season:

There's something special about senior quarterbacks in East Lansing. That has been true since the Spartans played their first Big Ten game 58 years ago. In their final collegiate seasons:

- Tom Yewcic took the 1953 team to an 9-1 finish, capped by a Rose Bowl win over UCLA in the program's first opportunity.

- Coming off a 3-6 season, Earl Morrall led MSU to another 9-1 mark in 1955, including a second win over the Bruins in Pasadena.

- Jim Ninowski helped the Spartans to be 8-1 in 1957 and the College All-Stars to beat the NFL Champion Detroit Lions the next summer.

- In 1959, Dean Look switched from halfback to quarterback, was an All-American and placed sixth in the Heisman Trophy voting.

- Six years later, Steve Juday handled the snaps for a 10-1 MSU team that owned the Big Ten and shared the national title.

- Charlie Baggett was in charge when the ground-bound Spartans went 7-4 in '75, including their first win in South Bend in 10 years.

- In his fifth season, heady Eddie Smith steered a probation-slapped team to an 8-3 finish and a share of the Big Ten title in 1978.

- Eight years later when Lorenzo White was injured, Dave Yarema hit 202 of 297 passes for 2,581 yards, smashing Smith's marks.

- Dan Enos directed an 8-3-1 team in 1990, earned a Big Ten ring and became the only MSU quarterback to start two bowl wins.

- Three years later, Jim Miller completed a then-school-record 215 passes in the Spartans' lone bowl season from 1991-94.

- Coming off a year with forfeits and firings, Tony Banks stunned Michigan and took Saban's first team to a bowl game in 1995.

- It was Bill Burke's turn in 1999, Saban's farewell. After sitting home the year before, 10-2 MSU beat ND, U-M, OSU, PSU and Florida.

- Overcoming substance abuse, Jeff Smoker broke school records for completions, air yards and TD passes en route to a bowl in 2003.

- And Brian Hoyer helped the Spartans go 9-4 in 2008, the first time in 43 years that they'd beaten the Irish, the Wolverines and Purdue.

Combined, those 14 seasons with senior quarterbacks produced a record of 109-45-2, five Big Ten titles and five Top 10 finishes in the polls.

When you consider that MSU was a sub-mediocre 238-239-9 over 43 seasons from 1967-2009, you can see what a senior quarterback has meant. And the program has never had a better leader than Cousins, soon to be named its first three-year captain in 63 years.

Speaking of leaders, Dantonio is about to enter year five as the Spartans' head coach, a modest milestone that only eight of his 25 predecessors reached.

If he's here for the start of the 2012 season, as everyone expects, he'll trail just Duffy Daugherty (19 seasons), Charlie Bachman (13), George Perles (12), Chester Brewer (8) and Biggie Munn (7) for longevity.

Fifth years have been as good to MSU coaches as they have been to quarterbacks. Bachman's team reached the Orange Bowl. Munn's and Perles' teams won Rose Bowls. And Saban's team was just the second in school history with double-digit wins, with help from Bobby Williams and a staff that stayed and won the Florida Citrus Bowl.

Winning a bowl of any kind would be a breakthrough these days. Can that happen? Absolutely. Even if a postseason losing streak is two games longer than the habit of hoisting Paul Bunyan again.

AUGUST 3, 2011 • WEDNESDAY

LARGER THAN LIFE

HE WAS A GAME CHANGER, a program changer and a position changer.

He was Charles in charge.

And he left Michigan State University a much better place for having been there.

Charles Aaron "Bubba" Smith died Wednesday at his home in Los Angeles at age 66.

No one who saw him play college football will forget a then-mammoth 6-foot-7, 280-pound defensive end – and occasional nose tackle.

No one who saw Smith smile on campus or in commercials can quite appreciate the frightening chants of "Kill, Bubba, Kill" in the mid-'60s.

And no one who heard him speak through tears about a Texas-to-Michigan migration can doubt how much East Lansing meant to him.

He was big enough to have three nicknames: "Bubba," "The Beaumont Tower" and "The Ambulance." Why the last two? Because the Beaumont, Texas, native drove a lot of quarterbacks to the hospital.

No. 95 was big enough to be one of just three Spartan players to have his number retired, joining tackle Don Coleman (78) and roverback George Webster (90), his partner in crunch.

And Smith was big enough to be one of only two MSU athletes to rank among the Big Ten Network's top 50 Big Ten Icons – No. 26 on the list last fall, 24 spots behind Magic Johnson.

Long before that honor, the two-time consensus All-American had been seared into our consciousness as one of the best of the best. He was inducted into the College Football Hall of Fame in 1988 and was a charter member of the MSU Athletics Hall of Fame in 1992.

He was No. 6 and No. 8 on two lists of the Top 10 Greatest Defensive Players of All-Time, according to collegefootballnews.com. And his memory will be preserved this fall with the Big Ten's first Smith-Brown Defensive Lineman of the Year Award, an honor he shares with Penn State end Courtney Brown.

If MSU defensive tackle Jerel Worthy isn't able to win any other award this season, he ought to make sure he's worthy of that one. It belongs in a case in the Skandalaris Center – a few feet away from the Paul Bunyan Trophy and new Big Ten Championship hardware.

Worthy doesn't remember Smith. How could he? They never met.

I remember him very well. How could I not?

I remember the first time I heard much about him. A disappointing 4-5 program in 1964 began the following season with a 13-3 win over UCLA and a 23-0 triumph

It was "Thrill, Bubba, Thrill" one last time at Spartan Stadium

at Penn State. The best was yet to come.

The '65 Spartans can make a case for being as good as any defense in college football history. In separate interviews, Hall of Famers Joe Paterno, Bump Elliott and Ara Parseghian have told me they'd testify to that fact.

Duffy Daugherty's greatest team held seven opponents to seven points or less – including Michigan, Ohio State and Notre Dame – and never allowed more than 14 in any of its 11 games. The average yield? Try 6.2 points.

MSU's only close call in a 10-0 regular season was a 14-10 win over sixth-ranked Purdue and quarterback Bob Griese in West Lafayette.

But what really separated Hank Bullough's defense was its demolition of rushing attacks. In an era where few schools could pass, it held the defending Rose Bowl champion Wolverines to -51 rushing yards, Woody Hayes' ground-bound Buckeyes to -22 and the fourth-ranked Fighting Irish to -12 – a three-team total of -85.

That 12-3 win in South Bend on November 12 came after a fan assault on the Spartan Marching Band and a subsequent de-hinging of the door to the visitors' locker room. It also wrapped up at least a share of the national title, since the final UPI poll was taken before the bowls in those days.

Even in a bizarre 14-12 loss to UCLA in the Rose Bowl, the MSU defense was amazing. The Bruins rushed 41 times for just 65 yards, 139 less than the Spartans managed. But three interceptions and a fumbled punt at the 6-yard line fueled a humongous upset.

I remember watching that game in total disbelief. But I remember my first trip from Detroit to East Lansing the following spring even clearer.

I'd gone to lots of U-M games as a kid but didn't get to MSU until a ninth-grade trip to the state capital included a stop on campus. There, I wandered into the basement of the Union and heard the crashing of pool balls. As I blindly turned the corner, I ran smack into Smith's lower extremities.

He stood up – and up and up some more. If he'd asked me my name, I wouldn't have remembered. Suddenly, he smiled. I was never so happy to see a jolly green giant with a pool cue about the size of a pencil.

From that day on, I followed the Spartans and eventually chose MSU over Northwestern as my school-of-choice in 1969. By that point, Smith had helped one of the best senior classes the NCAA has known earn a slice of another national title.

Actually, he may have been a bit too good – or so Daugherty always believed. Smith's first-quarter crush of ND quarterback Terry Hanratty knocked the sophomore All-American out of the '66 "Game of the Century" and changed momentum completely.

The Spartans had Hanratty scouted perfectly and believed they could blank the Irish. In fact, they did lead 10-0 until backup QB Coley O'Brien took over and led his team to a TD and a tying field goal.

On the game's final series, Parseghian wisely chose not to pass, protecting the ball and the slimmest of No. 1 rankings. But with Smith lined up directly over a backup center, you can imagine the verbiage when the visitors stopped trying to score and "Tied One for The Gipper."

At 9-0-1, MSU couldn't return to Pasadena or play in any bowl due to the Big Ten's no-repeat rule. But in early 1967, it contributed an unprecedented half of the first eight selections in the first combined AFL-NFL Draft.

Smith's dominance was duly rewarded when the Baltimore Colts made him the No. 1 overall choice. Minnesota took halfback Clinton Jones No. 2 and split end Gene Washington No. 8, while Houston gladly grabbed Webster with the No. 5 pick.

Smith spent nine years in the NFL – five with Baltimore, two with Oakland and two with Houston. After being stunned by Joe Namath and the New York Jets in Super Bowl III, a game he always suspected had been thrown, he earned a championship ring in Super Bowl V when the Colts edged Dallas.

Individually, Smith was off to a great start with back-to-back Pro Bowl appearances in 1970-71. But while with the Raiders, he suffered a horrific knee injury when he nearly impaled himself on a down marker. His career and, in many ways, his life was never quite the same.

Bubba Smith prepares to crush Notre Dame's Terry Hanratty in 1966

Making the best of a bad situation, Smith took up acting and seemed to be a natural. It's hard to say which made him more famous, his Miller Lite commercial for "the easy-opening can" or his role as Moses Hightower in all the "Police Academy" films.

I remember seeing him in L.A. in late December 1987. MSU was making its first appearance at the Rose Bowl in 22 years. And Smith couldn't have been prouder at the annual Big Ten Club of Southern California Dinner, hosted by Bob Hope.

I remember talking my bosses into sending me to New York City the following year when Smith was inducted into the College Football Hall. He must've thanked me three times for coming and gave me bear hugs and handshakes. All I wanted was my right hand back.

There, we talked for close to two hours as former teammates like opposite end and close friend Robert Viney stopped by. Smith was bitter at the way he felt his younger brother, Tody, had been treated at MSU – though not as hurt as he would be 20 years later over a rejection by then-Spartan head coach John L. Smith.

He had an up-and-down relationship with Daugherty, who never seemed to understand the tickets that gravitated to a hard-to-hide Buick Electra. And in a test of wills, Smith and the other defensive stars inserted themselves back into a game to save a shutout after Daugherty had pulled them.

But there were more laughs that night in Manhattan than in all his commercial and comedy roles combined. Equally impressive was his undying love for Bullough, the only college or pro coach he respected without question in their days at MSU and in Baltimore.

Then, as was true until the moment he died, Smith was proud of what his university represented. He spoke of the racial barriers that were obliterated in Mid-Michigan, as opposed to life in East Texas. And he loved to wear his green-and-white gear in Hollywood when he was active in acting.

We saw that love again in 2006 when Smith came back to campus one last time for his number retirement and the 40th anniversary of the 10-10 tie. If he could've suited up one more time, he would have.

Perhaps that's why one of his last objectives on earth was to try to set up a scholarship in his name in East Lansing. Marcia Livingston, a nurse and a 45-year friend of Smith's from his campus days, had just returned to Michigan from California the day before the end came.

Pending an autopsy, the initial reports are that Smith died of natural causes. He had just found the Lord, according to devout Christian and longtime MSU football friend Fred Tinning, and had received daily scriptures. Of all the places Smith could pass away, sitting in his chair and reading the Bible, then dying instantly has to rank high.

Maybe he was just ready to go home – and that doesn't mean Beaumont. Smith had just had back surgery. And he needed a new knee very badly. The last time I spoke with him on the phone, he told me how much pain he was in and how he could barely get around.

Tinning had just made a request to the MSU football staff that they get a football signed and send it to L.A. to help lift his spirits. I don't believe that ever happened. But as Smith would know, defensive linemen aren't handed the ball. They have to go get it.

He's headed where his father, Willie Ray, is probably about ready to start practice and where Tody loves and respects his coach. Best of all, he'll be back in a huddle with a lot of departed Spartan stars from a defense that went 19-1-1 in two seasons.

Middle guard Harold Lucas went first. Then, defensive back Jess Phillips, linebacker Charlie "Mad Dog" Thornhill, Webster and cornerback/captain Don Japinga all joined him. Maybe Daugherty needed a little more pass rush.

If you believe in omens, it could serve MSU well this season. The last time the Spartans went to Pasadena, Daugherty died that September, the day before the Florida State game. George Perles has always believed that had something to do with USC's last fumble.

Either way, Daugherty is slowly getting all his old players back.

Let's hope they play their home games in heaven. With Smith in the lineup, they'll still be a helluva team.

AUGUST 13, 2011 • SATURDAY

THREE IS A MAGIC NUMBER

WHEN ESPN3 adapted an old Schoolhouse Rock! song for its promos, it wasn't thinking about Edwin "Rock" Baker or Michigan State football.

But it could've been. "Three is a Magic Number" this season – and not just because Dan Conroy was 14-for-15 in three-point tries as a sophomore.

Three things need to take place for the Spartans to take their place as back-to-back Big Ten champions, something that hasn't happened since 1965-66 and never occurred before that:

ONE • Mark Dantonio's fifth MSU team needs great play or a fair amount of good fortune.

After playing games 1-7 and 10-11 in the state of Michigan in 2010, the Spartans will face five tough or tricky road tests: Notre Dame, Ohio State, Nebraska, Iowa and Northwestern. Each of those teams believes it can beat MSU.

Likewise, the Spartans will have to win some big road games – bigger challenges than their two most impressive W's outside Ingham County last year, a 34-17 thumping of Michigan and a 28-22 title-clincher at Penn State.

And they need to win the majority of their close games, just as they did last season. In an 11-2 breakthrough, a team that majored in resiliency trailed in the second quarter in eight games and in the fourth quarter five times.

To do that again, MSU must stay reasonably healthy, especially at a few key positions. Yes, there's way more depth than the program has seen in some of its players' fathers' lifetimes. But if the Big 11 – the Spartans' 11 most essential players – stay in uniform, maybe this won't be the season when an improved team has a worse record, as almost everyone expects

TWO • MSU's stars have to shine like Alpha Centauri on a clear night.

That means big-time players have to make big-time plays to repeat as Big Ten titlists. The Spartans have as many of those performers as any team in the conference, perhaps even more than we realize.

MSU placed five players on ESPN.com's preseason All-Big Ten team – the same number as Wisconsin and more than 10 other programs: Baker at running back, Joel Foreman at guard, Jerel Worthy at defensive tackle, Trenton Robinson at safety and Keshawn Martin as the punt returner.

Baker, Foreman and Robinson were also on the CBSSports.com list this week. Martin almost assuredly would've been if a return specialist had been named. And though Worthy didn't quite crack the lineup, quarterback Kirk Cousins did, beating out Michigan's Denard Robinson, Northwestern's Dan Persa, Nebraska's Taylor Martinez and Wisconsin's Russell Wilson.

If Cousins is the first-team All-Big Ten choice at the end of the regular season, not just the beginning of it, the Spartans will be playing in Indianapolis and will have a great shot to get to Pasadena.

THREE • Five more players should say, "Hey, what about us?" And the only sane answer is, "You're really good, too."

Some are largely unknown. Some are known but unproven. And others are just unsung. They've already made sizeable contributions on the field, including one senior I'd take over any current Big Ten player at his position.

Let's start that role call with cornerback Johnny Adams, a fourth-year junior with the potential to be

B.J. Cunningham makes a tough grab look easy at Northwestern

one of the best pass defenders in the conference.

At 5-foot-11, 175 pounds, Adams doesn't strike fear into enemy receivers. Actually, that can be a good thing for MSU's defense. He's as quick as any corner in the league, stronger than he appears and better than opponents remember.

He has gotten beat at times. Who hasn't? But long passes against Michigan, Northwestern and Purdue weren't entirely his fault. Plus, Adams has the big-play ability to save or turn a game at any moment.

With MSU struggling in the first half against Notre Dame, Adams came off his receiver and made a leaping interception to keep the game within reach. Three weeks later, his goal-line interception in Ann Arbor kept the Wolverines at bay.

The best news about Adams is his steady improvement. We saw that last spring, when he showed he had the makings of a shutdown corner – except when mugging Draymond Green. If No. 5 wins the first Tatum-Woodson Award as the league's best DB, in honor of OSU's Jack Tatum and Purdue's Rod Woodson, don't be surprised.

No. 4 on our list of underrated players is fourth-year junior Chris McDonald, who started 12 of 13 games at right guard last season. That McDonald is fully capable of moving out to right tackle shows his strength and versatility.

Though Foreman will get all the hype up front, and justifiably so, McDonald isn't far behind him. Now 6-5 and 300 well-packed pounds, he looked different at Media Day. You should expect him to help give the Spartans the best guard tandem in the conference.

Don't worry, Alabama isn't on the schedule this season. And in the unlikely event it shows up there in January, Tide destroyer Marcell Dareus won't be in uniform. The Buffalo Bills choice with the No. 3 overall draft selection has other things to do than sit and study his sacks against MSU.

No. 3 among the Spartans who'll surprise you is sophomore middle linebacker Max Bullough, who has fended off a challenge from teammate TyQuan Hammock. He also has light years to go to make fans forget Greg Jones or stop waiting for freshman Lawrence Thomas to be handed the position.

At 6-3, 245, Bullough has size, speed, range and incredible instincts. He also has exceptional bloodlines over three generations, representing the first family of MSU football. And if he were ever needed at tight end, which he won't be this year, Bullough could do the job there, too.

It's probably appropriate he wears No. 40. He most resembles a bigger Jim Morrissey, the Spartan-turned-Bear and the player Bullough's dad, Shane, backed up in 1983-84. Morrissey was the program's last solo captain in George Perles' second season. Look for Bullough to share that honor in 2013.

No. 2 on the list of MSU's unknown players around the conference and unproven contributors locally is true sophomore defensive end William Gholston, a 6-7 bookend for often-ignored junior Tyler Hoover.

It was Hoover who came up with a strip and recovery near the goal line that kept the Spartans in the game at Northwestern. And a healthy Gholston will give Big Ten offensive coordinators a lot of sleepless nights, as they try to come up with new ways to block him.

No. 2 had two-and-a-half sacks Saturday in his team's first jersey scrimmage. At 6-7, 280-plus, he'll have opponents thinking there are two of him in the lineup all season. Enjoy him while you can in East Lansing. Everything Gholston does screams NFL.

And No. 1 on this list is No. 2 among active Big Ten receivers, No. 3 for a few more weeks on MSU's career catch list and one of the top six all-time Spartan pass catchers with Andre Rison, Charles Rogers, Kirk Gibson, Gene Washington and Plaxico Burress.

Very few people understand how good B.J. Cunningham has been or how good he'll be over the next few seasons. At 6-2, 215, the fifth-year senior plays a similar game to Muhsin Muhammad, No. 16 in pro football history with 860 receptions.

Cunningham has a highlight tape the pros will love, incredible touch from playing trick-catch games with Mark Dell in their apartment and more speed than people expect. Without his fourth-quarter touchdown grabs, MSU would've had three more losses last year.

This season, look for Cunningham to lead a deep receiving corps and leave some opponents at a loss for words. We'll leave you with five to help you remember him.

3 is a magic number.

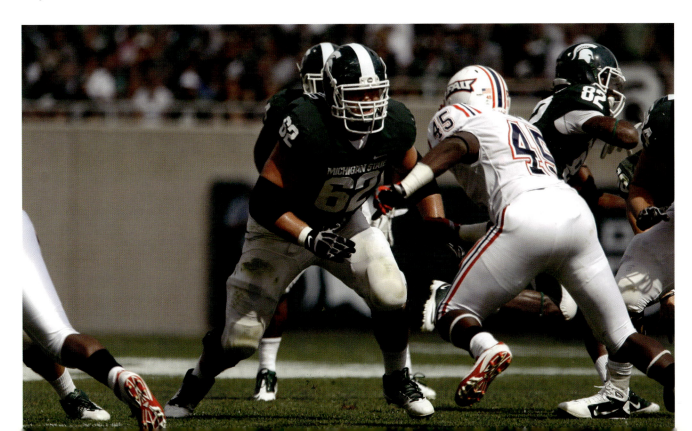

Right guard Chris McDonald picks up the pass rush

QUITE THE CATCH

B.J. CUNNINGHAM REELS THEM IN

HE COULD BE the least-known truly great player in Michigan State football history. Only his family, a few close friends and rabid fans can tell you his real first name.

But in four incredibly productive seasons, not counting a redshirt year, B.J. Cunningham – short for Bryan Junior – shattered school records for career catches and receiving yards. He made countless key plays and tough grabs in big games. And his teammates voted him their MVP for 2011 – no small feat when a group is 11-3 and the Big Ten Legends Division and Outback Bowl champions.

The Westerville, Ohio, native caught 218 balls for the Spartans, 70 more than second-place Matt Trannon and the seventh-highest total in Big Ten history. He also gained 3,086 yards through the air, 94 more than MSU legend Andre Rison for ninth-best in league annals.

Somehow, Cunningham never earned first-team All-Big Ten honors from the coaches or the media, even when he had a school-record-tying 79 catches for 1,306 yards and 12 touchdowns as a senior, as many scores as any receiver in the conference.

A lot of prima donna wideouts would've grumbled and groused about a lack of respect. All Cunningham did was keep working and winning. The more you watched him, the more you loved him.

The problem was that a lot of people didn't watch him closely enough.

Not as a three-star recruit at Westerville South High, less than 15 miles from Ohio Stadium.

Not when he was his state's MVP in the Big 33 Football Classic between Ohio and Pennsylvania.

Not in 37 wins as a Spartan or 49 games when he caught at least one pass.

And not as an undervalued pro prospect at 6-foot-1 3/8, 211 pounds – a possible steal as a sixth-round pick of the Miami Dolphins.

"I just want to show people what I can do," Cunningham said prior to the NFL Draft. "I've been working hard to improve my speed and vertical push. I know I can catch the ball and block downfield. I think I've shown that."

He proved it to quarterback Kirk Cousins right away. The most prolific pass-catch combo to play in East Lansing spent 2007 on the scout team in the first year of the Mark Dantonio era.

"I always knew what B.J. could do," Cousins said three years later. "He had talent back then. And he has never stopped getting better. He has made some amazing catches for us. As a quarterback, he makes my job easier."

As a redshirt freshman in 2008, Cunningham started 12 times and had 41 receptions, two behind team leader Blair White. He had five catches in his MSU debut at California, an acrobatic snare for 41 yards vs. Eastern Michigan and a key first-down grab to set up the tying score in the third quarter at Michigan.

But his best game as a rookie was a six-catch performance against Georgia in the Capital One Bowl, with five of those grabs resulting in first downs. It was a sign of things to come when Cousins took snaps in the second quarter. The Bulldogs should've paid closer attention.

As sophomores Cousins and Cunningham connected 48 times, including a 73-yard TD in the fourth quarter of a 40-37 win at Purdue. Two months earlier, Cunningham had seven catches at Notre Dame and followed with five in back-to-back games

B.J. Cunningham hangs on for the catch vs. Northern Colorado

HEART OF A **SPARTAN**

B.J. Cunningham and Mark Dell made a great combination

against Michigan and Wisconsin. But the season didn't end as well for him or his depleted team.

After being a spectator at the Rather Hall disturbance, Cunningham was part of a mass suspension that probably cost the Spartans a win over Texas Tech in the Alamo Bowl. But without those absences, Keith Nichol might not have switched from quarterback to receiver. And Cousins wouldn't have had to arrange secret throwing sessions with Cunningham and Mark Dell at an area church.

The chemistry they developed was off the charts. And before Cunningham was back on the roster, he and Cousins knew what could happen in 2010-11 if the pieces fell in place. After the next year's Green-and-White Game, a smiling Cunningham thanked everyone he knew, especially Dantonio, for a second chance.

His production increased to 50 catches and nine scores, including some of the biggest plays in the school's first 11-win season. Cunningham had seven grabs for 101 yards vs. Notre Dame, including a 24-yard tying TD in the fourth quarter after being pushed out of bounds. And he had eight for 113 yards at Northwestern, including the winner on a juggling reception with 2:00 left. To put it another way, without No. 3, "Little Giants" and "Mousetrap" would still be movie titles.

Heading into his senior season, Cunningham was 10 catches from becoming MSU's all-time leader. After tying Trannon with nine grabs for 130 yards against Youngstown State and passing the 150 mark with five against Florida Atlantic, he left no doubt with 12 receptions for 158 yards at Notre Dame.

Cunningham left the Buckeyes wondering, "Who was supposed to be recruiting Westerville?" In front of his own cheering section, he had nine catches for 152 yards. That included his team's only TD, a 33-yard snare in traffic, in the Spartans' first victory at OSU in 13 years.

Two weeks later, lost in all the "Rocket" replays, it was easy to forget that Cunningham kept MSU close to Wisconsin with six grabs for 102 yards. A 35-yard catch-and-run on a fourth-and-2 curl and a diving snare on a two-point play belonged on anyone's YouTube highlights, as did his postgame piggy-back ride.

After being bullied and blanked at Nebraska, just the second time he hadn't caught a pass for the Spartans, Cunningham answered his critics with three catches for 104 yards against Minnesota. Then, he began a sensational stretch with nine scores in the next four games by finding the end zone twice in a payback at Iowa.

He had six grabs for 132 yards and two TDs against Indiana, six for 120 and two tallies at Northwestern and five for 115 and three scores vs. the Badgers in the rematch in Indy – a 30-yard cross on fourth-and-inches to start the second quarter, a lateral-and-lunge after a catch by Nichol and a 44-yarder in the fourth quarter.

That effort earned Cunningham National Wide Receiver of the Week acclaim. But it wasn't enough to send MSU to Pasadena in his final opportunity. Still stunned nearly an hour after the game, he expressed his deep frustration. And if we didn't understand his commitment to winning, we learned it shortly after midnight.

"Man, we got here and really wanted to win," Cunningham said, answering questions that stung like salt on an open sore. "But I'm proud of this team for playing a hard-fought game to the very end ... It was a sick feeling. I was just trying to get to the locker room. I still feel that we're the best team in the Big Ten and deserve a BCS bowl bid."

Instead, the Spartans wound up at the Outback in Tampa. And without Cunningham's seven catches, they never would've beaten Georgia in three overtimes and won their first bowl in a decade.

Later that winter, after moving to Arizona to train, he ran a 4.59 40 and measured in with the smallest hands of any receiver at the NFL Combine. They didn't measure his heart or see why his hands were as soft and strong as any that MSU has had.

They couldn't tell that B.J. also stood for Brightest Jewel.

No one fires up the troops like strength coach Ken Mannie

AUGUST 20, 2011 • SATURDAY

KOOL-AID? JUST A HOT TEAM

THEY START THE SEASON ranked 17th in the Associated Press writers poll and the *USA Today* coaches poll. In fact, the Michigan State Spartans have been 17th in everything this month but the Iowa Straw Poll.

Yet, that rational rating hasn't registered with Vegas oddsmakers. The over-under win total for MSU has been set at just 7.5 games. For some strange reason, an improving program that won 11 times in 2010 is projected to plunge from champ to chump.

Far be it from us to encourage gambling on college football (choke, choke), but you may want to explore that possibility a bit further. So much for gold and Treasury notes ...

To win fewer than 7.5 games this season, Mark Dantonio's best team would have to lose all five road games (Notre Dame, Ohio State, Nebraska, Iowa and Northwestern) or stumble at least once in Spartan Stadium (probably against Michigan or Wisconsin).

For the record, last year's team won four games in white jerseys and was 7-0 in East Lansing. This year's squad is bigger, faster, deeper and smarter – "BFDS". And it doesn't have to Google "Big Ten champions" for a basic understanding of the concept.

So while casinos have been built with the billfolds of suckers like yours truly, 42 years of following Big Ten football on a daily basis say MSU is likely to win at least eight games. I'd bump its over-under number a full game to 8.5. And I'd be sorely tempted to bet the over.

Since the day the Spartans went splat like a bug on Alabama's windshield, the prediction here has been a 9-3 mark for the 2011 regular season. A lot has changed since January 1, including hairlines and waistlines. That football forecast has never wavered.

For those who've watched MSU tease and disappoint for decades, the first impulse is to say, "They're supposed to be good this year ... That probably means they'll be 6-7."

It's easy to understand that skeptical outlook, even among diehards. It's called operant conditioning. The Spartans couldn't be a better example if they were coached by B.F. Skinner this season.

Likewise, it's predictable that some would get giddy at the prospect of back-to-back years with double-digit wins, something that has never happened at MSU. It hasn't happened for the Detroit Lions, either, even with 16-game schedules. . . . I know, misery loves company.

But there's legitimate cause for optimism for both teams – the Spartans and the Liedowns. That's what a four- or a five-win improvement does for a dormant program and its long-tortured fan base.

After the winningest season in school history, you don't have to be chugging lemon-lime Kool-Aid to forecast nine MSU victories this season. And you don't need a sobriety test if you dare to predict a 10th triumph.

In Mid-Michigan, "BFDS" finally represents size, speed, stability and experience. It's the maturation of a program, as Big Ten Network analysts Gerry DiNardo and Howard Griffith saw during Friday's tour stop for a half-hour preview that will air Tuesday evening.

Bigger? It doesn't take a scale to see that the Spartans are better put together this year. A lot of that credit goes to strength and conditioning coach Ken Mannie, now in his 17th season. He came to MSU with Nick Saban in December 1994. And there's a reason Saban tried to hire him at LSU and Alabama for boatloads of money.

There's "bad big" and "good big" in college football.

It all starts with practice, as Mark Dantonio tells the media

We see that all the time in Dantonio's program, often with the same player two years apart. If a recruit arrives at 6-5, 300, he'll be torn down, then built back up till he's ready to compete at a Big Ten level.

Faster? The Spartans have always had a few fast players. Today, they have a quicker team. Their tight ends aren't lightweight tackles. Their Sam linebackers can also play Star. And they have a 237-pound running back who can gain 75 yards on one carry, not after 25 of them. Dion Sims, Chris Norman and Le'Veon Bell, take a bow.

Deeper? Nothing shows the difference between Dantonio's program and some others we've seen than a glance at the depth chart. MSU's second team is better than it has been in 45 years. For the first time since before George Perles arrived as an assistant in 1967, the Spartans aren't four injuries away from being a losing team.

Smarter? It helps to have seen and felt how football should be played in January. Thanks for the growing pains, Bama. And with a fifth-year senior quarterback who could go down as one of the three best in school history, MSU should be able to handle any surprises.

What does it all mean in late August? Not enough to make hotel reservations in Indianapolis, let alone Pasadena. That's all up to the players and coaches.

As leaderback Kirk Cousins suggested in a speech you'll soon see on ESPN and read about in the New York Times, one of the biggest barriers to success is a false sense of privilege and entitlement.

"From everyone who has been given much, much will be demanded; and from the one who has been entrusted with much, much more will be asked," the passer with all the passages quoted from Luke 12:48.

If that reads like a solution for a recent political stalemate in this country, it certainly could be. But it's just as true as a mandate for athletic excellence. Or as the great philosopher Linus van Pelt said, "There's no heavier burden than a great potential."

Some people don't see it that way. Detroit Tigers manager Jim Leyland has said at least a dozen times, "I'll take talent (over chemistry) any day." And he couldn't be more wrong.

Of course, talent is a good thing. But it means nothing if it's wasted. Talent only matters when it leads to performance. And performance as a team usually requires skill, sweat and smarts.

This year's MSU football team has talent – maybe more than it has had in many of our lifetimes. It seems to have the necessary will, as we've seen since the first winter workout at 5:30 a.m. And it appears to have the scent of success and the scars it took to get that.

If, indeed, that's the case, the 7.5-win hurdle could be cleared by Halloween – certainly by mid-November. Nine wins in 2011 and a school-record 20 over a two-year span are definitely possible. So is a chance to go down in history as the first Legends Division champ and 12-team Big Ten titlist.

If ...

By now, everyone has an idea of how the season will play out. You do. I do. The Spartans do. And so does Vegas.

It isn't drinking anything – whiskey or Kool-Aid – to think MSU can do what is has done before. Beating Michigan four straight times and winning back-to-back conference titles would fall into that pile of overdue accomplishments.

But it's silly to assume that something will happen just because it can. Some people make things happen. Some watch things happen. And some wonder, "Huh? What happened?"

When I say 9-3 or better, I'm betting on more than talent. I'm betting Spartans Will. Vegas should've talked to Kirk Cousins.

SEPTEMBER 3, 2011 • SATURDAY

RAY OF HOPE

IT WON'T BE REMEMBERED for B.J. Cunningham's nine catches or Max Bullough's 15 tackles.

It won't go down in Spartan football history for its sloppy tackling and silly penalties.

Instead, a 28-6 win over Youngstown State Friday should be filed forever in the joy department.

It was the first time a simple, 7-yard pickup on a team's first snap was its Play of the Day.

But that's what happened when a fifth-year senior, fourth-year starter and first-year captain made the Call of the Year.

And when its No. 1 beneficiary – No. 73 in green – made us smile and cry at the same time.

Together, as always, Joel Foreman and Arthur Ray Jr. shared an unforgettable moment.

It was Foreman's inspiration to end his 22-game starting streak so Ray could have what he richly deserved.

It was Ray who continues to inspire us all by thinking he should beat cancer by three touchdowns.

At first glance, they couldn't be more different in terms of race, background and collegiate success.

That much is black and white.

Ray, a Chicago native, and Foreman, from Highland, Mich., and Milford High, are teammates, roommates and soulmates.

While Ray was battling for the use of his left leg, enduring tumor removal, three bone-graft surgeries and five other procedures, Foreman was blocking Wolverines, Hawkeyes and Nittany Lions.

The guy who was supposed to be a star had to learn how to stand again and to take his first steps. The player who was signed with zero fanfare became a fan, a friend and a force at left guard.

So it was only natural that Foreman made what seemed to be an unnatural choice by stepping aside

Captains Trenton Robinson, Joel Foreman and Kirk Cousins lead "The Walk"

HEART OF A SPARTAN

Everyone's hero, Arthur Ray (73), and Spartan brother Joel Foreman (67)

for a moment – ideally, the first of many.

No. 67 didn't lay his jersey on Mark Dantonio's desk in a scene out of "Rudy". Rather, he laid out a new definition of leadership.

Foreman stepped to the forefront and showed us a different way in an era of me-first – often second and third, too.

"Words can't describe what Arthur has done," Foreman said. "Not only has he been an inspiration to me, but he has inspired this entire team. It's the least I could do. I wish I could do more."

When Foreman watched Ray defy all odds and participate in 11 spring practices, he made up his mind that MSU would have a new left guard for at least one play.

"When I'd see him run the stairs every day this summer, I knew what I wanted to do," said MSU's first four-year starter on the offensive line in the last 17 seasons. "But it's not something I did. It's all Arthur."

Not quite. First, Foreman kept the idea to himself for four-and-a-half months. Then, last Tuesday, he told Dantonio how he wanted the season to begin.

"I said, 'It's your decision, Coach,'" Foreman explained. "He said, 'No, it's really our decision.'"

A delighted head coach could've said, "Let's wait and see." But Dantonio left it up to one of his first and best recruits.

"I said, 'It's your football team. What do you want to do?'" he said of a moment just as satisfying in its own way as "Little Giants." "I wanted to make sure our players understood it wasn't Mark Dantonio being a nice guy. It was Joel Foreman being selfless. And that's a big step when you have people like that on your football team who care about others."

Foreman cared enough to keep the secret from Ray, though his smile nearly gave it away.

And when the announcement was made to the entire team Friday afternoon during pregame, a standing ovation of love followed.

Whether the Spartans win four games or 14 this season, they sealed the deal that they're a football family.

If you don't think solidarity matters, if you don't believe the whole of championship teams is greater than the sum of their parts, you didn't watch MSU basketball soar in back-to-back postseasons, then splinter and sputter last winter.

That cohesion carries over to the fan base. And in this case, the significance wasn't lost on a crowd of 75,910, the largest for a season opener in Spartan Stadium since 1987 – another significant year.

As Ray lined up next to Foreman and swayed to "The Star Spangled Banner," tears streaming down his cheeks, he was every bit as emotional as you'd expect before his first real snaps in 56 months.

"Coach (Ken) Mannie grabbed me and said, 'You've got a game to play. Get composed!'" Ray remembered. "I thought, 'God is real.' If anyone is a walking miracle, you're looking at him."

His mother and sister in the stands didn't know what was coming. But they definitely knew where a fighter had been.

Three months after appearing in the Offense-Defense All-American Bowl in Fort Lauderdale and two months after signing his National Letter of Intent in February 2007, Ray began chemotherapy.

He didn't enroll at MSU until spring semester of 2008, then had to leave campus when his lower leg became infected.

Ray's spirit was infectious from Day 1.

"I was glad to be here, especially when we won the Big Ten Championship," he said. "But I kept thinking, 'How much longer am I going to have to wear these warm-ups?' Today, running out of the tunnel and seeing the student section go crazy, it was just the way I dreamed it."

Dreams do indeed come true when people believe and persevere. Ray did that and more with help from his faith, his family, a network of friends and a strong sense of self.

As he answered every question in the interview trailer, he made me think of so many other survivors – and of some whose memories will never fade.

I thought of Brian Bemis, who lost his leg to childhood cancer and became a golf pro and a teacher at Hawk Hollow.

And I thought of Brandon Gordon and James Stanley.

Gordon, one of the bravest youths Mid-Michigan has known, inspired the entire MSU hockey program in its National Championship season before passing in 2009.

Stanley, a junior at Holt High, missed three years of school with his ordeal. But he couldn't have been happier Friday night as a stat crew volunteer in the press box.

Ray was a brother to both boys and wore a wristband with their pictures to honor them Friday.

He also gave us the answer to an all-time trivia question: Aronde Stanton and Andrew Johnson.

If anyone asks, "Who did Ray block on his first play?" you might get a lunch or a beverage out of it.

When a false start would've been understandable, Ray flew out of his stance at the snap, hit Stanton (52) first, then spun back to bump Johnson (44) off his pursuit of Kirk Cousins.

And when Cousins hit Brian Linthicum with a completion, Ray's night was also complete – a grade of 100 percent, blocking two players on one play.

"This is just the beginning," he said. "Everyone else's expectations of Arthur Ray have never been mine. Coach (Mark) Staton is a great coach. And I want him to coach me fairly. I don't want to be given anything."

Ray has given his all and given his team a lift more often than he knows. When he gave Foreman a smile and a "Thanks" Friday, all paybacks were complete.

"I didn't come back to play one or two plays," Ray said. "I've got a taste of it now. And it want it all."

If that's not possible or not likely, you tell him.

As someone whose cancer disappeared in a comparative blink of an eye last December, I'm not about to doubt him.

Like virtually everyone who has met him, I'm too busy smiling.

ALWAYS
PROTECTING

JOEL FOREMAN LOOKS OUT FOR EVERYONE

HE WAS TOLD he wasn't big enough, good enough or strong enough to play in the Big Ten or the Mid-American Conference.

Joel Foreman didn't listen. And he certainly didn't forget.

"That's something that I put in the back of my head during my time at Michigan State," said a four-year starter at left guard. "I think one of the biggest motivators for people is being told you're not good enough to do something. I just used that as something to prove myself."

Foreman took the road less traveled to play for the Green and White. He didn't even play football until his freshman year of high school. His mom was afraid he'd get hurt. And he loved to play baseball. Looking at his 6-foot-4, 315-pound frame today, those reasons sound humorous.

But the team aspect and pure physicality of football couldn't keep Foreman off the field for long. The only problem he had was learning how to put his pads on straight.

Foreman's natural talent didn't go unnoticed, as he committed to play for Mark Dantonio at Cincinnati. When Dantonio became a Spartan, so did Foreman. It was his childhood dream to play at MSU. And a strange first recruiting trip with the previous staff didn't change his decision.

"I went there for junior day, and I don't think one person talked to me because I wasn't a big recruit," Foreman said with a laugh. "But I just told my dad, 'This is where I want to go.' I knew it right away. Luckily, Coach D honored that scholarship offer at Michigan State. And I committed before he could finish the sentence."

Everyone knew who Foreman was by the time he graduated. He left MSU tied with linebacker Eric Gordon for the most starts in school history (49). He holds the record for the most starts by an offensive lineman. And he was the first four-year starter on the offensive front since tackle Shane Hannah from 1991-94.

He also had a handful of wins over Western Michigan, Eastern Michigan, Central Michigan and Purdue, four universities that told him he couldn't play at the next level.

"Regardless of what you're doing, you face challenges and obstacles," Foreman said. "The world tells you you're not good enough to do anything. You really have to do it on your own. You have to be proactive and believe in yourself. If you don't, how can you expect anyone else to believe in you?"

Foreman was quick to point out that any adversity he faced was dust in the wind compared to what his teammate and close friend Arthur Ray Jr. went

Joel Foreman shows how to slow up two Purdue pass rushers

HEART OF A **SPARTAN**

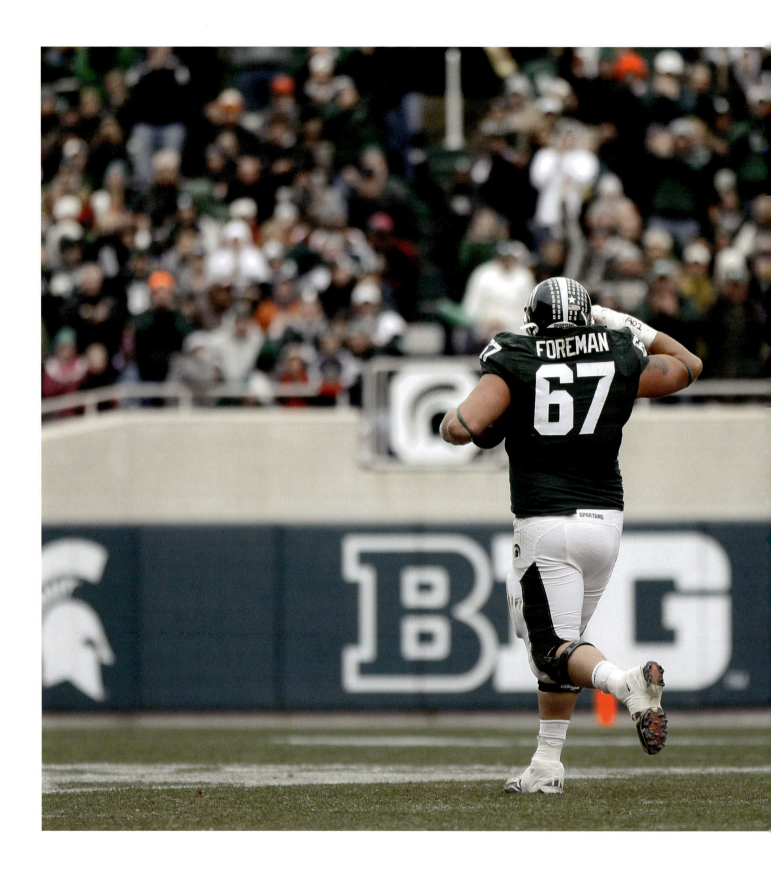

With a senior salute, Joel Foreman says goodbye to football

through. And he turned those words into actions.

Last summer, Ray Jr. participated in team workouts after years of bone cancer treatments. When they ran the stairs at Spartan Stadium, Ray Jr. was behind Foreman every step of the way. And every time they reached the top, huffing and puffing and dreaming of lying poolside, Ray Jr. would utter a few words that had an impact.

"He'd tell me, 'Everyone told me I couldn't do it, but I'm here doing it right now,'" Foreman explained. "That was unbelievable. You'd see the scar on his leg, then see him running up the stadium stairs. He was just loving to be running around again. It really makes you realize what's important."

Foreman knew what was important. He requested that Ray Jr. start in his place for the first game of the season against Youngstown State.

It wasn't a favor. It wasn't for attention. It was just the right thing to do.

"It meant a lot," Ray Jr. said. "Once I found out, I was so excited. And I appreciated it from him because he started a lot of games for us. I'm sure if he didn't start, he would've broken the starts record. For him to want me to have that opportunity to play that first snap, it meant a lot."

Records, minutes, stats, snaps – none of those numbers mattered to Foreman. He did what he thought was right and never gave it a second thought.

"The attitude he has while he's playing and now after he did it is just unbelievable," Foreman said. "I can't say more about the guy. I don't think it was something I did. I think it was something Arthur earned. It was the least I could do to give him the opportunity to do that. He's going to go down as one of the greatest Spartans to ever come through Michigan State in any sport, at any time."

Foreman has his brother-in-law, Dave, to thank for his selfless and positive attitude. Dave is one of Foreman's closest friends. And he almost lost his life in a motorcycle accident that left him without an arm and leg.

"We thought he was going to die. They thought he was going to die ... but he didn't," Foreman said. "He came back and by the end of the week was cracking jokes in the hospital. You wake up and your left arm and left leg are gone, how are you going to react to that? He chose to use it as a positive to help impact other people."

Foreman mirrors himself after those who inspire him, hoping to impact others by his strong character, not by any numbers on the stat sheet. His teammates obviously felt his influence was important, electing him as one of the team's three captains in 2011.

It was just another dream come true.

"I had always hoped to be able to do that by the time I left, and it's obviously something you can't campaign for," Foreman said. "To be thought of that way by your teammates is quite an honor. Like in any leadership position, not just when stuff is going right but when stuff is struggling, you have to be able to lead your team through it with a good attitude and think positively."

It's not hard for the country boy to be positive. Foreman played football at his dream university, spends his free time hunting and listening to country music, is surrounded by supportive friends and family and is engaged to his high school sweetheart.

Who couldn't be happy with that?

Foreman chose not to pursue a career in pro football, though he certainly would have deserved a look. And if he can't protect quarterbacks any more, his dream of being a police officer will allow him to provide safety on an entirely new level.

"That's something I have a passion for," Foreman said. "If I was doing that, I wouldn't be working, because I think it's the coolest job I could possibly have. It mirrors a lot of things about football. There's a huge team aspect, a brotherhood that goes into it, and it's just a very honorable job."

It's not surprising that Foreman chose a career as selfless as he is. From his home to the field to the streets, Foreman considers himself one of the luckiest people in the world. But there's no doubt that the world will be a better, and safer, place with the Spartans' No. 67 on patrol.

SEPTEMBER 10, 2011 • SATURDAY

ON SECOND THOUGHT...

ONE WEEK AGO, the Michigan State Spartans were seen by many as a sloppy, sluggish bunch that couldn't block or tackle at a championship level.

They were also 1-0.

Today, the same players, led by the same coaches, are sending writers and fans scurrying to the MSU record book.

Their winning percentage is still 1.000.

What changed between a 28-6 win over stubborn Youngstown State and a 44-0 suffocation of outclassed Florida Atlantic?

The Spartans were infinitely more focused Saturday afternoon than they were eight days earlier. That led to far greater efficiency on offense and defense and optimistic projections for the 2011 season.

But I'm reminded of one of the smartest things George Perles ever preached: "You're never as good as you look when you win and seldom as bad as you seem when you lose."

MSU didn't lose its opener. It only felt that way for a team with a Big Ten title to defend and the stench of a bowl obliteration to erase.

Likewise, the Spartans weren't a perfect team in Game 2. They didn't have to be to dominate a team that already had lost to Florida, 41-3.

So let's hold off on the plans to visit Pasadena this winter, just as we should've waited with the suicide-prevention calls after Week 1.

We didn't expect to know much about Mark Dantonio's team after two weeks. And we still don't, though that's about to change.

We do know that it's not good enough to play the way anyone wants when it's not sharp and sure of its mission.

Against the Owls of 77-year-old Howard Schnellenberger, MSU looked a whole lot better than it did when the teams met 52 weeks ago at Ford Field.

The Spartans won 30-17 that day, allowing 256 yards through the air and 20 first downs. In the rematch, they yielded just 26 passing yards and one first down.

It was the first time in NCAA history that a team had 16 times as many letters in its coach's last name as first downs.

And it tied the MSU record for fewest first downs allowed, matching the singular output by Maryland in an 8-0 game in 1944.

Even if you subscribe to the oft-stated theory of Spartan defensive coordinator Pat Narduzzi that "Stats are for losers," the numbers told the story much better than they usually do.

FAU managed just 22 yards on 20 rushes. It averaged 1.1 yard per carry and 2.0 per pass attempt. And without turning the ball over in the third quarter, it had the ball for just 1:46.

MSU's only takeaway all day – and let's nitpick by saying that total has to change against Notre Dame, the reigning master of football philanthropy – came midway through the fourth period. It also resulted in seven points when recently converted running back Jeremy Langford went 37 yards with an airborne fumble.

Meanwhile, the Spartans were turnover-free, had only three penalties for 20 yards and were 11-for-21 on third- and fourth-down conversions.

Compare that to the Owls' 0-for-10 success on those plays and it's surprising the margin on the scoreboard wasn't larger. If not for a 53-yard kickoff return, the guests wouldn't have had a snap beyond their 38-yard line.

With that performance on defense, MSU is allowing just three points per game this season, its lowest yield at this point since starting with a 13-3 win over UCLA and a 23-0 victory at Penn State in 1965, Joe Paterno's last year as an assistant coach.

Obviously, YSU and FAU aren't in the same category as UCLA and PSU. They're barely in the same alphabet. But they do provide a bit of perspective in relation to a year ago.

A 72-6 combined score against the Penguins and Owls compares favorably to the Spartans' 68-31 edge over Western Michigan and FAU in 2010, a record-setting season despite a pair of projectile vomits vs. Iowa and Bama.

Yet, none of that matters when MSU visits South Bend this week. If the Fighting Irish don't turn the ball over nine times against South Florida and Michigan, they're a Top 15 team instead of September's biggest disappointment.

Watching ND gag away a 24-7 lead in the fourth quarter in Ann Arbor left several vivid impressions – many more than you'd expect from a matchup of the nation's No. 36 and 37 teams (AP) or No. 42 and 36 (*USA Today*).

No. 1 – Any secondary other than the Jets' or the Eagles' is going to have a devil of time with ND wideout Michael Floyd and a difficult challenge with receiving mate Theo Riddick.

Last year in East Lansing, Riddick had 10 catches for 128 yards and a touchdown, while Floyd had six grabs for 81 yards and two scores.

No. 2. – The Irish defensive backs must never have played basketball. If they did, they could've been the first multi-sport athletes to airball their rebounds.

ND finished with three interceptions of Denard Robinson and should've doubled that total. Its futility on fair-catchable deep balls made Jaren Hayes-on-Braylon Edwards in 2004 look like textbook coverage.

No. 3 – Irish head coach Brian Kelly must not be spending enough time at the Grotto. There's no other way to explain a vein-popping debut or Saturday's night's sickening collapse.

When they talk about the luck o' the Irish, no one said it would always be good. When Robinson scooped and scored on a goal-line fumble to put his team back in it and ND QB Tommy Rees whiffed on a pass attempt inside the U-M 10, maybe it just wasn't their night.

You can judge for yourself over the next 20 years as ESPN and the BTN show lowlights and replays of a game that was 15 minutes – OK, maybe 30 seconds –

Jeremy Langford returns an interception for a score vs. FAU

from being all-but-forgotten.

The trick for MSU isn't to top those theatrics, just to finish one point ahead of the Irish after 60 minutes – or maybe a bit longer if it takes a sequel to "Little Giants."

Style points won't matter at this point. If the Spartans win by 22 again, the critics will say, "So what? You beat a terrible 0-3 team." If they lose by one, they'll be ridiculed for not being ready for the big stage.

I think I know how MSU will play in Kirk Cousins' chance to return to the scene and silence the echoes of a 2009 collapse.

Dantonio's team will play well, regardless of which ND shows up. The question is whether the Irish will still be traumatized by their trip to Washtenaw County or will have worked out all the kinks in time for a season-saving opportunity.

If they haven't solved those problems, season over. It would take 25 hours a day of "Hail Marys" – and I don't mean the passes – for Kelly's team to make a BCS bowl as an independent after an 0-3 start.

Thus, you're going to see the best that ND has at 3:30 Saturday, whether you're there or watching on NBC. And it'll take everything the Spartans have to make it seven wins in eight visits to South Bend.

It's finally time to see if they have the stuff to scare the rest of the Big Ten. That's entirely possible. But it's just as likely that Irish will have 10 times the total offense that FAU did.

SEPTEMBER 17, 2011 • SATURDAY

MAXIMUM EXPOSURE

THIS MUCH WE KNOW about Michigan State's football fortunes in 2011: The Spartans won't go 14-0. And when they play the way they did this week, they won't score 14 points against a good team – yes, that includes Notre Dame when it isn't into self-mutilation.

Everything else is still up for grabs, much like a pass from Denard Robinson. MSU isn't as bad as it looked in a bumbling, humbling Saturday in South Bend. How could it be? But it isn't nearly as good as it needs to get to keep October from making November irrelevant.

As we said last week, the surest bet on the board wasn't the winless Irish giving significant points and winning by triple that spread. It was that people would draw conclusions, positive or negative, from one performance and assume they know where MSU will be in 11 weeks – bound for Pasadena or in postseason purgatory.

The good news – and let's get that out of the way in the first few paragraphs – is that the Spartans have been in worse predicaments than they are today after a 31-13 thumping. In fact, in 1987, MSU needed a late touchdown and a two-point conversion to trim the Fighting Irish's final margin to 31-8.

The following Friday, Duffy Daugherty died. And the afternoon after that, George Perles' fifth team fell to Florida State 31-3 in a game that wasn't as close as the score. We're talking about two L's by a combined 62-11 count. But Lorenzo White and "Gang Green" never lost again that season and beat USC a second time to finish 9-2-1.

No one is saying that this year's Spartans are destined to return to the Rose Bowl, where they haven't been in nearly a quarter-century. They'd need to have their individual and institutional IDs checked to set foot on that hallowed ground.

All it means is that Mark Dantonio was right about at least one thing Saturday. The most important thing his team has to do is "weather the storm" – in this case, one with a lot of wind but not a great deal of structural damage. The program's foundation is still in place. Its players just need to come inside. In Week 3, they stood on the porch and did a rain dance.

Some thought MSU was beaten the second Michigan downed ND in a Week 2 seven-on-seven scrimmage. But when the Irish went 0-2 with 1,055 yards of total offense, you have to consider the law of averages, especially when a visiting team is way below average in every phase of play.

Yes, we've heard that stats are for losers. In a way, Brian Kelly's program deserved the two defeats that it got against South Florida and a smug group 63 miles to the southeast that gets all its smiles in September lately.

So maybe it's fitting that MSU had edges in many of the meaningless numbers. In the second half, when the game was already lost, the Spartans led 204-80 in total offense, 11-6 in first downs and 18:04-11:56 in time of possession. That belated arrival meant about as much Saturday as when ND beat M.A.C. 34-6 in 1897.

Here's what did and always does matter – all you need to know about Week 3 and something most fans forget when they try to predict or evaluate an outcome: Football success is almost always a matter of making big plays and avoiding key errors. More games are lost with mistakes than won with brilliance. Cue the "Notre Dame Victory March."

When a team has an 89-yard kickoff return for a touchdown and an 82-yard interception runback to set up a closing field goal, as the Irish did, game over.

When a visitor tries to pull an upset with 12 penalties, lowlighted by pass interference when a short completion would've led to a punt and by three holds by the offensive line in the span of 10 snaps, it's spitting into a 30-mph wind.

When a group that preaches physical football and offensive balance is outrushed 112-13 in the first half and winds up with 29 yards on 23 attempts, none

longer than 8 yards, good luck – especially when the left tackle's ole´ move leads to a sack/fumble and the right tackle is carted off with a possible broken foot.

And when a coach who should know better outsmarts himself and tries a high-risk, low-reward fake field goal just before halftime, virtually the opposite of last year's game-winning play, it was hard to imagine how his team could win.

After a three-and-out to begin the third quarter – including a ridiculous play call with a poorly protected, overthrown deep ball on third-and-1 – and a quick ND TD made it 28-10, it has hard to believe the right team was No. 15 in both polls.

This one was over before the first of Kirk Cousins' 34 completions for 329 of the most misleading yards you'll ever see. The script was set when the Irish won the coin toss, aggressively took the ball and quickly asserted their will.

Cierre Wood had 59 yards on his first six carries (-2, 10, 16, 2, 11, 22) – more than twice the visitors' total – as Brian Kelly's much maligned team went 76 yards in eight plays. In contrast, after Wood's last scamper made it 7-0, MSU counterpart Edwin Baker immediately carried twice, each time for 1 yard.

When the Spartans got a field goal four series later, it was their only points off back-to-back takeaways. Of course, ND answered with George Atkinson III's TD runback to make it 14-3, as one blocker took out two defenders. There went the idea that special teams were supposed to be an MSU strength in the matchup.

Searching for mismatches, the Irish found one with No. 3 receiver T.J. Jones against Mitchell White, the Spartans' backup corner. A well-thrown, 26-yard strike from quarterback Tommy Rees made it 28-10 late in the third quarter and ended any thoughts of a comeback.

For all the talk about a terrific Irish receiving corps with All-American Michael Floyd, Theo Riddick and Jones, B.J. Cunningham outplayed them all. MSU's career receiving king had 12 grabs for 158 yards, while ND's threesome combined for 10 catches and 131 yards. Still, the only stats that matter today are the records: 2-1 and 1-2.

"I was very surprised," senior free safety and

captain Trenton Robinson said. "We knew everything that they were going to do. We've just got to stop the run. That's all there is to it. If you don't execute and make plays and you have 12 penalties, you're not going to win the football game."

When Dantonio said he had "a bit of a concern" about the offensive line, he won something, too: The Understatement of the Week Award. The Spartans ran for 203 yards against the Irish last year. And they were on a pace to do that again Saturday. All they had to do was play 28 quarters.

That problem should disappear when Central Michigan comes to town next weekend. One more pratfall against CMU or even a scare in the first half will have a lot of people wondering why they picked MSU to make it to Indy as anything other than auto racing fans.

It's the Spartans' last chance to prepare for the Big Ten opener at Ohio State, another team that lost by 18 points to an early-season underachiever. If they win there and get two more W's next month, people will barely remember 31-13. If they get pushed around and lose their poise again, they'll lose a more important game.

They already lost a Golden Dome opportunity.

SEPTEMBER 24, 2011 • SATURDAY

CHIPPING AWAY

IT WAS ALL ANYONE could ask – a good win in a no-win situation. Michigan State was supposed to pound Central Michigan: "Hammer, meet your new friend, Nail." And if the Spartans didn't bludgeon the Chippewas for 60 minutes, they did more than enough to make some despondent fans drop their sharp objects.

It's easy to totally dismiss Saturday's 45-7 score with the chant: "It's only a MAC team! It's only a MAC team!" But when CMU had won three of the seven previous matchups in East Lansing, when Toledo's seniors had beaten Michigan and scared Ohio State and when Western Michigan was about to remind Illinois that it wasn't ready for the BCS Championship, a 38-point victory was better than OK.

It was a confirmation. After three tune-ups and a reality check, MSU is as ready for Big Ten play as it's going to get. Sure, it'd be nice to have a couple more healthy offensive linemen. It'd be nice to have a 100,000-seat stadium, too. The bottom line is the Spartans have enough players to win at OSU and beat U-M two weeks later – the "Big Two, Little State" portion of their schedule.

That opportunity shouldn't have been in question. MSU can go toe-to-toe with any team in the league, even Wisconsin on October 22, and be 3-0 when it travels to Lincoln, Neb., for the toughest game on the schedule. It can also be 0-3 if it plays as poorly as it did at Notre Dame.

It used to be about the opposition. For years, the Spartans were several players short – and maybe a coach or two, too. The only way they could win a big game was for something strange to happen or for their opponent to contribute to the outcome in a significant way.

The most significant change after 4 1/3 seasons under Mark Dantonio is that that's no longer the case. With the exception of bowl games against Alabama, it's all about what MSU does now.

Just what did it do Saturday on a near-perfect afternoon for football? Not enough to erase the stench of a 31-13 loss at Notre Dame but more than most people, including the Vegas wise guys, expected.

First, MSU rushed for 197 yards. If that wasn't an eye-popping total, it was nearly seven times as much as a measly effort at ND. And the Spartans did that with new starters at center and right tackle and a surprise contributor at left tackle. More on Micajah Reynolds later.

It got solid play from the backs, especially Le'Veon Bell and Larry Caper, another great catch-and-run for 54 yards from B.J. Cunningham and 7-for-8 passing from backup quarterback Andrew Maxwell. On a similar note, when Brad Sonntag is your leading

Le'Veon Bell can't be stopped by a diving arm tackle

receiver with four grabs, it's either a very good day or a very bad one.

Defensively, MSU yielded just 21 yards on the ground, 8 fewer than its offense managed against the Irish. Aside from one 15-yard scramble, it didn't allow a rush of more than 6 yards. And in contrast to the opener against Youngstown State, the Spartans got off the field in a hurry, permitting just two conversions on third or fourth down in 13 attempts.

The best stat of all was four interceptions from three safeties and a middle linebacker. More than half of CMU's passes fell incomplete – even with the four that wound up in MSU's hands. The Chippewas gained just 91 yards through the air, 16 more than the Spartans had on runbacks. And Isaiah Lewis' 37-yard swipe-and-sprint gave the defense as many points as it surrendered.

Aside from a three-TD yield to the Fighting Irish, MSU's defense has allowed a total of 13 points in its other three games. It would've had a second shutout Saturday if not for a blocked punt that gave CMU the ball on the 13.

As many complaints as we've heard about this year's defense, some legitimate and some not, the Spartans stand at or near the top nationally in several key areas. They were No. 4 in total yards allowed and No. 3 in pass defense coming in and could be No. 1 in the country in pass defense efficiency this week.

Yes, those numbers came with plenty of help from lesser opponents. But MSU did hold the Fighting Irish to 275 yards of offense. And a lot of other FBC teams have played four pushovers this month, not three.

No one is saying that the Spartans have crossed a bridge to greatness or even guaranteeing that they're good enough to have another 3-1 record next month. If they can't run the ball effectively and contain OSU quarterback Braxton Miller, they'll enter their bye week at 3-2 – the worst of the season's three possible scenarios.

For some inexplicable reason, I never for a moment thought MSU would win at ND this year. But since the day Jim Tressel stopped having a vested interest in the Buckeyes, I've never thought the Spartans would lose in the 'Shoe. I don't think that today, either.

Why not? Why should the Spartans be picked to win in Columbus for just the fourth time in 45 years? Because I still think they're a nine-win team with the four things it takes to be successful: talent, depth, leadership and character.

The first three attributes are well-documented. MSU has enough skill in important spots, enough quality backups to survive the usual injuries and enough key seniors and coaching to compete for the conference championship in Indianapolis.

It also has enough questions to answer that it could finish anywhere from first to fourth in the Legends Division. The schedule-makers didn't do Dantonio's team any favors.

But there's another reason I'm sticking with by post-spring projection of a 6-2 league finish and a share of the first Legends crown with the Cornhuskers. There's something about this team that makes me think it has more character than characters.

The latest example came when Reynolds learned last Sunday that he'd be switching back to offense, his fourth move since arriving as a guard in 2009. A lot of players would've grumbled or worse a long time ago. And we can question the wisdom of previous moves all we want. None of that mattered this week.

The 6-foot-5, 320-pounder from Lansing dove back into the playbook, picked up the tackle assignments and watched more tape than some head coaches to try to prepare for the challenges ahead. The only thing he wouldn't do was leave the video on while he slept for subliminal coaching. Micajahs need their quality rest.

"I had a lot of support from the coaches and guys like Joel Foreman," Reynolds said of his neighbor at left guard. "I had a lot of faith, too. I didn't allow any sacks and had a couple of key reaches. On a 10 scale, I'd give myself a 7 or a 7-1/2.

"I really only had three practices. But when you stay after and watch another two-and-a-half hours of film, it helps. All I know is if the coaches tell me I'm starting at Ohio State, I'll put in as much time as I ever have in my life. If not, I'll do what I can. It's not about me."

For winners, it's almost always about we. And at 3-1, the Spartans could be who we thought they are.

Mark Dantonio and his former assistant, ex–MSU quarterback Dan Enos

Jerel Worthy prepares to wreak havoc back in Ohio vs. the Buckeyes

OCTOBER 1, 2011 • SATURDAY

SACK YOU VERY MUCH

B.J. CUNNINGHAM just had to make one final leaping grab Saturday.

He rose higher than any Lambeau leap – and landed in the laps of jubilant Spartan fans in a nearly empty Ohio Stadium.

There was only one problem. He had to get down. And when Michigan State's MVP for the first five weeks of the season came back to earth, he was caught by Defensive Coordinator Pat Narduzzi.

That was only fitting after a 10-7 "program win" that should've been a shutout, if not a 20-point victory. Narduzzi's D-line and linebackers and DBs had caught Ohio State quarterbacks Braxton Miller and Joe Bauserman more often than people catch colds in Columbus.

Nine sacks and 13 tackles for losses, not counting those that were replaced by penalties, sent 70,000 booing Buckeyes to their cars before their team had a drive of more than 29 yards. It was an exodus much like a haunting 2006 humiliation in East Lansing.

No, it wasn't a perfect day. It didn't have to be. That was the beauty of an often-ugly game. So what if MSU's ground game ran on empty again, netting 71 yards in 31 tries? Who cares if Kirk Cousins threw two more interceptions and was lucky a third toss wasn't a pick-six?

That's nit-picking after the visitors were clearly superior in beating their 10th different Big Ten opponent since 2008 – completion of "The Dantonio Slam." Cunningham was brilliant again. Kickers Mike Sadler and Dan Conroy were heroes. And the defense delivered a frightful beating.

More on Cunningham in a minute. But if Sadler doesn't retrieve an errant snap and turn a 25-yard loss into a 37-yard gain with the first of several good rugby punts, his team probably falls behind early. And if Conroy doesn't drill a 50-yard field goal into the wind in the fourth quarter, the defense may have had to win it in overtime.

Consider that done. Aside from an irrelevant extra-point, the Spartans never let OSU call signals in the red zone. How could they? Until the final 1:51, the nation's leaders in total defense had allowed just 112 yards and nine first downs in 57 snaps – 1.96 yards per play.

For a program that hadn't blanked the Bucks in 39 previous tries, a missed tackle and a 33-yard touchdown with 10 seconds left spoiled a spectacular opportunity. Still, it was a Narduzzi of an effort, even if a second shutout this season – something MSU hasn't had since 1965 – remains on the to-do list.

It also brought back memories of its three best defensive efforts in the series. If you weren't around for a 32-7 stomp in 1965, when George Webster, Bubba Smith and Co. held OSU to minus-22 yards rushing; for a 13-7 mashing in 1987, when the Buckeyes scored on the game's first play, then rushed for exactly 2 yards in the final 59:45, or for a 23-7 suffocation in 1999, when a Nick Saban/Dantonio defense bounced back from its only two losses to leave John Cooper at a loss for words, it was a memory trick Jerry Lucas would try.

It was "Gang Green" revisited. And there was nothing lucky about what happened in "The Horseshoe." No brief return to the banks of the Olentangy had ever been more enjoyable for a group of Ohio escapees.

Native sons Cunningham, running back Le'Veon Bell, defensive tackle Jerel Worthy, defensive end Marcus Rush, outside linebacker Denicos Allen and cornerback Johnny Adams all turned some heads in the briefest of homecomings.

"Today meant a lot to all of us," said Adams, a chirper on the field whose words to the rest of his team spoke volumes. "We wanted the shutout. All of us did. But a victory here … it's just as good."

Cunningham, the best receiver in the Big Ten, was an improved version of Muhsin Muhammad again,

HEART OF A SPARTAN

Linebacker Max Bullough plants OSU quarterback Braxton Miller

grabbing nine balls for 154 yards and soaring to score his team's lone TD on a 33-yard ad-lib.

As longtime play-by-play broadcaster George Blaha mentioned at halftime Saturday, if Cunningham will never get the recognition of past receiving greats Gene Washington, Kirk Gibson, Andre Rison, Plaxico Burress and Charles Rogers, he belongs in the discussion.

Bell played better than his 67 yards of rushing and receiving would indicate. He did a nice job of penetration pickups in pass protection and was solid on special teams. And Worthy, Rush, Allen and Adams were worthy of all the praise they'll receive.

They were in the Buckeyes' backfield more than presidential candidates plan to be in the country's No. 1 battleground state. The battle for State supremacy ended quickly, as OSU ran just 49 plays on its first 12 possessions, including five three-and-outs.

It wasn't the first time the Buckeyes have been tattooed recently. But it was as painful and permanent as any ink job could be. And if Narduzzi still thinks "Stats are for losers," a big reason he never told his players they were No. 1 in the nation in key yields, they were for winners Saturday, too.

The Spartans did their own version of "Script Ohio," marched around the Field Turf and dotted the hosts' favorite formations with superior defense, not sousaphones. You half-expected a crowd that began with 105,306 on hand to start a new cheer – "O-H!" ... "Oh, no!"

When the celebrations in the north end zone and the MSU locker room ended, Dantonio framed the day another way. Part of the reason he's the right coach for a program that has long been drenched in self-doubt is the way he never forgets.

"Let's see," he said, recalling a first-try formula that kept his team from traveling to Pasadena. "Three teams were Big Ten champs last year. We beat Wisconsin. Now, we've beaten Ohio State ... I'll leave it at that."

Leave it to "The Best Damn Band In The Land," as it's billed, to add the perfect P.S. After singing "We don't give a damn for the whole state of Michigan! We're from O-hi-o!" one distraught musician couldn't resist. As the players left the field, he dropped his instrument from his lips and hollered, "Hey, Spartans! ... BEAT MICHIGAN!"

With the Buckeyes staring at a four-game skid, including trips to Nebraska and Illinois and a visit from Wisconsin, their only hope of avoiding total disaster is beating U-M themselves on November 26 in Ann Arbor. But if MSU can start the Wolverines on another freefall, that'd be fine, too.

Senior free safety and free-thinking captain Trenton Robinson was well aware of that. His endzone interception on the opening drive in last year's battle of unbeatens made him the best Robinson in Washtenaw County that day. And the mere mention of October 15 made him want to grab a helmet.

"It's going to be crazy!" T-Rob said. "We're going to be so excited. We'll have to try to control that a little bit – but not too much. I can't wait to get out there in those black uniforms. None of us can wait."

The Spartans will just have to. First, they have a bye week and a chance to get as healthy as possible. And as MSU's first win over OSU in 12 years proves beyond a shadow of a doubt, good things are well worth the wait.

OCTOBER 15, 2011 • SATURDAY

FOUR-EVER YOURS

NO SPARTAN headgear ever looked better than the Nike Pro Combat model did ... atop Paul Bunyan in the winners' locker room.

Bunyan, a Michigan State senior, laughed at the notion that he'd been thinking of transferring and did everything except count off his team's points and shout the lyrics to its fight song Saturday.

It was OK to be the strong, silent type. His friends had done all the necessary talking with a 28-14 triumph over previously unbeaten Michigan, actions that spoke much louder than words.

Edwin Baker, an aptly named "Rock", rushed for 167 yards – the Spartans' fifth-best total vs. U-M and 2 yards more than Wolverines offense Denard Robinson managed rushing AND throwing.

Or whatever you want to call some passes in desperate need of a GPS.

Robinson ran for just 42 yards, in large part because U-M had 69 yards in losses. Meanwhile, Baker had 49 yards on MSU's first possession alone.

"We had to keep fighting and believing," Baker said after an emotion-packed, on-field soliloquy. "We felt it all week. Every time we play Michigan, it's personal."

He wasn't referring to the personal fouls that kept the Wolverines in the game until late in the fourth quarter, instead of in danger of a blowout.

But Baker aside, the Spartans were far from a solo act. They were a team that fulfilled one improbable

Johnny Adams' blitz on fourth-and-inches nails Dennard Robinson

HEART OF A SPARTAN

dream and took giant strides toward several more in Year 5 of the Mark Dantonio era.

"D-Rob" play-alike Keshawn Martin had a pair of nifty tightrope runs and pylon tucks after catches, his first scores against a school less than a half-hour from home that had overlooked him.

A much-maligned offensive line won a veto-proof majority of its battles, helping MSU outrush the Big Ten's top ground game, 213-82. For the 39th time in the last 42 seasons, those were the only numbers you needed.

Ah, but there were many more – statistics and standouts.

Leaderback Kirk Cousins played his best game this season in becoming the first Spartan QB to start in three straight wins over the Wolverines.

"I saw a different Kirk today," Martin said. "He was more confident and wasn't worried about making mistakes, just plays."

Don't be fooled by the numbers: 13-for-24 for 120 yards and two TDs amid winds that blew away entire tailgate parties. Cousins had four balls dropped and never made the big mistake that gets teams beat.

Instead, sporting facial hair at the podium for the first time, there was no mistaking his passion and purpose.

"You're looking at three seniors right here from the state of Michigan," Cousins said, including safety Trenton Robinson and guard Joel Foreman in a clipped cadence that would've worked under center. "And for the rest of our life, we will walk the streets of this state – for the rest of our life! ... That's satisfying."

It also shows the motivation for MSU to inflict another physical pounding on a program that's still regarded as inherently superior in Cousins' hometown and most others.

"To go 4-0 against them is as special as anything we've accomplished here," Cousins said. "I feel we've been overlooked and underestimated for most of our careers."

Not any more. At least not defensively. The nation's No. 3 scoring defense and leader in yards allowed had seven more sacks of Robinson and wayward scrambler Devin Gardner.

That's 16 sacks in the last two games. For the record, and MSU is fast approaching a lot of them, the defense produced 20 sacks last season in 13 games.

Linebackers Chris Norman and Denicos Allen and DBs Johnny Adams and Isaiah Lewis led the feeding frenzy, while punter Mike Sadler and tight end Garrett Celek made big plays on special teams.

U-M had six first downs from Spartan penalties, the same number it managed through the air. And

while we're talking about the gift that kept giving, the Wolverines' best plays were sloppy MSU fumbles.

But becoming the sole leader in the Legends Division of the Big Ten was more a matter of will than skill.

The Spartans showed their resolve by answering U-M's challenge with a tying TD on their first possession, a statement score to start the second half and an insurance tally – just the second points the Wolverines had surrendered in the fourth quarter in seven games.

Perhaps they failed to grasp the full meaning of "CONTROLLED aggression." Obviously and maddeningly so. But if you're going to have 13 penalties for 124 yards in walkoffs, you'd better leave with a pound of flesh.

MSU left with a couple of tons of it, finishing with more sacks than Meijer. Once again, the Spartans

Edwin Baker leaves six Wolverines behind during a 167-yard day

HEART OF A **SPARTAN**

were Heisman-busters and reality checks for the U-M's championship plans.

"Any time you get a win over a top 10 team or what they are – or were – it's special," MSU defensive coordinator Pat Narduzzi said shortly after receiving a Gatorade shower.

He was willing to trade an offside penalty or two and a couple of late hits for the constant indentations the Spartans were making in the Wolverines' hides.

"We try to do 60 minutes of unnecessary roughness," he said only slightly metaphorically. "That's what we try to do on every play."

By the fourth quarter, there was residual damage, as there always is when a defense delivers more blows than Manny Pacquiao. And Saturday was a time for crunching, not cuddling.

Adams had arguably the most important sack, a blindside blitz – "Green Pony," as it was called in the huddle – when U-M tried to get cute on fourth-and-less-than-1 in position to make it 21-all.

Kirk Cousins leaps onto Keshawn Martin and Chris McDonald after another TD

Johnny on the spot, it turned out.

And Lewis provided the icing with a 39-yard pick-and-prance when the Denarderines went to the air once too often.

"Hail to the Victims," indeed.

U-M was just 3-for-15 on third-down conversions. And to their credit, "D-Rob", safety Jordan Kovacs and defensive tackle Mike Martin all refused to whine that the Spartans hadn't played nice.

When asked if MSU had played dirty, a battered Robinson said, "No, they were playing football. It's a dirty game."

Afterward, there was plenty of whining elsewhere. One Spartan fan summed it up in the closing seconds, hollering "I thought it was RichRod's fault?" and chanting "Four more years!"

By that point, the MSU students had already made middle linebacker Max Bullough laugh with a "Little Sis-ter!" serenade. Moments later, they were joined by defensive end William Gholston, tight end Brian Linthicum, Baker and Cousins, who'd all leaped into the crowd to celebrate.

The funniest moment of the day came shortly after that, when Gholston was trapped in the stands behind a gate to the field. Consider it his punishment for two personal fouls and taking the Combat part of the uniform too literally.

"I am in so much trouble right now!" he said when finally freed as he raced toward the locker room.

By then, the Spartan family had already celebrated. And returning players like 2008 All-American Javon Ringer could barely contain themselves.

"I was there when it started!" the Tennessee Titans running back said of an entire-class winning streak some never thought they'd see. "And I'm proud of it, man – so proud to be part of it."

When Dantonio arrived in the interview room, his smile was as wide as the media had ever seen it. And a question about having so many players back for the game produced a long, emotional answer.

"They ARE the program," he said after his team had outrushed the Wolverines for a fifth time, including one season under Lloyd Carr, three wish-they'd-been-vacated years under Rich Rodriguez and the latest game under Brady Hoke.

Pressed for personal reflections, Dantonio said, "Anybody who has ever worn a green shirt can feel it's personal. For every player and every coach, that feeling is strong. And it lasts a lifetime."

Over the life of the series, U-M leads, 67-32-5 – a lead that will never totally disappear. But since 1950, the first season after the Spartans had been accepted into the Big Ten over the Wolverines' objections, the margin is just 34-26-2. Only Ohio State has more sets of gold pants.

Hoke now stands 5-6 against MSU, counting his days as a Western Michigan and U-M assistant. And defensive guru Greg Mattison sees his record against the Spartans dip to 5-15 with stops all around the Midwest.

The one thing that wouldn't stop Saturday and may not have stopped yet was the smile on defensive tackle Jerel Worthy's face. The mid-season first-team All-American will be a perfect subject for a "GameDay" piece when ESPN goes live next weekend.

"I feel even better about getting that tattoo now," he said of a full-bicep graphic of a Spartan stepping on a Wolverine. "But it's not about what's on your arm."

It's all about what's in your heart. MSU proved that after a lousy performance at Notre Dame. And it'll have to do so again when mighty Wisconsin visits for a payback opportunity.

But when asked if he knew the last time the Spartans had beaten U-M five in a row, Worthy's expression changed from joy to bewilderment – if only for a few seconds.

"Never?" he repeated when told the answer. "Well, that gives us something to look at for next year."

There's no assurance that Worthy will be here – unless that game is on an NFL bye week. But there's no guarantee that he won't be, based on the fun he just had and one simple fact.

The drive for five is still alive.

WORTH EVERY SECOND

JEREL WORTHY'S FOOTBALL JOURNEY CONTINUES

IF HE WEREN'T cracking helmets, he'd be cracking jokes.

"I'm a comedian," Jerel Worthy said with a laugh few quarterbacks could ever appreciate.

"Comedy Central" will have to wait. The next stage Worthy will walk on is the green grass of a fortunate NFL team, the powerful Green Bay Packers.

The junior defensive tackle chose to forgo his senior year at Michigan State to enter the 2012 NFL Draft. It was a decision many Spartans were dreading but one Worthy felt he had to make.

"It was just a lot of family and financial issues," Worthy explained. "But at the same time I felt like I did a lot of things and accomplished a lot individually. It was the right time to go."

Worthy comes from a close-knit family that has supported him since the first time he picked up a football. He feels fortunate to be able to support them in return.

"It's a blessing," Worthy said. "It's something that I just have to continue to get better at, to provide for them and make them happy. If they're happy, I'm happy."

They're happy. They're proud. And so are his teammates.

"I couldn't be more excited for him," teammate Arthur Ray Jr. said. "We developed a good relationship ever since I was on crutches. After everything we've been through, I'm really happy for him right now. It's a time we always dream about. Now, it's real."

Worthy was the anchor of an MSU defense that led the Big Ten in total defense, rushing defense and sacks. And yes, he had a few individual accomplishments.

No. 99 was named a first-team All-American by the Associated Press, American Football Coaches Association, Walter Camp Foundation, The Sporting News, CBSSports.com, NBCSports.com and Yahoo! Sports. He was the first Spartan defensive lineman to earn that AP honor since Bubba Smith in 1966.

That was just the 2011 season. He had enough tackles, tackles for losses, blocked field goals, quarterback hurries and sacks in his career to make anyone's head spin – especially those on the receiving end of his hits.

But the 6-foot-3, 310-pounder isn't known only for his statistics. What makes Worthy such a unique player is his burst off the ball. Yes, he's quick – sometimes a little too quick.

Fans used to groan when yellow flags were thrown to the ground, catching Worthy jumping offsides. But after a conversation with an official after a crucial call in the Big Ten Championship game, the penalties might not all be Worthy's fault.

You remember the play. Wisconsin faced a third-and-5 at the MSU 40. And Spartans and Badgers were shaking Lucas Oil Stadium. But when Worthy fired into the backfield, nailing Montee Ball for a loss, a yellow flag flew at a critical moment.

With a first down by penalty, Wisconsin quarterback Russell Wilson hit Jared Abbrederis moments later for a 42-yard touchdown that pulled their team

Jerel Worthy enjoys life in the spotlight en route to the NFL

HEART OF A **SPARTAN**

within a point. What followed wasn't funny to anyone.

"He told me I was too fast and didn't really know if I was onside or offside, so he just kind of called it offside," Worthy said of the official's uncertainty. "I was a little upset. But you just have to roll with the punches a little bit and keep going."

That's exactly what he did. Despite a heartbreaking loss that night, Worthy helped his team to a historic triple-overtime victory over Georgia in the Outback Bowl, ending a 10-year postseason drought.

Now it's on to the next opportunity. Reaching the professional level in sports is a goal many athletes can only dream of achieving. Even standing on the sidelines as a redshirt-freshman, Worthy wasn't convinced he could make it to the NFL.

"It was just kind of like a hobby at that point," Worthy said. "Once I got to start, it was something that I really wanted to pursue and something I felt I could be. I worked on trying to become the best I could be and be in the position where I am now, just trying to achieve goals and set the standard high."

He has done just that, for himself and for others. The Huber Heights, Ohio, native understands that if he can be overlooked by the powerhouse Buckeyes, help MSU to back-to-back 11-win seasons and have an opportunity to be an early pick in the 2012 NFL draft, it's important to show others that no dream is out of reach.

"There are people who didn't have the same type of guidance that I had, so it's important to be able to give back," Worthy said. "I can teach them a lot of things that I recently learned."

Four years in a Spartan uniform gave him more than just quick feet.

"It taught me to be a better person and become a better man," Worthy explained. "Coach Dantonio always said, 'When you leave Michigan State, you want to be a man and be a better person than when you came in. I feel like all the ups and downs I went through, all the good times and bad times, molded me into the person I am today."

There are a few things that will never change.

One, his passion.

"The passion I have for the game is just being able to go out there and do something I love," Worthy said. "I've always been competitive. Whether it's school, football or anything else, I'm always trying to win. I think that's the same passion you have to have in life in order to be a success."

Two, his friendships.

"They're lifetime relationships," Worthy said of the teammates he has had over the last four years. "We've been through a lot of ups and downs, a lot of good times and a lot of bad times. But those good times and bad times developed great friendships. And it's something I can take with me for the rest of my life."

Three, his education.

One of the stipulations in Worthy's contract was that he would finish his degree in Child Development this summer.

"It's very important because football won't last forever," Worthy said. "As much as a lot of people would love it to, it's not. You always have to have something to move on with after your career is over, and that's what I'm going to do."

Four, his record against the school down the road.

4-0.

He only needed one word to describe it.

"Splendid."

There's no doubt in his mind that he'll miss MSU. He'll miss Spartan Stadium, the fans that filled its seats every week, his coaches, his friends and the college atmosphere. But there are bigger things in life than football. And Worthy understands the need to help those who have been his biggest inspiration.

Plus, he'll have a few more years playing the game he's always loved as a second-round pick and the first MSU player taken – projected as a 3-4 defensive end.

"Being in a position to put a smile on my face and see the smiles on the faces of my family members, being able to do something you love . . ." Worthy said. "I think that's why it's just a blessing I'm able to pursue a professional career."

He is certainly Worthy of it.

OCTOBER 22, 2011 • SATURDAY

HAIL, YES!

THEY USED THEIR HEADS in all the right ways – in ways that few imagined they could.

Not as battering rams or criminals' tools. As secret weapons that proved they could think, not just thump. And as a way to keep a last pass alive until "Rocket Man," Keith Nichol, could catch it and carry it for the longest yard they'll ever gain.

When not-so-instant replay finally fixed a mistaken spot with no time remaining, it was time for one of the crazier celebrations East Lansing has seen.

The Michigan State Spartans were ahead of the pack in the Legends Division of the Big Ten – 37-31 winners over Wisconsin in one of the wildest games imaginable.

Or in this case, in four football games Saturday night:

- In an "Oh, no!" start that saw the fourth-ranked Badgers lead 14-0 on the scoreboard and 110-5 in total offense before MSU received its second snap.

- In amazing stretches that saw Mark Dantonio's players answer with 23 unanswered points and a stunning 31-3 stretch of dominance.

- In a furious Wisconsin charge that tied the game with two late touchdowns and left most people thinking the Badgers would win, either with a field goal off a turnover or with momentum in overtime.

- And in a bizarre final sequence, a 78-yard drive that included a fumble recovery by Dan France, six completions from Kirk Cousins, a third-down conversion from a second-and-20 crater and, finally, a play that works a lot better against air at the end of Thursday's practices than against half the population of Wisconsin.

So what if ESPN entertainer Lee Corso, one of four finalists to succeed Duffy Daugherty as MSU's coach in 1972, was wrong on his 200th headgear selection on "College GameDay." His record was still a sterling 137-63. And his network had just enjoyed 3 hours, 23 minutes of a non-scripted instant classic.

As I mentioned to the *Lansing State Journal's* Joe Rexrode after all the interviews had ended, it was a part of "The Fantastic Four" – the MSU home football finishes for the ages.

It earned its place on the program's Mount Rushmore of endings with a 16-13 upset of No. 1 Ohio State in 1974, a game without a winner until 45 minutes after a chaotic last scrum; a 26-24 victory over Michigan in

2001, when T.J. Duckett fair caught Jeff Smoker's final flip into the end zone, and a 34-31 OT triumph over Notre Dame in 2010, when Aaron Bates and Charlie Gantt were the biggest "Little Giants."

How does that happen? With incredible determination, instinctive play and a little luck. When a 315-pound offensive tackle falls on a slippery loose ball at the Spartans' 24-yard line in the final minute, a 34-31 loss was closer than anyone wants to remember.

But if you remember anything but the feeling of euphoria 10 years from now, remember this:

MSU proved what can happen when a team plays smart, plays tough and plays together through 60 minutes and a few seconds more.

It illustrated the value of walk-ons like punt blocker Kyler Elsworth, whose all-out effort helped the Spartans lead 23-14 at halftime.

And it showed the importance of developing depth, as backup Denzel Drone and others filled in for suspended defensive end William Gholston.

Surely you remember Gholston. He was in the news more often than executed murdered Muammar Gaddafi this week and was painted with a similar brush as one of world's worst menaces.

When the Big Ten finally said Gholston would have to sit out the game after volunteering to help his pals prepare on the scout team, MSU had one more rallying point.

It already wanted to show it was every bit as Worthy of a Rose Bowl berth as the Badgers were last season. And if the Spartans couldn't undo a tiebreaker change that cost the school its first BCS bid, they could show that there's more than one deserving candidate to represent the league in Pasadena again.

Perhaps most important, even more than a win that won't send MSU to California, was the way its players rallied and represented themselves when countdown clocks had been replaced by penalty-yardage calculators.

After committing 13 penalties for 124 yards against the Wolverines, the only reason the score of last week's game wasn't closer to 49-7, the Spartans were penalty-free and happy to be.

If anyone would've predicted that Wisconsin would have six more walkoffs than MSU, he or she would've faced a sobriety test before finishing that sentence.

Likewise, if anyone had said the Spartans would go from 14 down to nine points ahead with a safety, a blocked field goal, a double-reverse, a long TD reception-and-run and a snuffed punt for a score, it would've defied all logic.

But then, when was the last time a team had fewer extra points AND field goals and was on the left side of the final score? None in any of the 500-plus games these eyes have covered since 1978.

And if we're going back that far, we may as well flash back another 80 years. It had been 113 seasons since a team had defeated two Big Ten opponents with 6-0-or-better records. The University of Chicago

Kirk Cousins' pass deflects off Wisconsin's Jared Abbrederis and B.J. Cunningham before it lands in the hands of game-winner Keith Nichol

did that in 1898, handing Northwestern and Wisconsin their first losses late in the year.

Ironically, it was Chicago's departure from Western Conference athletics that created an opening for MSU to make the league a Big Ten again.

Arguably the best defensive teams in the conference's proud history, the 1965-66 Spartans, were honored at their 45th Homecoming celebration. And football-track All-American Gene Washington was saluted for his induction into the College Football Hall of Fame with a place of honor on the stadium's east upper deck. Afterward, all he wanted to talk about was the performance of this year's team.

"To do what they just did and score on the last drive and the last play, that's special," Washington said. "That's very special and says a lot. It also says, 'Thank God for replay!'"

Appropriately, the biggest hero was another physical receiver: Nichol, a converted quarterback and Oklahoma transfer who has never whined and only cared about winning. If he didn't have to survive the segregation in Texas and in all of college football that Washington did, Nichol's perseverance was still duly noted.

Today, it's almost time for Nichol and his teammates to put a magic moment behind them. When Dantonio said, "Where do we go from here?" the correct answer was, "To Lincoln, Neb., a trip of 733 miles, for a Legends Division showdown next Saturday at noon that's more important, if not nearly as glitzy."

"We will carry this forward," senior safety and co-captain Trenton Robinson said with an all-business expression. "Before we can think about facing Wisconsin again in a championship game, there's a long road ahead. We have to go to Nebraska first. And let's go!"

There's no choice but to go there for a team that shows no signs of stopping in the hunt for red (and a little blue) October.

Kirk Cousins fires another completion vs. the baffled Badgers

OCTOBER 29, 2011 • SATURDAY

"O" NO!

THEY DIDN'T GAIN 622 YARDS and still lose a game by 35 points. That was Baylor at Oklahoma State.

They didn't have a 250-yard rusher and a 100-yard receiver in an unimaginable upset. That was Iowa at Minnesota.

The Michigan State Spartans had a different problem Saturday in a 24-3 loss at Nebraska.

In a word, MSU was strangely . . . ffensive.

You could say their performance was offensive to the senses. And you'd be right. But that wouldn't be entirely accurate.

The Spartans had no "O".

When a defense holds the Huskers to 270 yards in Lincoln, allows 0 yards passing in the first half and sets up a score with a slick interception and runback, it's usually singing the fight song in a jubilant locker room.

When MSU's defense did that, it was almost speechless. The scoreboard did all the talking. And when an opponent gets as many touchdowns as your team has points, it's going to be a long day.

It wasn't surprising that the Spartans lost. History, the oddsmakers and the schedule all suggested that would happen. The shock was that they were so impotent against a disappointing Nebraska defense.

MSU had just one snap inside the hosts' 11-yard line. And that line of scrimmage immediately moved backward when Le'Veon Bell was thrown for a 3-yard loss.

On the topic of throwing, a lot of people were at a loss to explain what happened to the Spartans and quarterback Kirk Cousins, who went from hero to zero in less than seven days.

In the worst game of a distinguished career, Cousins completed less than 41 percent of his passes and averaged an anemic 3.6 yards. His first throw deep into double coverage fell incomplete. And his second toss was intercepted, setting up Nebraska's first score.

William Gholston leads the charge against Nebraska running back Rex Burkhead

With sacks subtracted, Cousins produced 65 yards on 31 throws or aborted attempts. The Huskers got more than that in the last two quarters from quarterback Taylor Martinez, whose javelin-style motion made Denard Robinson look like Aaron Rodgers.

It didn't help that tight end Dion Sims dropped a ball that could've made a major difference or that B.J. Cunningham, who was on pace for 98 catches this season, was blanked for the first time in 42 games.

And we can't help but wonder what coordinator Dan Roushar was thinking. After Bell carried four times for 29 yards in the game's first five snaps, he rushed just eight more times. The best play MSU had, running between the tackles, was largely abandoned.

Thus, it shouldn't be a shock that the Spartans failed to convert a single third-down situation in the

HEART OF A **SPARTAN**

first, third or fourth quarters.

Of course, it didn't help that MSU had nine more penalties for 90 yards, including a rare offensive facemask flag against Bell. His cross-country run that could've set up a first-and-goal at the Nebraska 1 turned into second-and-22 at the 30.

That wasn't the only blown opportunity. Nick Hill's 62-yard kickoff return went for naught when Dan Conroy was short with a 52-yard field goal. And Johnny Adams' 25-yard swipe-and-scamper could only produce three points.

No one can blame the Spartans' lack of discipline

Strong safety Isaiah Lewis delivers another big hit vs. the Cornhuskers

on William Gholston this time. After sitting out the win over Wisconsin for a retaliatory punch against Michigan, Gholston had a career-high 15 tackles. And fellow defensive end Marcus Rush added 13.

This time, the ends didn't justify the means.

Their superior efforts weren't nearly enough, despite holding workhorse running back Rex Burkhead to 3.7 yards per carry and the slick Martinez to 1.9.

None of that mattered when MSU had to play its best game to win and turned in one of its worst, for whatever reason.

Instead of channeling the dominance we saw at Ohio State and against the Wolverines and Badgers, the Spartans looked more like the team that forgot to show up at Iowa and against Alabama last season and at Notre Dame this year.

Maybe it's something about road games on Halloween weekend. MSU lost 42-34 at Minnesota on October 31, 2009, and 37-6 last October 30 in Iowa City.

Maybe it's something about facing Nebraska. The Spartans aren't just 0-6 in the series. They've never scored more than 14 points against the Huskers. And they've never allowed less than 17 – a bad recipe for success.

Or maybe it was just the emotional whirlwind of a 3-1 month that almost anyone would've taken before it began. If Keith Nichol sees "Rocket" one more time, he's going to think he plays for NASA.

But when people say it's the coaches' job to get their players ready to play each week, they're forgetting one thing. The players have pulses. They bleed. And even if they're quarantined, they hear what's being said.

One week ago, we couldn't believe the finish. In Memorial Stadium, there was never a start.

That brings me back to something a lot of you are sick of reading – a truth that was explained in the first column that ever ran in this space.

You're never as good as you look when you win and seldom as bad as you seem when you lose.

MSU won lots of close games and got everything it could out of the 2010 season, winning a school-record 11 games and being blown to bits in two of them.

The season, we could see something similar, though the implosions have come a little earlier on the calendar.

"This is about the long haul," Mark Dantonio correctly reminded us. "This isn't about one football game."

Except ... in one way, it was.

Unlike the suffocation of the Buckeyes or the stunning of the Badgers, the MSU-Nebraska game was the key game in the Legends Division race in the Big Ten.

If the Spartans had lost to Wisconsin and beaten the Huskers, no problem. MSU would've had head-to-head and three-way tiebreaker advantages over U-M and Nebraska.

Now, it'll take a 4-0 November and a slip by the Huskers for the Spartans to make it to Indianapolis for the first Big Ten Championship Game.

MSU definitely can do that, starting with a win over Minnesota in a game that won't be played for a bronze pig.

Then, we'll see if the Spartans remember Game 9 last year in Kinnick Stadium, a house of horrors where they haven't won since October 7, 1989, more than six-and-a-half months before Jerel Worthy was born.

The regular season will end with a Senior Day visit from Indiana and a return trip to Northwestern, teams that combined to score 94 points more than MSU did Saturday.

If the Spartans play the way they can, they'll be 10-2 and will have an excellent shot of getting to Indy, even it takes some help from U-M.

If not, they'll wonder what happened and ask themselves how they can look so good for so long and suddenly turn into pumpkins.

They need to start asking that question today, just to make sure there isn't a slip-up. If they think the Golden Gophers can't spring an upset, they can tweet the Hawkeyes.

Better yet, they can take care of business this week, then get ready to win once at Iowa.

The MSU basketball team will be facing No. 1 North Carolina the day before that in San Diego. The Spartans-Hawkeyes football game is suddenly much more important.

HAPPY HOMECOMING

KEITH NICHOL KNOWS
THE KEY IS GETTING IT RIGHT

LIFE IS A GAME of quick decisions. We don't always have days or weeks to react.

But when there's a chance to correct an error, when we can hit the reset button or right a wrong, we would be silly not to take advantage of that opportunity.

Sometimes it just takes the courage to do that. Sometimes a player and a referee have more in common than anyone realizes.

Keith Nichol knows all about that.

It turned out to be the wrong call when he reneged on a 17-month commitment to Michigan State and suddenly enrolled at Oklahoma. With a coaching change in East Lansing and a chance for stability and stardom in Norman, it was an enticing option. It just wasn't the right one.

After a year at OU, Nichol knew it was time for an audible. Facing skepticism and scorn from some fans, he showed all kinds of character by coming home, competing for a job that easily could have been his, then switching spots to make the team better.

Of all the players Mark Dantonio has had, none has displayed a better change of direction than a can't-miss quarterback who became a can't-do-without wideout and a free agent with the Washington Redskins.

Of all the positions Nichol could play, including a couple he hasn't tried yet, the two labels that fit him best are football player and first-string winner.

And of all the people to be a Homecoming hero, of all the guys to benefit from instant replay, Nichol deserved to score a game-winning touchdown against Wisconsin that we'll be watching for years.

It's all about getting it right.

"I don't look back," Nichol said. "I'm proud of the player I've become."

As well he should be. Instead of falling victim to pride, Nichol had an amazing, down-and-up ride with the Spartans. And chances are, he isn't done playing or representing.

It all started in high school with the Lowell Red Arrows, where Nichol went 33-3 as a three-time all-stater. He threw for 76 touchdowns and ran for 56 more as one of the nation's top dual-threat quarterbacks.

After battling for the starting job at OU in the spring of 2007, Nichol spent his freshman season as a third-team QB. Knowing he was stymied behind eventual Heisman Trophy winner Sam Bradford, it was time to transfer, sooner rather than later.

That was made easier by a conversation he'd had with Mark Dantonio in December 2006. Though it was tough to lose a prospect like Nichol, MSU's new head coach wished him well but said the door would be open if he ever changed his mind.

When Nichol arrived, he had to sit out the 2008 season under NCAA transfer rules. But the following spring and summer, he and sophomore Kirk Cousins had one of the closest competitions in school history. In the 2009 Green-White Game, amazingly, each threw for 357 yards and four TDs.

Though Cousins was named the starter, Nichol had some chances. He threw for two scores in the opener against Montana State, led the Spartans to a win over Illinois in his only start under center and tossed two TD passes, including a 91-yarder to Keshawn Martin, in relief at Wisconsin.

But after the Rather Hall suspensions, MSU was is desperate need of anyone who could catch a pass in an Alamo Bowl matchup with Texas Tech. Nichol could

Keith Nichol proves he can still throw the ball, too

HEART OF A **SPARTAN**

catch, run, block and learn the assignments as well as anyone on campus, though he may have been even better as a safety.

He caught two balls for 11 yards that night and scored his first collegiate TD on a 7-yard keeper from the wildcat formation. In the spring of 2010, "Mr. Versatility" became a full-time wideout. Nichol started eight games as a junior and caught 22 passes, including a 42-yarder at Michigan.

His senior year was one of big moments. And no one did more with limited touches than Nichol. Three of his 26 catches created vivid memories. Two of them led to spectacular victories.

Say the words "Rocket Man" in East Lansing, and as many people will answer "Keith Nichol" as "Elton John." A 44-yard Hail Mary heave on the game's final play gave the Spartans a 37-31 win over the Badgers in an ESPN prime-time telecast and was one of college football's lasting images in 2011.

With the game tied at tied at 31 and :04 remaining, MSU lined up with three receivers split to the left. But Wisconsin coach Bret Bielema called a timeout. If he hadn't done that, who knows what might have happened?

The Spartans switched their alignment to trips-right and went with the same "Rocket" call. Nichol was flanked furthest from the ball and was quickly shoved to the Badgers sideline. Actually, that probably helped the play's timing, as he trailed for exactly the kind of deflection he found.

When Cousins fired from his own 45, the ball grazed the fingertips of Wisconsin receiver and last-play safety Jared Abbrederis, then bounced off the helmet of B.J. Cunningham in the end zone. It caromed directly to Nichol two feet short of the goal line, where the real fun began.

The head-high catch was the easy part. Nichol still had to twist his body just enough to push the ball over the goal line, as Badgers linebacker Mike Taylor fought for every inch. The ruling on the field? No TD. But replay official Tom Herbert saw what Nichol knew.

"After further review," referee Dennis Lipski announced, "the runner did cross the line, the goal line ..."

Before he could finish that sentence or raise his arms, pandemonium erupted. Cunningham leaped on Nichol's back. Dantonio jumped just as high, his heart racing. And a team that played a full 60 minutes without a single penalty raced to celebrate as one, sharing that joy with the student section.

"We've won some close games around here with big plays, but that might be the biggest," Dantonio told sideline reporter Erin Andrews.

Error correction can be a beautiful thing, as Nichol realized before anyone else.

"It came down to a battle between a linebacker and a receiver to see who wanted to win the game more," analyst Kirk Herbstreit said. "And Nichol, the former quarterback, had just enough, literally two or three inches."

"We practice it every week," Nichol said. "You never know when a situation like that is going to happen ... To come out here in front of all these fans and win the game that way is incredible. I think it sums up how the whole game went."

A whole career, too. Never easy. And never out of reach.

But Nichol wasn't done, saving the best for the final six weeks of a five-year odyssey. He showed his option skills with a sweet catch-and-lateral to Cunningham for a TD in a Big Ten Championship rematch. And his 7-yard grab gave MSU its first lead, 20-19, in a triple-overtime Outback Bowl win over Georgia.

"Our guys outlasted theirs," Nichol said. "It shows how our careers have been, facing adversity every day and fighting for everything we've gotten. Coach Dantonio had a heart attack. That didn't stop us. Nothing did, even when it seemed that we were playing against the refs sometimes. We kept our mouth shut and went to work.

"To go out this way is the best. It means more than beating Michigan. We know how to do that. It's part of our culture. But we didn't know how to win a big bowl game. We do now."

Change is a powerful force. So was No. 7.

NOVEMBER 5, 2011 • SATURDAY

T-ROB-BERY ... T-RIFFIC

AFTER SINGING the "MSU Fight Song" in front of the student section Saturday afternoon, Trenton Robinson had unfinished business.

He had to throw a few Frisbees to his friend, Zeke III, at Spartan Stadium. Luckily, his incompletions to a yellow lab didn't matter. His interceptions and intensity did.

"T-Rob" had just saved the Big Ten Legends Division leaders with picks late in the third and fourth quarters of a 31-24 win over Minnesota. That first play set up a game-tying field goal. The second sealed a surprisingly tight victory.

But before he left the field, the senior free safety from Bay City and defensive captain had a little more work to do. He bounced from teammate to teammate, shouting "One more! One more! One more!" in reference to a two-season unbeaten streak at home.

With one more win against Indiana in two weeks, MSU can stretch that string in East Lansing to 14 games. Already, it's the longest sustained success since 19 straight triumphs on the banks of the Red Cedar from 1950-53.

And if the last "W" was anything but artful, it looks great in the latest Big Ten standings. If the Spartans can win at Iowa for the first time since October 7, 1989, the first year of the first Bush administration, they'll be in position to play Penn State, Ohio State or Wisconsin in the first Big Ten Championship Game on December 3 in Indianapolis.

Depending on what happens with Nebraska, MSU might still have to beat the Hoosiers on Senior Day and survive another trip to Northwestern, where Mark Dantonio's conference co-champs were extremely fortunate to win last season.

If you don't believe the Wildcats can be dangerous, address all inquiries to Lincoln, Neb., where they just clawed the Cornhuskers – the same 10th-ranked team that had beaten the Spartans by three touchdowns a week earlier.

The fact is, as much as we want to say this team is better than that one, upsets happen. They did to the Big Red and Big Blue in adjacent states Saturday. And they nearly got MSU and OSU, too.

Robinson may have been the biggest reason the Spartans escaped. His enthusiasm finally jolted a team that was outgained, 415-402. The hosts also allowed 22 first downs, 34:28 in time of possession and 7-for-15 third-down success.

"I always go to the sideline and say, 'We've got to keep going! Somebody has to make a play!'" Robinson said, not realizing that someone was him.

But it's easy to jump around and holler. It's harder to deliver a game-turning play – the kind that "T-Rob" did against "D-Rob" with an end-zone interception on the game's first series at Michigan Stadium and delivered again vs. Gophers quarterback MarQueis Gray.

"He just brought a lot of emotion and was all about making the play," MSU middle linebacker Max Bullough said. "It's less about what people say and more about what they do."

Here's what the Spartans did in a C-/D+ performance: They survived another sluggish start and made just enough plays to get to 7-2 overall and 4-1 in the conference, something they wouldn't have done in a lot of other years.

For the fourth straight week, MSU gave up a TD on its first defensive series. But after surrendering scores on drives of 82, 83 and 80 yards, the Spartans got serious. Minnesota's last five possessions ended with two interceptions, two three-and-out punts and a turnover on downs.

How many times over the last three decades have we seen the opposite occur? How many times have we seen the Green and White blow a game it had no business losing or botch a seemingly simple play in the fourth quarter? Too many to list here.

This year's team is different that way. Actually, so was last year's group when it came to close games,

MSU wouldn't have beaten Minnesota without Trenton Robinson's two interceptions

245

one of the major trends of the second half of the Dantonio era.

Since an excruciating 15-13 loss to Iowa on a last-play breakdown in 2009, MSU has played 27 games. Seven have been decided by seven points or less. And the Spartans have won all seven of them.

Eventually, the law of averages will come into play. But if you believe that the mark of a successful program is to win the majority of its close games, MSU has done that as well as any program could over the past two-plus years.

The four games the Spartans have lost in the last two seasons have been by 31, 42, 18 and 21 points – an average margin of four touchdowns. As infuriating as those no-shows have, there's a more revealing number.

MSU has won the other 18 games, a record that's second-to-none among Big Ten schools. And its 11-2 conference mark is the best in its league, one game better than the Buckeyes and Badgers.

So what does that mean when Robinson & Co. make a repeat appearance in Kinnick Stadium, a place their school hasn't won since Jerel Worthy was still in the womb? Maybe a little. Maybe a lot. Maybe nothing.

It all depends on which team shows up – the one that was blown out by Iowa and Alabama and was basically inept at Notre Dame and Nebraska, or the one that wears a league championship ring and could be in line for better jewelry.

It's one thing to have swagger, especially when it has been earned. It's another to turn receiving nemesis Marvin McNutt into Marvin McNope and to make star runner Marcus Coker just another back.

Can the Spartans do that? Of course they can. Kirk Cousins, Le'Veon Bell, B.J. Cunningham, William Gholston and Isaiah Lewis were only in uniform for one of the setbacks in Iowa City and can't be held accountable for the rest.

But there's no guarantee that MSU will win because it's the better team, because it's due, because of the revenge motive or because it just beat a team that defeated the Hawkeyes seven days earlier.

The better team doesn't always win. The better team that day usually does. And so what if it's due? So are a lot of mortgage payments that won't be made this month. Each game has to stand on its own.

As far as paybacks are concerned, if owing a team a pounding meant anything, the Spartans wouldn't have won 17 straight against Minnesota from 1977-97. And if Michigan's anger at a stronger sibling didn't matter in 2009-10, surely its countdown clock would've said it's time to play winning football against MSU this fall.

Finally, the transitive law – if A > B and B > C, then surely A > C – doesn't work in a sport where luck is part of the winning equation. Thus, the Spartans > Gophers > Hawkeyes hierarchy in head-to-head matchups means nothing. A heads-up performance means more.

That means avoiding the silly interceptions we saw when MSU trailed Iowa 30-0 at halftime last year. It means no more fumbles from a running back who was All-Big Ten a year ago. And it means eliminating some silly penalties – or at least limiting the walkoffs to one per play.

Maybe Cousins' personal foul for spiking the ball in frustration Saturday was a wake-up call. Maybe Robinson sounded the alarm on defense. But the Spartans have a chance to throw more than Frisbees now. They can throw their critics and doubters for a loop.

Winning at Iowa and being victorious in a bowl game are the last two obstacles to putting "Same Old Spartans" into the same dumpster as its old feelings of in-state inferiority.

NOVEMBER 12, 2011 • SATURDAY

A WEEKEND SALUTE

FROM ANCHORS AWEIGH to Demons Away – all in the span of 20 hours.

The Michigan State Spartans have had a lot of great weekends in football and basketball. In hockey, too. MSU is the only school with multiple national championships in all three sports. But it's hard to remember a more important two days for two teams than the Carrier Classic in San Diego and the Cornfield Clobber in Iowa City.

The first event was Mark Hollis' dream-come-true. The second was Mark Dantonio's team-come-through.

To understand the relevance, you have to know the relationships. It started in 1983 when Tom Izzo was a graduate assistant and Hollis was a first-year student manager. Before Izzo's first game as a head coach in 1995, Dantonio had been hired as a Nick Saban assistant. And when Hollis left for other jobs, then returned and became director of athletics, he knew two things.

He wouldn't rest, nor should anyone else in the department, until MSU had played in the Rose Bowl. And when it was finally time to hire a football coach, he wanted someone as committed to winning the right way as Izzo had been – and still is.

Flash forward to 2006. John L. Smith is a coaching corpse. And Hollis is scouring the country to find an ideal replacement in a program that was 14-21 the past three years. But of all the decisions he made, the best was to listen to Izzo and wait to talk to Dantonio, who was tied up at Cincinnati for a few more weeks.

By the time their plane returned from Ohio, they both knew they'd found the right guy. And before the final amazing memory on the deck of the USS Carl Vinson, as close to a triumph as a setback could be, Hollis and Izzo were thinking about the next day's developments.

Like Dantonio, they remembered every painful play against Iowa the previous two seasons. They saw Marvin McNutt's touchdown on a last-chance slant route in 2009 and Micah Hyde's cross-country interception return in 2010. They watched the Spartans get stunned 16-13 and slaughtered 37-6.

So it was no surprise that Hollis, the No. 1 non-military hero or White House guest on the ship, and Izzo, who always thinks of championships, were on the same boat that way, too. They knew a football win this weekend was the more important outcome.

Dantonio, his players and his staff didn't disappoint them. Returning to the scene of a serious mugging, they delivered a 37-21 beat-down and allowed MSU to celebrate in Kinnick Stadium for the first time in 22 seasons.

The last time that had happened, Keshawn Martin, Jerel Worthy and Trenton Robinson were embryos. This time, they were embracing at the end of the game as if they'd won the Big Ten's first Legends Division title. They were one week premature.

Fifty-four weeks after the embarrassment of a 30-0 halftime deficit, the Spartans scored 31 points in the first 30 minutes. They finished with the same total Iowa had in handing an undefeated team a 31-point pasting – a game that left MSU as a co-champ in Orlando instead of an outright titlist in Pasadena.

This time, the Spartans left nothing to chance. They were the better team in every way – and not because Kirk Ferentz's players were still celebrating their win over Michigan seven days earlier.

Le'Veon Bell was far superior to fellow sophomore Marcus Coker at running back, outrushing him 112-57 and adding 49 yards on two receptions. Bell's 25-yard carry with 1:57 left in the first half made it 24-7 and gave the Spartans all the points they would need.

Time-share back Edwin Baker, never known as a receiver, made a highlight-video, 17-yard grab at the right edge of the end zone. Wideout B.J. Cunningham caught the other TD passes on pickups of 6 and 22 yards. Martin had a 67-yard catch-and-run. And tight end Brian Linthicum had a team-high five receptions for 71 yards.

You had to feel good for quarterback Kirk Cousins, a Hawkeyes fan growing up in Iowa. It wasn't that he threw for 288 yards. It was that he threw the hosts for a loop with his leadership and mistake-free play on the same field where he had been intercepted three times.

On defense, cornerbacks Johnny Adams, Jeremy Langford and Tony Lippett had takeaways – an interception and two fumble recoveries. And middle linebacker Max Bullough had 13 tackles, albeit none as big as a goal-line stop his father, Shane, helped make in a one-point win over the Hawkeyes 27 years earlier.

The special teams were special, too. Punter Mike Sadler averaged 46.2 yards and put three kicks inside the 20. Worthy blocked a field goal. And Dan Conroy drilled three three-pointers, icing the game from 48 yards.

Even the coaches had moments to savor. Up 31-7, Dantonio called a reverse pass, and Martin hit Linthicum for 28 yards. It was better execution of a play the Hawkeye tried unsuccessfully with a 30-0 lead the year before.

Four plays later, on fourth-and-6, holder Brad Sonntag picked the ball up on a fake field goal and ran for 8 yards and a first down. The trick play was called "Gold." But while the media was searching for the name, *Detroit Free Press* columnist Drew Sharp announced, "That one's called 'Payback's a Bitch!'"

Indeed, it was a perfect play on a near-perfect day. As alumni from Pacific Beach to Pompano Beach gathered to watch, MSU showed its heart in what had long been a house of horrors.

"I remember coming off the field last year when we were No. 5 in the country," Robinson said. "It sickens me to think about it. I just remember the fans yelling 'Overrated!'"

Not this time. Not this team.

With the most points the program had ever scored at Iowa, the Spartans registered their 34th win in a four-year span, the most by any senior class in the school's 115-year football history.

More important than numbers were a new mindset and a different image. Gone was the MSU program that couldn't quite answer its critics. In its place, we saw what happened when talent and tenacity took the field at the same time.

The visitors didn't just leave with a victory. They flew home with vindication.

"We talked about either weathering the storm or being the storm," Dantonio said. "We didn't know which it would be."

For one destructive day, his team was a cyclone. And unlike the Cyclones from Iowa State, MSU can make a championship statement, starting with the first Legends title.

The Spartans still have to beat Indiana on Senior Day and win at Northwestern to post double-digit wins for the fourth time. But their latest triumph was a classic, too.

Hollis, Izzo and Dantonio all knew it could be.

Cousins, Bell and Bullough proved it would be.

It was a weekend to savor. And there was nothing corny about it.

Jerel Worthy delivers a big smack in Iowa City

NOVEMBER 19, 2011 • SATURDAY

SENIOR MOMENTS

THEY DIDN'T WANT TO LEAVE THE FIELD.
Finally, the Michigan State Spartans did that and headed off to their locker room. There was another version of the "MSU Fight Song" to sing, a B1G Legends Division trophy to receive and a bright football future to embrace.

At day's end, they had three games left to play when the schedule had only guaranteed one.

But whatever happens next Saturday at Northwestern, the following week in Indianapolis and on January 2 in Pasadena or somewhere in Florida, some things are cast in State-stone:

- With a 55-3 autopsy of Indiana, the Spartans became the first team ever to win a Big Ten divisional crown and lock up a berth in the league's new championship game.

- MSU completed its second straight 7-0 campaign at home and boosted its four-year record in East Lansing – before crowds of all sizes and degrees of support – to 24-4.

- At 6-1 in conference play and 9-2 overall, Mark Dantonio's fifth-year program climbed to 20-4 over the last two seasons and won its 35th game in the last four years – both all-time bests.

- A class with class said goodbye to its turf in all kinds of ways – with classic fakes and solo trips to the end zone, with terrific catches and breathtaking runs, with a guard-around ramble and reward and with a logo salute from a leader we'll salute for a long time.

The result of the game was never in doubt. Indiana was In-trouble and In-over-its-head long before the In-troductions.

Forty-five years from the day of the biggest football game ever played in the state of Michigan, the 10-10 "Game of the Century" with Notre Dame, the Spartans welcomed another visitor from the Hoosier State the way the Harlem Globetrotters treat the Washington Generals.

And when they were all done leaping – into the air, into each other, into the crowd and into their families' arms – they should be remembered for their most important leap.

For a program-turning leap of faith.

Those who came to campus in 2007, when Dantonio's staff took over after the John L. Smith error, could only take stock in a promise. MSU had just finished a 22-26 rainstorm of folly and futility. Now, those fifth-year seniors could experience 23 triumphs in the span of two seasons.

Those who arrived 12 months later and finished their careers without being redshirted will be remembered forever on the banks of the Red Cedar. They could finish with 38 wins in four years – the same number of victories the Spartans had in seven seasons from 2000-06 under three confused head coaches.

The true beauty of what MSU has done is the lesson it has taught us all about perseverance: There are very few things in life so severe that they can't be overcome.

Mistakes in judgment, understandable skepticism and physical blows – including bone cancer and a heart attack – can all be overcome with faith, family and the right kind of fight.

That faith can take a lot of forms. For leaderback Kick Cousins, the most successful signal-caller and captain the Spartans have known, it always starts with crediting his lord and savior, Jesus Christ. But it doesn't have to, as much as Dantonio supports that thinking.

Different players have different beliefs. The successful ones have three things in common: They all believe in something. They all have someone who believes in them. And at Winning Time, they all believe in themselves.

It's often a cliché, if not a recruiting gimmick, when coaches talk about "family" to try to promote their programs. For Dantonio, it's a firm commitment. Any more so and he could add 105 players a year as dependents.

Not that the vast majority of his players don't have families and friends waiting outside the stadium on Saturdays. They do. And especially after a crushing defeat, that's comforting to see.

But there's an extended support system and an all-for-one, one-for-all attitude that I haven't seen with the Spartans in successive seasons since the mid-1960s – ironically, the last time they sustained this level of success.

How has that happened? More often than not, it hasn't been with gifts of greatness. MSU has won 13 of its last 15 conference games with will just as much as skill. In a way, that makes its success more rewarding.

The fact is, this team has been knocked flat several times. Somehow, just when cynics were sharpening their swords, a group that hasn't cared who hasn't believed has scraped itself off the ground, then managed to stay grounded.

Before Dantonio's "Keep Playing" mantra could have real meaning, his players had to keep working, almost non-stop. They had to put in the extra time and extra sweat so a demeaning "S.O.S." abbreviation stood for "S'never Over, Spartans!"

That's one of the two greatest accomplishments with this team – far greater than four straight victories over Michigan and back-to-back wins over Wisconsin.

MSU hasn't just changed the composition of its roster. It has managed to change the culture, an incredibly difficult thing to do.

As was the accumulation and assimilation of players into a successful system. Together, they improved, then proved a lot of people wrong.

Maybe Cousins said it best, as he often does – and not just when he's representing the players from all 12 teams with an often YouTubed speech at the Big Ten Football Luncheon.

"We talked about it when we first got here in 2007, back when we were all at McDonel Hall," he said. "We said we were a bunch of two-stars with an extra heartbeat. And we said, 'Our two- and three-

Keshawn Martin and Joel Foreman share a day to remember

Jerel Worthy does his best Le'Veon Bell impression, minus the football

stars are coming to get your four- and five stars!'"

Consider them devoured like a helpless steak on Jerel Worthy's plate. But Cousins' point was well-taken after he'd just helped to post 55 of them.

If No. 8 was an afterthought in Dantonio's first class, the No. 1 thought Saturday was just how close he is to quarterbacking the Spartans in the Rose Bowl, a stadium he couldn't even talk his way into as a visitor last summer.

With a win in over next week's Penn State-Wisconsin survivor, Cousins could become the first MSU QB to have the paint of roses on his cleats since another No 8, Bobby McAllister, won there in 1988. And it'd be great to show that being in the Rose Bowl isn't all Luck.

It's love for one another, too – the kind displayed by receivers B.J. Cunningham and Keshawn Martin. Cunningham hosted Martin, a virtual unknown and a recruiting steal, on his official visit four years ago. Saturday, they combined to catch 14 passes, including Cunningham's 200th, for 231 yards and three touchdowns.

But the image I'll treasure from Saturday was the reaction to rock-solid, fifth-year guard and captain Joel Foreman's career-only 3-yard run. You'd have thought he'd scored on a Hail Mary when he reached the sideline with a ball he wasn't surrendering.

The first person there to greet him? His good friend, Arthur Ray Jr., a cancer conqueror who started the season-opener at Foreman's insistence and whose appearance on the field against the Hoosiers again showed how far a band of brothers has come.

No surrender. No pretenders.

Just another trophy to tote around and display near Paul Bunyan, an old spittoon and a land-grant award they may as well compete for in Lucas Oil Stadium.

They'd also find room or make room in the Skandalaris Center for two more prizes, the spoils that go to Big Ten playoff and BCS bowl champions.

For all that has been done the past two seasons, three challenges remain. Complete teams complete their mission.

NOVEMBER 26, 2011 • SATURDAY

THE BIGGEST 10

THE NUMBERS TELL a terrific story. And the counting continues for the Michigan State Spartans:

- Ten wins for just the fourth time in 115 seasons of football.

- Back-to-back years with double-digit victories for the first time.

- A 21-4 mark in the past 15 months, with a chance to have more triumphs in 16 than any Division I team in state history.

- A 14-2 Big Ten record in 2010-11, the best for any school in that span.

- Three Big Ten road wins over bowl-bound teams, the most of any program this season.

- Excellence that would've brought two Rose Bowl trips under the previous years' rules.

- Thirty-six wins in less than four seasons, three more than MAC/MSC/MSU had ever had.

- A 5-1 record vs. Michigan and Ohio State since 2008, the best four-year mark since 1950-53.

- A fifth straight bowl bid for the first time in school history, with the last four games on January 1 or 2.

- Sixty-two career touchdown passes for Kirk Cousins and 206 grabs for B.J. Cunningham, among a slew of individual school records.

But this year isn't about individuals. It's all about a team.

And it isn't about statistics. It's about stories – the kind that'll be told at tailgates in 2051 and beyond.

The first team to lock up a berth in the first Big Ten Championship Game doesn't care that it's a double-digit underdog this Saturday in Indianapolis.

The Spartans don't mind that Wisconsin is the popular pick – some would say the logical one – to represent their league in the Rose Bowl.

All they know is that they're 60 minutes of football away from a site they've only seen on TV.

They're four quarters from having the paint of roses on their shoes, the stated goal when Mark Hollis became athletic director and again when he hired Mark Dantonio.

But if MSU's path to Pasadena began that day in December 2006, it became a 10-lane expressway when Dantonio and an unusually stable staff began a two-part plan.

Half construction. Half instruction.

The Spartans became a championship team – to nearly everyone's surprise – by pursuing that prize with laser-like focus.

That started with a winning philosophy, an approach that was shaped by successful stretches under Nick Saban and Jim Tressel.

Both those coaches knew that you win by getting the best players you can and making them better, whether it's at Toledo, Youngstown State, MSU, LSU, OSU or Alabama.

The first two of those schools have a great deal in common, as do the last three. The group that's presented with a different set of challenges is the one Dantonio inherited.

Unlike the Tigers, the Bucks and the Tide, the Spartans can't count on an endless stream of top-10 classes. Unlike the Rockets and Penguins, success and continued employment depend on the ability to beat teams with top-10 talent.

MSU has done that primarily with GP3 – good players and great people with growth potential.

Aaron Bates, Charlie Gantt, Eric Gordon and Greg Jones are gone. Kirk Cousins, B.J. Cunningham, Joel Foreman, Keshawn Martin, Trenton Robinson and Kevin Pickelman are going.

Of those 10, one name doesn't seem to belong

Keshawn Martin has clear sailing for a score against the Wildcats

HEART OF A **SPARTAN**

with the rest. What matters is that he belonged in this program and belongs on the field for the Big Ten's best defense.

Pickelman belonged in the Northwestern backfield last weekend, sharing the team lead with eight tackles – all solos – including a sack of dangerous quarterback Dan Persa.

For the year, No. 96 has 37 tackles, 7.5 for losses. He also has a pass deflection and a forced fumble. But it's what he represents that matters more than his stat line.

"When I say I'm a Spartan, I think of all the hard work – the summers, the 5 a.m. workouts and the players who played before me," Pickelman said. "That's who I'm playing for, the guys who've given so much to this program."

Pickelman wasn't picked for that privilege. He persevered and earned every bit of it.

As a senior at Marshall High, just 51 miles from the MSU campus, he may as well have been five time zones away. A tight end with 12 receptions and a linebacker with D-line speed, he didn't think he'd ever play in January.

The *Detroit Free Press* ranked him as the state's 25th-best prospect in 2006. *The Detroit News* wasn't nearly as optimistic, rating him 56th in the senior class.

Jerel Worthy puts the hurt on Northwestern quarterback Dan Persa

He was rejected by John L. Smith & Co. Twice. So he finally committed to Central Michigan, where he'd probably be an All-MAC performer today if Dantonio hadn't been hired by the Spartans and Brian Kelly hadn't succeeded him at Cincinnati.

If Kelly had stayed in Mount Pleasant, it wouldn't have mattered if Dantonio had treated Pickelman like a five-star recruit. A promise had been made. A promise would've been kept.

But with Butch Jones taking over at CMU, a scholarship offer disappeared. Finally, Marshall coach Rich Hulkow, a backup defensive lineman at MSU in the early '70s, decided to give it one more try.

When "Hulk" called Dantonio, whom he'd known from summer camps and four-star quarterback Ryan Van Dyke's recruitment, the message was more than "Congratulations! Welcome home."

It was a request for a brief meeting – one more chance to pitch a favorite player and four-year mainstay to his favorite school.

Ten minutes ... If that was all the time Dantonio had during a hectic transition, it would have to be enough. And it was.

Talk about your time well-spent! Pickelman will make his 10th start this season at defensive tackle Saturday night in Lucas Oil Stadium.

"I love being able to dominate someone," said Pickelman, a product of the coaching of Ted Gill and Pat Narduzzi and the conditioning of Ken Mannie. "D-tackle is the toughest position on the field. And I wanted to take that challenge."

At 6-foot-4, 288 pounds, he barely resembles the 240-pounder who showed up on campus 52 months ago and was named Scout Team Defensive Player of the Week for Dantonio's first game.

All-Big Ten? Only if you're talking Academic All-Big Ten, which he was in 2008. But Pickelman, a criminal justice major, gradually grew into a key player.

After redshirting in 2007, he played in 13 games, all as a backup, the following year. He made two starts as a sophomore and seven as a junior before becoming Jerel Worthy's sidekick this season.

Proving numbers don't tell the whole story, Pickelman has 14 more tackles than Worthy, a consensus first-team All-Big Ten choice. In at least one way, it's "Pick" over probable first-round draft pick.

"I don't talk much," Pickelman said. "But the coaches know I'm a consistent guy. If anybody needs anything, they can always count on me."

After the win over the Wildcats, with group interviews going on all around him, Pickelman gave a rare one-on-one interview – perhaps because everyone else in the media had gone elsewhere.

He didn't seem to need the attention. It's a good thing, because he hasn't gotten much of it. But he did get a sweet-looking ring this year. In a few months, Pickelman will get another one.

Like a lot of overlooked, underrated players on the league's highest-ranked team, he most wants a tag he can wear forever.

Back-to-back Big Ten champion and Rose Bowl winner.

"We're just going to work," Pickelman said. "Once you get a taste of that championship, you really want it again. And to put that rose in my mouth, that's all I can think about."

Picture that ... A career-ending celebration with a nice ring to it.

William Gholston is grabbed again as he's about to get a sack

DECEMBER 3, 2011 • SATURDAY

SO CLOSE ... ALL CLASS

THEY CHANGED A LOT of perceptions in the first Big Ten Championship Game. But the Michigan State Spartans can't change one thing.

A mystifying, maddening final score.

Despite dominating the Wisconsin Badgers as no opponent has this season, Mark Dantonio's team fell 42-39 late Saturday night in Lucas Oil Stadium.

With one too many mistakes and bad breaks, it went from Pasadena to parts unknown on January 2.

If the pain was etched on every player's face, that's what happens when roses die and you're left with a mouthful of thorns.

"In terms of athletics, I've never hurt more," fifth-year quarterback Kirk Cousins said. "I thought we played our hearts out and played a great game. We won the regular season outright and didn't wind up in the Rose Bowl."

The fifth-year senior was outstanding again with 22 completions in 30 attempts for 281 yards and three touchdowns. But a stadium he wasn't allowed to enter on a visit to California last summer will remain off-limits.

The same is true for his teammates, who were given pieces of rock from the site as a season-long inspiration. Today and for a long time, those rocks will be stuck inside their shoes.

"This is the most shocked I've even been in my sports career," senior safety and captain Trenton Robinson said. "I still can't believe that this happened, that we're here talking and not out on that field. This is hard. Real hard."

It was hard to fall behind 21-7 after one quarter and be outscored 14-3 in the fourth. But make no mistake, the Spartans were the better team for much of the night, whatever that's worth. Today, not a lot.

In a 22-0 second quarter, MSU gained 208 yards and held Wisconsin to minus 8. Dantonio took chances on a fourth-and-1 bootleg pass from Cousins to Cunningham for a 44-yard score and a fake point-after that Brad Sonntag ran in for two.

Remember those names for what they represent. They'll all be missed. And though the program is on solid footing, it's impossible to overestimate how much this group has contributed or minimize their loss.

Cousins has rewritten the school's passing records and displayed enough passion to make everyone better. He has been as good a leader as any team in any sport in any conference has had and will be missed more than anyone knows.

Cunningham, a Columbus kid who has become a man, has been through it all and has grown into arguably the best receiver the school has had. That's saying a lot with the list of MSU greats at that position.

And Sonntag, another senior wideout, is listed at 5-foot-8. There's no measurement for heart on the roster, just a guarantee that a lot of them were broken when their last chance to be recognized as undisputed champions evaporated.

"Everything was right in front of us," Robinson said. "Everything. Now, it's gone, and we have to worry about where some guys are going to send us instead of just being where we dreamed of being."

Oddly enough, the Spartans gained more respect in a gallant loss than they earned nationally the past two years. That was true for a fan base that out-traveled the Badgers and for a team that could have won a dozen ways.

"There were just some plays that you can't believe happened," Robinson said. "You see these plays, and you're like, 'Man!' They were the luckiest plays you can imagine. But they won for a reason, and we lost for a reason."

The Spartans lost because Wisconsin is an excellent football team, more resilient than it gets credit for being after back-to-back road heartbreaks of its own, and because they couldn't get the break they needed.

They lost the takeaway battle, 2-0, including

a fumble by Nick Hill on a kickoff return that soon helped the Badgers go up 21-7 thanks to touchdown machine Montee Ball.

They lost their momentum and surrendered a score a moment later when Jerel Worthy was called for a dubious offside penalty and Johnny Adams whiffed on a blitz of eel-like Russell Wilson.

Finally, they lost their last two opportunities when Keshawn Martin's toe stab was ruled out-of-bounds on a booth review, though another photograph clearly shows otherwise, and when his probably game-winning punt return to the 3-yard line was negated when Isaiah Lewis was pushed into a thespian punter.

Still, if you had said that the Spartans would outgain Wisconsin by 126 yards and average 5.6 yards per play to the Badgers' 3.4, few would've believed you.

If you'd added that the Big Ten's 12th-ranked rushing offense would gain 190 yards on the ground while the No. 1 running game would net 126, a sobriety test would've been ordered.

Yet, that's what happened. A 10-point underdog, despite having the B1G's only 7-1 conference record,

Keshawn Martin's punt return was called back, as was a trip to the Rose Bowl

acquitted itself extremely well and may have risen on a few AP, USA Today and Harris Poll ballots in defeat.

"We proved we belong with any team in the country," Cousins said. "Wisconsin is going to be a top 10 team and go to the Rose Bowl. Obviously, the way we played them twice, we belong right there with them. We're always trying to prove people wrong. They can think what they want. We played our hearts out tonight."

Meanwhile, another team from the Big Ten could be the big beneficiary of a non-champions bye. In a way, every team from the conference gains if a second team gets a BCS bid. But forgive Cousins from thinking head-to-head results and the standings should matter.

"Michigan sat at home on the couch tonight and watched us," Cousins said. "We played. You saw us. I don't know how you can get punished for playing. This is the way the system is. I think it's a broken system."

It's the way of the world. No one said that life is fair. In fact, it can be fairly cruel at times. But the Spartans didn't get to be Legends Division Champions by sulking, even when the two best teams in the league won't wind up with the two best bowls.

If not for a change in the tiebreaker formula, one that Dantonio endorsed, the Spartans would've faced TCU in Pasadena last season, instead of being served up to Alabama in Orlando. And eight league games lost their importance again this year, much to MSU's dismay.

"I know people like to make money, and it's about money," Cousins said. "This game brought in upwards of $20 million. Someone is getting that money. Not me. But someone is."

Forget that game and another shot at the SEC for a minute – and just for one as Cousins said, because, "That's the way we operate at Michigan State. This group will play hard in whatever bowl we get."

But anyone care for a rematch of the rematch – a best-two-out-of-three, if you will? ... The silence from Madison, Wis., today means the next replay will be next October 27.

Can't wait. And if there's another meeting next December 1 in Indy, that'd be just fine, too.

PERFECT PROGRESSION

KIRK COUSINS HAS SEEN IT ALL, GIVEN HIS ALL

HE COULD HAVE BEEN an Iowa Hawkeye.

Growing up outside Chicago with black-and-gold bloodlines, cheering for his do-it-all hero, that was Kirk Cousins' dream.

Or he could have played in Spartan Stadium and quarterbacked a Mid-American Conference visitor.

After being slow-played by the former Michigan State coaching staff, that seemed like a logical plan. But he who hesitates is … still available.

Better late than never, Kirk Cousins finally got a scholarship offer from new head coach Mark Dantonio in January 2007. And it's tough to say who got the better of that deal, a perfect blend of fate and faith.

This much we can say: MSU has never had a better leader under center or a better representative for the school, the conference and college football.

Still, the Spartans were perilously close to playing against Cousins, instead of playing with him and for him.

"I remember being in Kinnick Stadium for Homecoming in '95 and seeing Tim Dwight return a punt for a touchdown," Cousins recalled. "I was an Iowa fan from that day forward. I went to camp there to get on the radar. But they already had a quarterback committed, Marvin McNutt."

Just because the Hawkeyes were out of the picture, that didn't mean the Spartans were in it. Not yet. Not until the stars aligned.

It appeared that Cousins was headed to Western Michigan or Toledo. He also paid a visit to Princeton, which he promptly rejected due to distance and a level of play he called "glorified Division III."

"If Michigan State hadn't offered, I still don't know where I'd have gone," said Cousins, then an under-the-radar recruit from Holland Christian High. "John L. Smith's staff had been recruiting me. They said they'd like to take a second quarterback. But if John L. had stayed, you never know."

Cousins knows as much about football – and life – as any Spartan ever has. He became the program's first three-time captain since Robert "Buck" McCurry from 1946-48. Yet, he was perilously close to being a saint elsewhere.

The Spartans already had a commitment from Lowell High megastar Keith Nichol, dating back to July 2005. But when Smith was fired, Nichol visited Oklahoma in December 2006, committed on the spot and created even more uncertainty.

"I thought, 'Now, they really need a quarterback,'" Cousins said. "A week after Coach Dantonio took the job, they weren't sure if I was athletic enough. They weren't ready to offer me a scholarship. Then, they offered Nick Foles, who'd decommitted from Arizona State."

Cousins felt as if he had been shot in the gut, even before Foles arrived at MSU as a gunslinger from Texas. Never one to back away from a challenge, that snub only made him more determined to prove people wrong.

"I had a chip on my shoulder and said, 'I see the way it is!'" Cousins remembered. "But if you checked my bio on the recruiting services, it wasn't too intimidating."

It didn't have to be. Cousins just had to be Cousins. According to God's plan, that has always been enough.

"People want to know how it all happened," he said. "The short answer is God. John 15:5 says, 'I am the vine; you are the branches.

A surprise scramble helps MSU tie Georgia on a drive for the ages

Abide in me, and you will bear much fruit. Apart from me, you can do nothing.'"

Cousins stayed plugged into his power source and followed the path of greatest resistance. With an assist from former MSU receiver/return man Herb Haygood, his tape wound up back in front of Dantonio, who made arguably the best offer of his life – other than a marriage proposal to his wife, Becky.

Once on campus, Cousins began competing to become Brian Hoyer's backup and to convince everyone that he, not Foles, was the Spartans' future.

When the seniors drafted teams for the 2008 Green and White Game and chose Cousins first at his position, it was the first public indication. And when guest head coach Tom Izzo put No. 8 in the game for a final winning drive, even though it was Foles' turn to play, the vibes spoke volumes.

Spring ball and Nichol's decision to return home where he belonged were enough to convince Foles to transfer to Arizona, where he remained friends with Cousins and had a fine career.

With Nichol sitting out the 2008 season in accordance with NCAA rules, Cousins appeared in five games as a redshirt-freshman. The first clue of what he could do came against mighty Ohio State, when he hit 18 of 25 passes for 161 yards and a score in relief of Brian Hoyer. He finished by going 7-for-9 against Penn State and 4-for-5 vs. Georgia in the Capital One Bowl ... Remember that matchup.

Still, Cousins was an underdog in many people's minds the following spring. When he and Nichol each threw for 357 yards and four touchdowns in the Green and White Game, Dantonio had a tough decision. But when Cousins' teammates made him a captain before his first collegiate start, they recognized his leadership, too.

That was never clearer than after a frustrating 2009 season. It was Cousins who pulled a splintered team together, organized secret workouts with suspended receivers Mark Dell and B.J. Cunningham in a church gymnasium and made them believe in the team and themselves.

No other MSU quarterback was a starter in 27 victories. None led the Spartans to three wins over Michigan. And none could match his passing numbers: 723 completions, 9,131 yards, 66 TDs, 146.1 efficiency and 26 200-yard games.

Mistakes? He made a few, as he would be the first to tell you. But Cousins never lost the trust of his coaches or the respect of his teammates. That was obvious in the 2012 Outback Bowl, when he rallied the Spartans from a 16-0 halftime deficit to a 33-30 triple-overtime win.

None of those extra series would have happened if "Captain Kirk" hadn't driven his team 85 yards in 10 plays for a tying TD with :19 left. All he did in the final 1:55 was complete six passes to five receivers for 62 yards and pick up another 20 on a scramble, all without the benefit of a timeout.

But Cousins will be known for what he accomplished off the field as much as for all his statistics combined. A four-time Academic All-Big Ten pick with a 3.68 grade-point average, he became the handsome face of a resurgent program, one that turned years of ridicule into new respect. Suddenly, responsibility became trendy.

His greatest public moment may have been a 7-minute talk on behalf of all the league's players at the 2011 Big Ten Kickoff Luncheon. If you're one of the few who haven't seen that video, or even if you have, do yourself a favor and Google search: "Cousins speech." Fifteen seconds after he finished, he was the only person in the room who wasn't standing and applauding.

We'll never see a list of all the appearances Cousins made for charitable causes. Suffice to say, he won the Lowe's Senior CLASS Award (Celebrating Loyalty and Achievement for Staying in School) as his sport's outstanding graduating student-athlete.

Pro football is Cousins' next stop. And you have to like his chances. After that, the choice is all his. Medicine, media, politics ... it's amazing what someone can do when talent meshes with a strong belief system and humble meets hungry.

DECEMBER 25, 2011 • SUNDAY

... AND A HAPPY NEW YEAR

THE SANTA SUIT was redder than any referee's face. And the sack of gifts was stuffed like Antonio Jeremiah's old uniform.

It was Christmas Eve for a football program that was good more often than bad this season. Its last lump of coal is in Indy.

So what should Mark Dantonio and the Michigan State Spartans expect under the shade trees in sunny Tampa?

Green grass, for one thing. Green is always good this time of year, even when maize and blue have run together in the wash.

Another shot at respect, for another. With all that MSU has accomplished, it hasn't won a bowl game since Le'Veon Bell was in fourth grade.

This just in: No one could stop his spins then, either.

But if the Spartans can beat the Georgia Bulldogs – and they can if they play well – they'll have a bowl win over an SEC team for just the second time in seven chances.

MSU lost 6-0 to Auburn in the 1938 Orange Bowl, 34-27 to Georgia in the 1989 Gator Bowl, 45-26 to LSU in the 1995 Independence Bowl, 24-12 to the Bulldogs again in the 2009 Capital One Bowl and 49-7 to Alabama in the 2011 Capital One Bowl.

Counting a 37-34 win over Florida in the 2000 Florida Citrus Bowl, the Spartans have been outscored 192-109 in those postseason matchups.

That means absolutely nothing to this year's team, which already has 10 wins a-leaping.

If anything, seniors Kirk Cousins, B.J. Cunningham, Keshawn Martin, Joel Foreman and Trenton Robinson see this game as a chance to right a ridiculous wrong, just as they did this year at Iowa.

And fifth-year receivers Keith Nichol and Brian Linthicum see a return trip to Florida as a final chance to show everyone what they already know – that their decisions to transfer in from Oklahoma and Clemson, respectively, will rank with the best they'll ever make.

So let's see what ol' St. Nick (the jolly guy, not Saban) has in store for MSU this time with a wishful peek at his presents and the program's future:

- For Bell, arguably the Big Ten's second-best back: A chance at Lorenzo White's career records and a shot at the Heisman Trophy in 2013 after leaving more defenders dazed and dizzy.

- For Cousins, as fine a leader as you'll find in any sport: Recognition as the Spartans' most-accomplished quarterback, a school-record 27th win as a starter, second-round status in the 2012 NFL Draft and half as much faith from his next coach as a three-year captain has always had in his Lord and Savior.

- For Cunningham, college football's most underrated receiver: Touchdown catches 26, 27 and 28, erasing Charles Rogers' MSU career mark, and as good a pro career as Muhsin Muhammad had.

- For Martin, a cross between Devin Hester and Denard Robinson: A long punt return with no penalty flags and enough healthy days to show NFL teams just how explosive he can be.

- For Foreman, who ended his consecutive starts streak at guard so cancer conqueror Arthur Ray Jr. could take the first snap in the season-opener: A final start in a bowl win and many more in the NFL.

- For Robinson, a free safety who paid the price for

HEART OF A SPARTAN

Linebacker Chris Norman is congratulated after a play in Columbus

success: A game-saving interception on a fourth-down pass and a way to share his infectious spirit with future Spartans and other young people.

- For Nichol, the catcher and pitcher on MSU's most surprising scores of 2011: A life so rich that his Hail Mary grab against Wisconsin won't be in his top 10 moments, even if it's always in ESPN's.

- For Dantonio, who's just proud enough to prevent a program's plunge: Back-to-back bowl wins in Florida and California and a streak over Michigan of Tresselian proportions, minus the crash landing.

- For effervescent Defensive Coordinator Pat Narduzzi: Continued candor, no need for apologies and a great head coaching opportunity, probably in 2013 or 2014.

- For much-maligned Offensive Coordinator Dan Roushar: Credit it took Narduzzi four years to get and more play calls as successful as his fourth-and-1 bootleg pass for a 30-yard score in the Big Ten Championship Game.

- For quarterback heir-apparent Andrew Maxwell: A smooth handoff of the reins from Cousins on January 2 and proof that patience is a virtue after three years as an understudy.

- For running backs Edwin Baker, Larry Caper Jr. and Nick Hill: The confidence Baker showed last off-season with his 2,000-yard, 21-TD projection, another lasting image like Caper's overtime score against U-M in 2009, a longer stride for Hill and no more fumbles – ever.

- **For redshirt-freshman offensive tackle Skyler Burkland and senior defensive tackle Kevin Pickelman:** Complete recoveries from knee surgery, with Burkland's best football definitely ahead of him and Pickelman's memories heightened by one more post-game chanting of the "MSU Fight Song."

- **For Ray, an inspiration for all he meets:** Continued success against his toughest opponent, more opportunities to play for the Spartans and a start at some point because his coaches can't keep him off the field.

- **For All-America defensive tackle Jerel Worthy:** An Outback Bowl Defensive MVP effort before he turns pro a year early, an end to offside penalties and a Warren Sapp-like NFL career – ideally with New England, where he can flash a sweet tattoo to Tom Brady.

- **For second-year defensive ends William Gholston and Marcus Rush:** Plenty of meetings over fallen QBs, starting with Georgia's Aaron Murray, and just the right kind of recognition – praise for Gholston's flag-free play and appropriate pub for "Pass" Rush.

- **For sophomore middle linebacker and captain-to-be Max Bullough:** Enough tackles, takeaways and titles by January 2014 that no one can argue whether his career has been better than his grandpa's, his dad's, his uncle's or his brother's.

- **For sophomore outside linebacker and deluxe leaper Denicos Allen:** More big plays against Ohio State QB Braxton Miller and enough name awareness that big-time announcers stop calling him Allen Denicos.

- **For junior cornerback and risk-taker Johnny Adams:** A critical sack on a blitz in next year's B1G title matchup and more than enough big plays to back up his omnipresent on-field chatter.

- **For sophomore strong safety and game-changer Isaiah Lewis:** An indelible memory of his pick-six vs. the Wolverines, amnesia about his last game in his hometown of Indianapolis and a blocked punt for the winning tally next year at Wisconsin.

- **For junior placekicker and fake-play decoy Dan Conroy:** A 51-yard field goal at crunch time next December at Lucas Oil Stadium and a pass or a pitch on Dantonio's next trick play.

- **For redshirt-freshman punter and scholar Mike Sadler:** Pooch punts that die inside the 5, at least 4.9-second hang-time on boots from the back of his end zone and a continuation of his 4.0 g.p.a.

- **For next year's senior class, with a tough act to follow:** More than 37 career wins and a packed Spartan Stadium for Senior Day, especially in the student section when they say goodbye.

That should be more than enough gifts – for the recipients and all their followers. Besides, one more package and the reindeer will sit out longer than this year's NBA players.

Marcus Rush and Denicos Allen lived in the Michigan backfield

JANUARY 1, 2012 • SUNDAY

ON YOUR MARK ...

THEY WEREN'T RUNNING for anything Sunday in Tampa. They weren't running from anything, either.

Mark Dantonio and Mark Richt were about as comfortable in their skin as coaches could be the day before the Outback Bowl, a meeting of teams with a lot more in common than their head coaches' first names.

At their final pregame press conference, it was clear why Monday's matchup is as interesting as it is important – because 10-3 Michigan State and 10-3 Georgia have many more similarities than differences.

Both programs have relied on defenses ranked among the nation's best. Both have won with precision passing. Both have lost a non-conference game, one in league play and a championship test.

Both teams even enjoy being Dawgs in the best way possible.

And both leaders knew they were speaking on the Sabbath, with Dantonio's religion never far from his sleeve and Richt adding, "(I hope) my Lord and Savior is pleased with it. That's kind of who I'm working for."

But Dantonio and Richt are similar, not twins. Neither are the Spartans and Bulldogs.

Dantonio can look mad when he's not. Richt can appear happier than he is. But only one of them will be happy at about 4:30 Monday afternoon.

"The bottom line is we have to win the football game," Dantonio said. "That's why we play."

It doesn't matter that MSU is ranked 12th by the writers and 13th by the coaches or that Georgia is 18th in both polls.

All that matters now is which team that wanted to be elsewhere will leave happy they were here, a postseason champion of something.

And that's the biggest difference between the Spartans and Bulldogs, one shaped by January perceptions.

It doesn't matter that Georgia lost to Boise State by 14 points in Atlanta two weeks before MSU fell by 18 at Notre Dame.

No one cares that the Bulldogs lost at home to South Carolina or that the Spartans were spanked at Nebraska – teams that will meet up the road in Orlando.

And it's almost irrelevant now that Georgia blew a lead over LSU a few hours before MSU did the same against Wisconsin, or that each allowed 42 points that day.

What matters is what happens at 1:08 p.m. Monday at Raymond James Stadium in 65-degree weather – a projected 21 degrees warmer than in Athens, Ga., and 39 degrees warmer than East Lansing, for those keeping score at home.

The only numbers we need to care about are the ones both teams put on the scoreboard. A lot of eyes will be watching one of this season's best pairings. Opinions are sure to be shaped.

Despite winning 106 games in 11 seasons, Richt's biggest perception problem is in-state, where he hasn't been able to deliver the National Championship that Vince Dooley did.

Dantonio needs to educate the masses, particularly outside of Michigan, that no team has a better Big Ten record than the Spartans the past four years and especially the last two.

The difference is all about bowl games, as both coaches understand – Richt with a contented grin and Dantonio with a steely stare.

Maybe some of that is because Richt has great memories of facing Monday's opponent as a player and a coach. Dantonio, not so much.

On September 25, 1982, Richt filled in for injured Jim Kelly and quarterbacked Miami past MSU in the Orange Bowl, 25-22 – one of seven losses in Muddy Waters' last season by eight points or less.

On January 1, 2009, Richt led the Bulldogs – or Matthew Stafford did – to a 24-12 comeback win over the Spartans in the Capital One Bowl.

When Stafford wasn't throwing to NFL targets Mohamed Massaquoi and A.J. Green, he was flipping wheel routes to Knowshon Moreno in a 21-point second half.

Know-wonder Richt smiled.

Dantonio smiled, too. But it required a question about his senior class and another about the fun his players had been having all week.

"We've done some fun things, some I guess that are a little bit out there," he said. "I saw one of our guys laying there with a piece of bread on his back, trying to get the seagulls to take it. And one of our big offensive linemen put on a black Speedo and walked around the beach for a while."

If that doesn't sound like the Mardi Gras, don't worry. There's a job to be done. Dantonio knows that. That's one of the reasons he flipped the team's schedule to allow more rest and later workouts.

But none of that will matter if the teams follow familiar scripts. One coach has been great in bowls. The other, for all his successes, is winless.

In a way, it's hardly a fair comparison. Richt was an assistant at Florida State when the Seminoles couldn't lose a bowl game. Bobby Bowden's program went 14 years without a postseason setback from 1982-95.

A relaxed Mark Dantonio enjoys his final Outback Bowl press briefing

HEART OF A **SPARTAN**

Of course, it helps when you're finishing among the top five teams in the nation each year, as FSU viewed as its birthright.

And in his first 10 seasons at Georgia, Richt's teams went 7-3 in bowls. If that sounds pretty good to MSU fans, it should be pointed out that Richt's predecessor, Jim Donnan, won four straight bowls from 1997-2000 – and was fired in the process.

"7-3 is not bad," Richt said. "In a bowl you usually get a pretty good opponent. You should be evenly matched."

Ah, therein lies the rub for the Spartans, whose 7-14 record in bowls ranks ahead of only Northwestern in winning percentage among Big Ten schools.

One could make the case, as we're about to do, that MSU hasn't had an even matchup in a bowl game since January 1, 2000. A 37-34 win over Florida also happens to be the last time the Spartans beat an SEC team.

A win over Fresno State in the Silicon Valley Bowl 10 years ago was exciting and just what we expected.

Losses to Nebraska in the 2003 Alamo Bowl, to Boston College and No. 1 draft pick Matt Ryan in the 2007 Champs Sports Bowl, to the Bulldogs with another top NFL selection three years ago and to Texas Tech in the 2010 Alamo Bowl, with a dozen players suspended, were all uphill climbs, to say the least.

A 49-7 thumping by Alabama last New Year's Day was hardly a fair fight under any jurisdiction. MSU could have played that game 10 times and … actually, it couldn't, because it wouldn't have had any quarterbacks left.

So the fact that Dantonio and this year's sensational senior class is 0-4 in bowls is irrelevant today – unless they fall to 0-5.

It should be noted that George Perles' program didn't win a bowl game until his fifth season in East Lansing. The same was true for Nick Saban's teams. When they finally broke through, it was Bobby Williams on the sideline against the Gators.

Bowls are funny that way. Williams was 2-0 with the Spartans. And long before that, Bo Schembechler couldn't win a postseason game for more than a decade – with some incredible Michigan teams.

Dantonio has a credible team this time and a legitimate shot. It's finally a fair fight. It's also one of the last hurdles to clear.

When that happens, and it will very soon, the nation will start to see MSU football differently. And we'll all see a smile that'll make a serious coach seem like a stand-up comedian, not just a stand-up guy.

Leadership counts, as Kirk Cousins and Mark Dantonio showed

JANUARY 2, 2012 • MONDAY

BOWLED OVER

IF IT HAD BEEN EASY, it wouldn't have been Michigan State.

But there was no better way for a class with class to say goodbye than to shout, "Hellooooo, Bowl Win!"

In just the third triple-overtime game in bowl history, the Spartans rallied three times Monday to stun Georgia 33-30 in an Outback Bowl matchup of Big Ten and SEC divisional winners.

"We've been doing new things," Mark Dantonio said in a passable impression of Muhammad Ali, circa 1974. "We've been chopping trees. We done wrestled an alligator. We tussled with a whale. We handcuffed lightning and threw thunder in jail."

Escaping from the prison of their image, his players pushed decades of past disappointments to the bottom of Tampa Bay.

With a second-half flurry reminiscent of Ali at his finest, MSU got off the canvas and fought back with 30 minutes of amazing football, then summoned the strength for 25 more plays.

The celebration that followed was one of the most meaningful in a proud program's history and a warm, fuzzy feeling five years in the making.

"I kept thinking, 'It can't end with a loss. It can't! We're not going to allow it,'" said quarterback Kirk Cousins, as fine a representative as college football has

Kirk Cousins gets the fans fired up en route to a triumph in Tampa

Defensive tackle Anthony Rashad White delivers the biggest blocked field goal in MSU history

274

had. "But It was a couple of inches from happening."

When Dantonio talks about "a game of inches," he means the stretch Anthony Rashad White somehow summoned to block the last kick from the Bulldogs' Blair Walsh, the SEC's top career scorer.

He means the second and third efforts of Le'Veon Bell on the tying touchdown with 14 seconds left and no timeouts remaining, a play call that could've backfired with a lesser back.

He means the vertical leap of Keith Nichol on a go-ahead grab near the crossbar and the horizontal lunge on the first of two Darqueze Dennard interceptions, a momentum shift of seismic proportions down 16-0.

But a win like this one has so many heroes – from unheralded walk-ons to transfers to five-star recruits.

They all had MICHIGAN STATE on their chests.

How about "Who's he?"-holder Brad Sonntag, who handled a low snap on the Spartans' lone extra-point, then helped his team go 2-for-2 on field goals in overtime, while Georgia was 1-for-3?

How about Dan Conroy, who hadn't kicked all day, then coolly drilled a PAT to make it 27-all and hit from 35 and 28 in OT to join an exclusive bowl-winners club with Dave Kaiser, John Langeloh and Paul Edinger?

How about Mike Sadler, a 4.0 student whose educated instep set Outback Bowl records with a 50.1-yard average on eight kicks and a combined 401 yards in boots, including four that died inside the 12?

How about Brian Linthicum, a senior tight end who started at Clemson and ended his college career with seven catches for 115 yards, both career-highs, including his team's only offensive play of more than 25 yards?

How about William Gholston, who wreaked havoc with seven solo stops, two sacks, five hits for losses, a fumble recovery and a pass breakup? He wore No. 2 because Georgia thought there were two of him.

And how about MSU's Dennard, a two-star recruit from The Peach State who reminded his heralded homeboys that losing is still the pits?

"Everything happens for a reason," the sophomore cornerback said of being able to walk the streets of Dry Branch, Ga., for the rest of his life. "When I went home for Christmas break, I was really getting it. We were supposed to get our heads beat in."

Instead, the Spartans beat down another barrier, earning their first bowl win in a decade and ending a five-game postseason skid, the last four in unfair fights under Dantonio's leadership.

MSU was the only Big Ten team to win on the busiest day of the postseason. Penn State, Ohio State, Nebraska and Wisconsin are all 0-1 this year. And Michigan may join them when it plays Virginia Tech.

The Spartans aren't responsible for that. They are responsible to each other. We saw that again when players made mistakes and held themselves accountable.

You can count on this. MSU has just had the only two 11-win seasons in school history. No NCAA Division I team or NFL franchise in the state has done better, not even the one in Ann Arbor.

"I kept saying that this win would mean more than beating Michigan," said Nichol, a study in perseverance. "We know how to beat them. We've done it four years in a row. It's becoming part of our culture. But we didn't know how to win a bowl game."

Now, they do. And the recipe isn't much different. It's blending skill and will until the whole is greater than the sum of its parts, until the fingers all become part of a fist.

After a first-half rope-a-dope that saw a 2-0 deficit grow to 16-0 with the longest pass and punt return in Outback Bowl history, the Spartans began to punch back in a 4-hour, 10-minute battle of attrition.

From the start of the fourth quarter till the final blocked kick, MSU outgained the Bulldogs 237-79, had 15 completions to Georgia's five and marched through Georgia for 85 yards in 1:41 without the benefit of a timeout.

That tying drive will rank with a marathon push against the Wolverines in 1995, a series with 103 yards of offense, as one of the most patient, passion-filled possessions a coach could want.

Cousins-to-Nichol for 15 yards ... to B.J. Cunningham for 7 and again for 22 ... to Bell for 3, Nichol for 6 and Keshawn Martin for 11 and ... hmm, that's only 64 yards.

Ah, yes, we can't forget a 20-yard scramble by a quarterback who wasn't supposed to be run and a last-push, 1-yard smash by another unappreciated prospect.

"I got hit at the 1-1/2 and knew I had to get in," Bell said. "Everyone who was in on that play gave a little bit extra. Georgia thought we'd give up. But we weathered the storm. I couldn't be any happier for the seniors."

In many ways, their 37th win – four more than in any four-year period of MSU football – was the best. It was definitely the best description of why so many things have changed.

And it was exactly the way it would've been scripted. A group of lightly rated recruits with heavy burdens weighed in at just the right time, as Cousins noted. "K.C. and the Sunshine Band" were No. 1 again.

If the Spartans had won 31-14, it wouldn't have been as fulfilling. Or as fitting. They lost the game five different times. And won it six. But you can't keep good men down – unless they're willing to stay there.

Dantonio, his staff and especially their players have never seen themselves as incompetent. Just incomplete. That circle was closed in Raymond James Stadium, before a surprising number of true-green believers.

"Just believe and keep fighting the fight," Dantonio said of one of his five favorite triumphs. "When we got the first touchdown, it all started to change."

It's starting to change in another way, too. MSU has a one-game winning streak in bowls and a warmer winter ahead. Will it ever lose again?

WHERE THERE'S A WILL

GENTLE GIANT GHOLSTON GETS HIS WAY

HEART OF A **SPARTAN**

"I HAVE A REPUTATION?"

The 6-foot-7, 275-pound defensive end looked surprised. Yes, he's an aggressive player. But his hands do more than push opponents to the ground.

They write. You won't find Will Gholston writing about sports, though. He has another idea.

"I would do children's books and just let my imagination run wild," Gholston said. "I have this one little thing going on with the three ducks and the pigs."

Ducks and pigs?

"I can't let you know. I'm going to trademark it," Gholston said in an end-of-discussion manner.

It's hard to imagine a children's book author having a reputation. Let's just say he gets a little aggressive when he steps on the field.

"That's just football," Gholston said with a laugh. "You put the pads on and you have to expect to get hit."

Michigan State's opponents expect to get hit when he stretches out in a three-point stance. There's no trace of his pearly whites on the football field.

"I'm pretty sure that everyone in the locker room can tell when it's game time and when it's not game time," Gholston said. "I feel like I turn into another person during the game. I become more aggressive because I know I have to get a job done."

It's a job Gholston has been doing well ever since his days at Detroit's Southeastern High. The All-America linebacker was the No. 1 player in Michigan's class of 2010. His pile of scholarship offers was almost as tall as he was.

Ohio State, Oklahoma, Alabama, Tennessee, the school down the road – just to name a few.

It was MSU's coaching staff and family atmosphere that won him over in the end. Gholston also wanted to stay close to home. His family, especially his grandma, could still watch him play the game he loved.

But a verbal commitment to the Spartans didn't mean other schools stopped their pursuit. Gholston talked to some SEC players who compared the conference's winning history to that of the Big Ten. Though MSU's program was on the rise, it still wasn't considered elite.

It wasn't an easy choice to make. Gholston kept his word, however. He wanted to create his own legacy. He wanted to make his own footsteps. And he wanted to do it at MSU.

Spartans everywhere breathed a sigh of relief when the National Letter of Intent was finally signed.

It was official. Gholston was a Spartan. And he's more than happy with his decision.

"I think I made the right choice," Gholston said. "We had back-to-back 11-win seasons, won a Big Ten Championship my freshman year and went to the title game last year. It has just been great for me."

For the Green and White, too. Last season Gholston, the All-Big Ten second-team selection, led the team's defensive linemen with 70 tackles, including 29 in a two-game span. It was the first time in more than a decade that a Spartan defensive lineman had recorded double-figure tackles in back-to-back games.

Gholston was a hero in Mark Dantonio's first bowl win, a 33-30 triple- overtime victory over the Georgia Bulldogs. No. 2 did it all. He recovered a fumble, broke up a pass, tied a Spartan bowl record with five tackles for losses and had a career-best two sacks. The five stops behind the line of scrimmage tied for the third-highest, single-

William Gholston has turned the corner in more ways than one

HEART OF A **SPARTAN**

Few defensive ends show more emotion or ability than William Gholston

game total in school history. Gholston was just two tackles shy of Julian Peterson's record – pretty good company.

Not bad for a player who came to MSU as a linebacker.

How does he like the position change?

"I don't," Gholston said flatly. "I wish I played linebacker."

Watch out, Max Bullough.

"No, I'm joking," Gholston laughed. "Playing end is whole lot more fun. I know what I'm doing now."

It was a difficult transition from outside linebacker to defensive end. But Gholston can learn new skills as quickly as he tells jokes.

"It was a real tough adjustment mentally and physically," Gholston explained. "The mental standpoint was that I came here to play linebacker. I was an All-American at that position in high school. And the physical part was using your hands. It was a whole different type of technique, a different way to view the scheme. But I think it all came together."

Gholston knows there will always be room to improve mentally, physically and emotionally. The emotional aspect of his game is what got him into a trouble in mid-October 2011.

Michigan State led Michigan 21-7 as Denard Robinson took the last snap of the third quarter. As his pass was completed, a flag flew behind the play. After 45 minutes of hand-to-hand combat with Michigan tackle Taylor Lewan, a taunt and a downward shove of Gholston's head pushed him over the edge. As he got to his feet, Gholston struck Lewan in the head. A 15-yard penalty, his second of the game, turned out to be the least of his problems.

The Big Ten suspended Gholston for one game for violating the league's unsportsmanlike-conduct clause. The sophomore starter understood his response was inappropriate, even though it was provoked. It was an emotional learning lesson.

"You just have to be able to play within the scheme and control your emotions at the same time," said Gholston, reflecting on the suspension. "You can't let your emotions take over. You're still playing the game, and you can't take it too far."

Gholston watched the Wisconsin game on TV but was on his way to Spartan Stadium before it was over. He was jogging at first. Then, he heard the euphoric screams of thousands of fans. He thought MSU had kicked a field goal, so he started sprinting. Finally, he heard about the Hail Mary.

His reaction?

"'Oh, yes, we won!'" Gholston remembered. "I was having anxiety attacks because it was such a good game. It was so close! I turned into a spectator and started rooting."

He doesn't plan on watching MSU on TV again until his playing days as a Spartan are over. Those days could be cut short. Gholston has the potential to be one of the best defensive linemen in the country next season. If he plays his cards right, the NFL could come calling one year early.

He has a few friends who keep him from looking that far ahead though.

"There's a lot of people that help me ignore that," Gholston said. "When I talk to anybody from back home, they say, 'Well, "Too-Tall", you're still not good. You haven't done anything.' And I'm like, 'Yeah, I know. I haven't done anything.' Everybody helps me stay level."

But after a sophomore season that put him in the record books, Gholston still doesn't consider himself one of the nation's best. He expects more.

"I have no room for complacency, because I haven't done anything in my eyes," Gholston said. "I don't understand how I'm considered one of the best. I didn't do anything last year. I'm going to try to do something this year, though."

His goals are set.

"I have to have an All-American season and a winning season, a Big Ten title, hopefully get that crystal egg, too," Gholston said of the national championship trophy. "All of the above."

Gholston dreams big. He always has and always will. With that attitude, he should have plenty of golden nuggets in the future, whether they come from his ducks or the game of football.

JANUARY 5, 2012 • THURSDAY

PROGRAM WINS

IT'S FOOTBALL'S CATCH 22 – not the recruiting rankings we started in the *Lansing State Journal* nearly 30 years ago, but the dilemma college coaches face when they try to take it up a level.

They need to have very good players to win.

And they need to win to get very good players.

Of course, they can cheat. But if they want to risk probation, unlikely as that is, that's another problem.

Mark Dantonio wasn't willing to do that. And he wasn't the kind of flim-flam man who could sell snow to Eskimos – not that Nanook was a four-star anyway.

He had to build a championship program brick-by-brick.

He knew Michigan State had been up and down more often than a Case Hall elevator and was known as Team Schizophrenia.

He knew he had to beat Michigan and Notre Dame immediately and Ohio State eventually with talent those schools wouldn't touch.

He knew from six years as an MSU assistant he couldn't disregard Detroit or be a gimmick team, just one that used trick plays.

He knew his staff would have to evaluate and motivate as well as any coaches in the country, teaching and reaching at the same time.

He knew Spartan Stadium seated 75,000, not 111,000 – meaning he couldn't pay a defensive coordinator $900 grand.

Most important, he knew the culture. He knew it wouldn't be easy to win there. He also knew he could.

After five seasons, it's hard to find fault with much that Dantonio has done – though his Ali impression could use a little work.

As he continues in Year 6, Michigan State football is solid enough to withstand some storms, instead of being a lightning rod for turmoil.

Taking over a 4-8 team that majored in futility and minored in despair, Dantonio had the right answers to a lot of tough questions.

If he didn't have them, he found someone who did. The most important thing anyone can know is how much he or she doesn't. Dantonio never tried to BE the program, just the director of it.

Not so suddenly, several other questions have been raised and have become relevant, a victory in itself:

- When was the last time MSU had been to five straight bowl games? Not the 33 straight that U-M had from 1976-2008 or the 30 in a row that Florida State has now. Just five.

- When was the last time a class of recruits could say they played in four wins over the Wolverines? Or for freshmen who sat out 2008, that they're 4-0-and-counting?

- When was the last time the Spartans had double-digit wins in back-to-back years? Not the 11 of the last two seasons. Just 10. And you can include six National Champions.

- When was the last time MSU beat U-M, OSU, Wisconsin, a school from the mighty Southeast and a bowl opponent of any kind in the same season?

- And when was the last time the program had 37 wins over a four-year period? Or even 36? That's the football program, not the basketball operation.

The answer to all the above questions is the same. In a word: Never.

How has that happened? And what does it mean for 2012 and beyond?

By restricting his battles to the playing field and steering clear of politics, Dantonio has performed the toughest job of all as MSU's 24th head football coach.

He has reshaped the culture of the program, a feat accomplished only by Biggie Munn, 54-9-2 from 1947-53 after it had gone nine years with six wins or less.

While nearly everyone aspires to be in the pros

these days, Dantonio has made the most of the cons – a consistent message, continuity with his staff and confidence that every goal is within reach.

He has encouraged his players to dream. Yet, he has made them wake up in other ways. He has let them know a loss of consciousness is often followed by a loss of games.

He has challenged the bully on the block and punched him squarely in the solar plexus, knocking the wind out of people with a seemingly endless supply of hot air.

Yes, it helped that U-M became what MSU had often been with incompetence and infighting. But even before that, Dantonio accepted the challenge and stood up to the laughter and scorn.

No one is laughing at what the Spartans have accomplished the past two seasons. And only a fool would figure they'll shrink back to insignificance because the Wolverines are competitive again.

Dantonio has raised the floor for a program that found every trap door to the dungeon for decades. In some important ways, but not all till he wins in Pasadena, he has raised the ceiling, too.

There's no guarantee that MSU or any other school, even those with "We are ..." arrogance, will live in college football's penthouse.

But the outhouse? The Spartans were there long enough to know that smell is nothing like cocoa.

And The Big House? After winning there in 2008 and 2010, they know there's no better feeling than silencing close to 100,000 people and ruining their weekend – the next Monday at their workplaces, too.

It's all about hard work if MSU plans to be competitive with U-M and OSU – and, yes, Wisconsin – in the years just ahead. The Spartans seem to be embracing that challenge.

It's also silly to think the Wolverines and Buckeyes, perhaps even the Nittany Lions now, would stay down for long. They have too many resources to lose on a consistent basis.

Instead, it's up to MSU to be the best it can be, something we haven't seen yet. We've seen higher-profile recruits come on board, including the last three No. 1 prospects in Michigan. And we've seen a lot of players improve, something less sexy but just as important.

How has that happened? By believing in a course of action and making actions speak louder than words, by giving achievement a microphone and hype laryngitis.

Now, the challenge continues without an amazing group of seniors. Kirk Cousins, B.J. Cunningham, Keshawn Martin, Keith Nichol, Joel Foreman, Trenton Robinson, Kevin Pickelman and others came and conquered.

Their thumbprints will be there forever.

Most of those players were lightly recruited. It took a leap of faith to make a leap in the standings. But, oh, how Spartan spirits have soared.

A few bigger names – Nichol in 2008 and Tennessee transfer DeAnthony Arnett now – had to leave for a while before coming home. It says a lot about the Dantonio Way that those doors remained open.

Burning bridges is almost never good. Burning bad memories and burying the ashes of failure is almost always a plus.

A comeback for the ages against Georgia was an essential step for MSU's growth, just as an Elite Eight win over Kentucky after a horrible start was one of the final strides for Tom Izzo's basketball program.

That triumph happened in Year 4. The win over the Bulldogs took till Year 5. But building a football program is a tougher challenge, as Izzo has said.

Enjoy the journey. There are bumps in the road just ahead. But the right person is behind the wheel with more than enough horsepower.

The best is yet to come. And one last tip for those in the back seat who keep asking, "Are we there yet?": It's often more fun to get there than to be there.

In terms of being one of college football's best programs, we're about to find out.

A NICE RING TO IT

LE'VEON BELL A HEISMAN-TYPE BACK

IT WAS CUTE at first, then downright comical – three young kids doing pigskin pirouettes on the playground. Finally, one helmet-less player added his own play-by-play:

"Le'Veon Bell … spins … and he's in!" the boy broadcast to an audience of two. "Touchdown, Michigan State!"

So what if the youngster weighed barely a third of his hero's 238 pounds? Bell wasn't always the biggest, baddest running back in the Big Ten, either. But heading into his junior year, there's a good chance he will be.

Bell can pick a hole like a locksmith, splat defenders like bugs on a windshield and deliver a stiff-arm like a George Foreman jab. He can block. He can catch. And if you catch him smiling, it's never a shock – unless he's carrying the football.

From two-star recruit to too strong, Bell has been one of the best surprises of Mark Dantonio's first five seasons as head coach of the Spartans. If he does what he can, it won't be a shock if more baby boys in the Midwest are named Le'Veon than ever before.

Actually, that's more likely to happen in Michigan than Ohio these days. Growing up in Reynoldsburg, a few long runs due east of Columbus, it's stunning that Bell ever made his way to East Lansing.

"I've heard that whenever I've gone home," he said. "But it is what it is. Everything happens for a reason. God put me here. And I'm making the most of a great opportunity."

Bell almost always has. He started playing football at age 4 and never competed with his age group. That was also true when he enrolled at MSU a semester early and immediately turned his coaches' heads.

He had already done plenty at Groveport Madison High, the school that sent safety Eric Smith to the Spartans and eventually to the New York Jets. But the only other FBS schools to offer him a scholarship were Bowling Green, Marshall, Eastern Michigan and Colorado.

"I wasn't really a fan of any team," Bell said. "I had family members who were Ohio State fans and family members who were Michigan fans. I just really liked watching football. I had favorite players, not teams."

Though Bell wore No. 1 in high school, his two favorites wore No. 28 – one for Oklahoma and the Minnesota Vikings, the other at OSU.

"I really liked watching Adrian Peterson and Chris 'Beanie' Wells," Bell said. "They did a lot of things for their football teams. I just wish I could be as fast as Peterson. He's a freak. And he makes people miss. But I'm happy with the things the Lord blessed me with."

Exceptional patience and power, for starters. When you add a team-first attitude and a rare ability to block and catch, MSU might have its greatest gift from Ohio since another No. 24, "Jumpin' Johnny" Green, showed up unannounced to play basketball and lifted the Spartans to their first Final Four.

"When I was little, my uncle used to keep on the field, running routes and catching balls," Bell said. "But as a kid, I was actually a quarterback. I could throw the ball pretty well. And my older cousin was our running back."

Le'Veon Bell piles up more yards after contact

HEART OF A **SPARTAN**

When a lot of opposing coaches learn that, their first question should be: "Is it too late to recruit Bell's cousin?" The second could be: "Can I at least find someone with the same kind of killer spin?"

"It comes natural," Bell said. "I don't plan it. It just kind of happens. I really look to cut first. If I can't, I'll spin. It's a great feeling when you make a guy miss cleanly. It just comes over the course of a game. First, I might lower my head. Next, I might give him a couple of jukes. Then, I'll spin to keep him off guard."

Off guard, off tackle and around end, Bell rushed 289 times for 1,592 yards, 5.4 per carry, and scored 21 touchdowns as a freshman and sophomore. Battling shoulder injuries through the second half of his rookie year and backing up Edwin Baker until his first start in November 2011, his career's start has been amazing.

Bell debuted with 10 carries for 141 yards and two scores against Western Michigan, rushed 17 times for 114 yards vs. Notre Dame in his first night game and carried seven times for 78 yards at Michigan, putting his team ahead to stay with a 41-yard sprint.

His 35 catches last season were more than any MSU player except B.J. Cunningham or Keshawn Martin. And though Bell didn't have another 75-yard run, he went for 35 vs. Wisconsin, caught a 45-yard pass at Iowa and bulled 36 inches in the Outback Bowl for a tying TD with :19 left.

"I think that run against Georgia was my favorite," he said. "It was a pivotal play to put us into OT and help us win. I know that was the toughest yard I've ever had to get in my life."

If the toughest part of success is handling notoriety and hype, Dantonio tested Bell in spring ball by saying his job was up for grabs and reminding everyone that senior Larry Caper had started five games as a freshman.

By the middle of April, it was clear the Spartans had quality depth with four running backs, including one who answered the bell exactly the way his coaches had hoped.

"Le'Veon is having an outstanding spring," Dantonio said. "He's not complacent. And I think some other guys are showing they can do things as well."

Dantonio is understandably biased. So let's check with an expert on all-purpose backs, a player who scored an NCAA-record eight TDs in one game for Illinois in 1990.

"Bell should have a monster year," BTN analyst Howard Griffith said during a Pro Day visit. "I think he's the real deal. You saw that in the Big Ten Championship Game. He catches the ball. He has great balance. And arm tackles aren't going to bring him down. If they keep feeding him, he's really going to put up some numbers."

He could rank with a string of great 24s for the Spartans: Lynn Chandnois, Sonny Grandelius, Dean Look and Eric Allen. The player Bell probably resembles the most is No. 8, T.J. Duckett. But Bell knew more about the Spartans' last All-America running back and was all ears when their best ballcarrier was mentioned.

"I definitely knew who Javon Ringer was," Bell said of one of his favorites. "I watched him a lot when I was in high school. He was a tough player who'd get the ball 35 times a game and keep running hard. He didn't care about his body, just about helping the team win.

"And I know Lorenzo White was a great running back here. I never got to watch him, but I've seen a couple of highlights. I couldn't imagine carrying the ball that many times (56 for 292 yards in a title-clinching win over Indiana in 1987). He's probably the greatest back to ever come through here."

If there's anything Bell loves as much as animals, LeBron James and Twitter, it's meeting a challenge and finishing a job. His well-publicized January tweet about how Michigan and MSU stacked up last season quickly reached the Wolverines. And it's no spin to say Bell is fine with that.

"The job isn't done," he said. "It's all about keeping that chip on my shoulder, the one I had when I came out of high school. And it's up to me to make this team better. That's really why I'm here."